NAVIGATING THE UNKNOWN:

NAVIGATING THE UNKNOWN:

The creative process in contemporary performing arts

Edited by
Christopher Bannerman
Joshua Sofaer
Jane Watt

Middlesex University PRESS

rescen PUBLICATIONS

Middlesex University

NESTA Making Innovation Flourish

This project was supported by an award from NESTA, The National Endowment for Science, Technology and the Arts. NESTA is working to increase the UK's capacity for innovation. We invest in all stages of the innovation process, backing new ideas and funding new ventures that stimulate entrepreneurship: visit www.nesta.org.uk for further information.

First published in 2006 by
Middlesex University Press

Copyright © RESCEN – Centre for Research
into Creation in the Performing Arts,
Middlesex University

A CIP catalogue record for this book is available
from The British Library

ISBN 1 904750 55 9
ISBN 978 1 904750 55 0

Project administrator: Marianne Tyler
Designed by Struktur Design Limited
Printed in the UK by Cambridge Printing

Middlesex University Press,
North London Business Park,
Oakleigh Road South, London N11 1QS
Tel: +44 (0)20 8411 4162
Tel: +44 (0)20 8411 5734
Fax: +44 (0)20 8411 4167
www.mupress.co.uk

Picture Credits

All images copyright of photographers and artists
unless otherwise stated.

Cover, pp.2, 44-57, 238-239 (nos.55, 59)
Getty Images
pp.24-25, 26-27, 202-203, 223, 225, 238-239
(nos.2, 25, 48) Roger Fawcett-Tang
pp.238-239 (nos.7-12) Roger Fawcett-Tang,
based on diagrams in Keith Critchlow *Islamic
Patterns: An Analytical and Cosmological
Approach* (London: Thames and Hudson, 2001)
pp.70-89 Ghislaine Boddington
pp.102-103 *Talking to Tania 1, Day 6, Skyros,
Greece* (Richard Layzell on decorated moped).
Richard Layzell, 2003
pp.104-105, 120-121, 128-129, 137, 138-139,
144-145 Photographs of Stroud Valleys Artspace
by Richard Layzell, 2004-2006
pp.158-159, 184-185 Photographs of Rosemary
Lee at Chisenhale Studio by Nick Cobbing, 2005
pp.186-187 Hugo Glendenning
pp.200-201, 220-221, 233, 238-239 (nos. 4, 6,
20, 21, 23, 54-55, 56-58) Graeme Miller
pp.227, 229, 231 and 236 (upper left hand corner),
238-239 (nos.27-31, 41-47, 61-65, 72) Pau Ros
pp.238-239 (nos.32, 37) Alamy Images
pp.238-239 (nos.51-52) Cornelia Parker,
Pornographic Drawing 1996. Ink blot made with
pornographic videotape dissolved in solvent.
With thanks to HM Customs and Excise
pp.238-239 (no.53), 241 Dr Mark Carrington,
Cambridge University / Wellcome Photo Library
pp.238-239nos.70-71 Drawings by Adam McLean
pp.252-253, 270-272 *[h]Interland*, 2002 Video
projection still by Pete Gomes

CONTENTS

PREFACE

Since 2003, I have been privileged to witness the work of artists and researchers involved in ResCen, the Centre for Research into Creation in the Performing Arts, at Middlesex University, on their NESTA-funded project, *Navigating the Unknown*. This book is born of that rich, energetic mix of matter, mind, soul; individual and collective making, analysis and inward mapping.

Compass points

A brave, complex and thoughtful project, it has involved the core participants – the authors of this book – in making manifest some fundamental compass points in their enquiry.

First, they have created catalytic spaces for engagement, facing in (within themselves as individual artists, and in the core team) and facing out (with wider audiences). Time was stretched, and participation invited through unexpected and multiple entry points, enabling sharing of perspectives on the elusive process of creation experienced and made manifest. Engaging in dialogue with energetic high creators working in disciplinary areas as diverse as management, geography, psychology, psychoanalysis and neurobiology, the depths of the unknown were entered, new caverns and mysteries surfaced and explored, personal and shared hypotheses about the process of creation, offered.

Secondly, the navigation has reflected bold perspectives on knowledge as performance. Performance has been powerfully present, throughout, both when facing in, and when facing out. Whilst every session was documented in detail and catalogued in a growing archive (some of this made public through the ResCen website, providing enormous potential for mining the unknown at a level beyond performance), the element of the moment, and the making of knowledge in the moment through performance, was a continuous core. This text mirrors that process, offering a range of what my Harvard colleagues might call 'performances of understanding'.

Thirdly, the voice, ear, eye, hand and impulse of the artist have led the navigation, through clear and stormy waters, inward and outward. Tensions between directions sought, landmarks recognized, and means of propulsion, led to thickets, dead ends, wide open spaces and confused territory, as well as synchronous movement, mirrored experience and moments of individual and collective realization. Whilst interdisciplinary engagement was sought within and beyond art forms, the artist's impulse led this enquiry.

Navigating mystery

The three compass points; catalytic space, performance as knowledge, and the artist's impulse, provided a framework for the exploration shared in the pages of this text. The book walks the talk. It represents the multiple realities, perspectives and intertextual potentials, of *Navigating the Unknown*. It offers windows on the complexity of creation, mining intuition, conscious and unconscious, in making manifest. In doing so, it introduces the fourth compass point, the absence of which is also its presence. That fourth compass point is the persistence, depth and complexity of mystery in creation. It completes the book as representing a milestone, landmark and provocation, inviting the reader to engage in navigating mystery, within a vast, interdisciplinary catalytic enquiry.

My hope is that this multi-layered and non-linear book will stimulate in readers, participants in the text, what may be infinite exploration of the unknown.

Professor Anna Craft
University of Exeter
Visiting Scholar, Harvard University

July 2006

INTRO DUCTION

Navigating the Unknown represents a significant milestone in the development of ResCen, the Centre for Research into Creation in the Performing Arts. ResCen began in 1999 with the intention of forming a bridge between academia and the world of the professional performing arts and it proposed to focus on the creative processes of artists rather than performance. Six Research Associate Artists were appointed, each with a significant track record and, as a group, representing a variety of art forms and creative practices. ResCen enabled them to meet at regular intervals to reflect on the processes at play in their creative practice and looked for innovative and appropriate ways of representing and communicating these processes to a wider audience. At the same time, the ResCen artists continued to develop their professional creative practice.

One important aspect of ResCen's approach was in place from the beginning: to consider the artists as knowledge-holders, expert in their field, and therefore to afford equal weight to the voice of the artist in the research dialogue. This principle was felt to be key to the work of the Centre as it formed a central strand of the hypothesis that first-person reporting by artists could yield research findings that would contribute to our understanding. The privileging of the voice of the artist and the focus on process formed a distinctive mission that was intrinsic to spanning the divide between the world of artistic practice and academia. This represented

a departure from the traditional relationship between art and the academy and it was not universally welcomed. While this may be attributed to the focus on both first-person reportage and the slippery area of artistic process, it was also a disruption to the traditional academic practice in which interpretative analysis is used to posit meaning on the artwork as product, often without reference to either the artist or to the processes that formed and informed the work. In fact the perspectives of the academic and the artist should be complementary and ResCen has attempted to achieve this symbiosis; redressing the historical imbalance by privileging the voice of the artist and by involving theoreticians willing to engage with artists. In addition, the Centre has attempted to address a diverse audience made up of reflective artistic practitioners, those interested in the arts and artmaking, public policy, as well as academic research communities. This task has not always been easy and ResCen is grateful to NESTA, the National Endowment for Science, Technology and the Arts, whose support has been vital to the development of this work and this book, and to Middlesex University for the foresight to fund the proposed Centre in 1999 and for maintaining its commitment.

It is worth noting that the six artists who joined ResCen in 1999, are those who have contributed to *Navigating the Unknown*, demonstrating that their involvement in the project has stood the test of time. The artists' involvement did not imply an agreed artistic mission, or an approach that was common to the group; the interaction between them was allowed to develop according to their perception of what was most relevant to their interests.

This dialogic approach has continued with contributions from the ResCen artists, both individually and collectively, counterpointed by contributions from the editors as well as external experts. This allows a range of perspectives to be presented and the reader is invited to establish connecting trajectories between them, or to navigate the book by selecting their own path, following graphic signposts which identify the introductory essays which begin each section, artists' group conversations, individual artist's voices or guest essays. It is important to note that it would be an over-simplification to see the order of the book as proposing a linear artistic process by suggesting, for example, that intuition is only active in the early stages of the process. Some aspects of the design counter that interpretation by establishing non-linear pathways and offering random encounters as in the short observations interspersed throughout which are intended to be springboards to new ways of perceiving or thinking.

It is important to acknowledge that the ResCen project operates within wider reconsiderations of the relationship between artistic practice and research which are taking place across Higher Education in the UK and elsewhere. A range of formulations has emerged to characterise this relationship, including practice-led, practice-based and practice as research. The range of terminology indicates that the debate is not fixed and that there is no dominant definition of this complex relationship. The debate has also taken place at a time in which discussions of creativity have been widespread in public policy discourse in relation to primary and secondary education as well as in the economic and business sphere. This wider context has enabled the evolution to be multi-faceted and for the outcomes in one area to be relevant to other debates and disciplines. We hope therefore that this book will contribute to a range of debates and will be of interest to a wide readership.

Navigating the Unknown represents a significant strand in the work of ResCen, but it should not be seen as the totality of the work, please visit www.rescen.net for details of our other activities and publications.

Finally, we must thank all those who have contributed to this book, as well as those who have supported its production – without this support the work of ResCen could not take place. We all hope that you, the reader, will be engaged by this book and that it will enrich knowledge, understanding and debate.

Christopher Bannerman
Joshua Sofaer
Jane Watt

INVENTION

The Butterfly Unpinned

Christopher Bannerman

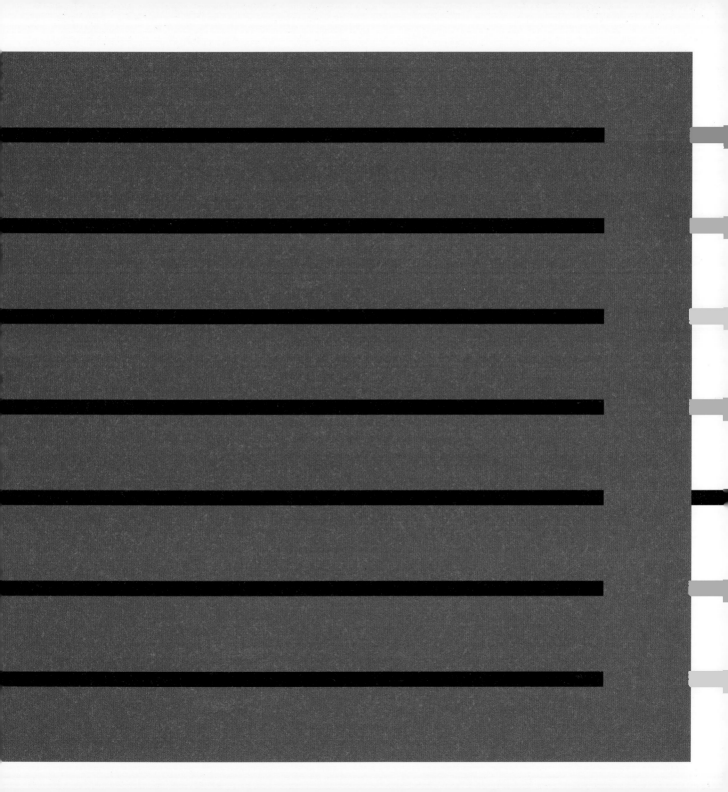

Part One of this book concerns the interplay of the conscious and unconscious in the creative process. It should be acknowledged almost immediately that the choice of the title In/Tuition raised certain issues which became part of the puzzle to be disentangled in the writing. One problem arose from the word 'intuition' itself. In 'Interplay', the roundtable discussion which follows, the ResCen artists discussed whether intuition might be better expressed as instinct. Ultimately, the former was the preferred term, as it seemed to denote a broader range of the phenomenon being explored. Instinct was felt to be a relatively narrow experience, perhaps stemming from nether regions, as in 'gut instinct', whereas the artists reported that the experience of intuition, especially in relation to intuitive insight, involved correspondence at a higher level. Of course the artists may be merely reporting on differing aspects of the same phenomenon, a point recognised by Guy Claxton when he noted that intuition is multiple and resists being boiled down to a single thing.[1] Other issues arose concerning the difficulties of discussing intuition due to its elusive nature and the role it plays in the work of the artists, a factor that inhibited discussion periodically.

Terminology and verbal articulation were also problematic when identifying the 'tuition' component of In/Tuition, and it is used here conditionally, as it proved difficult to agree a term which represented succinctly the aspects of creative process which appear to stem from the conscious, rational mind. It was felt that these aspects could be passed on; in other words, they were elements of the creative process that could be taught. This might include aspects such as strategies for generating and manipulating material, devices such as Graeme Miller's almost arbitrary selection of an overarching structure as a starting point, and decisions such as the location of the presentation of the work, or the

choice of collaborators. This conscious field of endeavour, comprising tools and strategies that could be learned and taught, contrasts with intuition, which was characterised as invisible, uncontrollable, sometimes available and at other times entirely absent, defying all attempts at engagement.

Another problem arose from the separation of the word intuition with a forward slash to constitute 'in/tuition'. This was intended to convey the separation of the conscious and unconscious processes that the artists acknowledged informed their work, but also to represent a unifying interplay between the two. This unity of the unconscious and conscious proposes that intuitive processes, which elude the direct gaze of the conscious mind and resist verbal explanation, are considered to be constituent elements of a field of knowledge and expert practice. To consider processes that can neither be consciously analysed nor verbally articulated as part of a domain of knowledge might be problematic itself and we will return to this theme. But the active relationship, the interplay, that 'in/tuition' conveys is especially significant, in order to avoid denoting the static, or the fixed, when the experience as reported by the artists was characterised by fluidity, movement and a dynamic interdependence.

The problems of terminology were considerable and they were located within a wider problem of words in general. But the first potential barrier was not terminology, rather it was the admission by the artists that they did not 'know' or could not always fully account for what they were doing. This was quickly dispelled in part through Shobana Jeyasingh's public admission that virtually all of her funding applications were works of fiction, as she could not possibly know at the point of writing what would transpire in the creative process.[2] The presence of the relevant officers from the Arts Council of England made this admission a declaration of artistic truth over the bureaucratic demands of arts funding. In fact, all the artists noted that the process of creating work almost always began by initiating a search for an unknown 'emergent premise'; or it involved the initiation of a strategy to find such a premise, which could be almost anything: literal, conceptual, or a concern stemming from the materials of the medium. The identification of the emergent premise often occurred through an intuitive insight, a moment that the artists frequently alluded to as a moment of recognition, acknowledging however, that this was often the 'recognition' of something that they had not previously seen. The apparent paradox of the new and emergent being 'recognised' in itself signals the problematic nature of this discussion, highlighting the potential for a collision of the rational and intuitive. The author Philip Pullman refers to 'fishing at night' in terms that match the notion of the search for the emergent premise. He notes that:

> There might be monsters there that could swallow hook, and line, and lamp, and boat, and you. These powers are not interested in any rationally-worked-out plans concocted far away on shore; none of the fish are interested in plans, or reason; the fears and delights of fishing at night have nothing to do with rationality.[3]

This might leave us wondering how he would recognise the 'fish' or emergent premise that he might catch and later he offers a hint when he notes that: '...he or she could catch a fish like that; could take a risk and write something true and meaningful.' So that is the measure by which Pullman judges the emergent premise; it must have the ring of the true and meaningful. The ResCen artists may use different words and at times have different expectations, but nonetheless, this test seems fit for purpose in artmaking.

A more potent barrier for the ResCen artists stemmed directly from the nature of intuition as they experienced it and its vital role in their work and their careers in general. Their willingness and even eagerness to discuss intuition was mediated at times by the reluctance to interfere consciously in a faculty which was beyond the control of the conscious mind, but which nonetheless was seen as vital to the production of their work. Rosemary Lee expresses this concern and links it to the difficulty of explaining it in words: 'Intuition is hard to talk about, by making it concrete I feel it's harder to find. The problem is partly semantic. I'm not sure I know what intuition is any more.'[4] The commitment to understanding and representing their creative processes overcame this inhibiting factor, but it is important to understand this reluctance, especially as the ResCen project was predicated on listening to the voice of the artist. Intuition was seen as vital to their creative process and in addition some artists reported that it also acts as a compass, steering them towards one path and away from another, even when the intuitively chosen direction seems inimical to their interests. Errollyn Wallen describes how she gave up a lucrative commission because it did not feel right.[5] In fact, intuition was often credited with a key role in their initial decision to be artists and was, therefore, not only vital to their current livelihoods, but also intrinsic to their identities as artists. This may be why, when asked to reflect on the role of intuition, a number of the ResCen artists refer to childhood experiences, implying that an initial experience of intuition has been formative and continues to resonate with their identities as artists.

This might be a perception common among artists generally as they rely on the power of intuitive processes in their working lives and therefore recognise its importance in everyday life. This experience of intuition as an unalloyed, almost childlike,

I relate

perceptive faculty might be what allows artists to see the everyday and mundane as if it were fascinating and mysterious – a kind of perception that the neuroscientist Mark Lythgoe termed 'bottom-up processing', adding that it seemed to be common to both children and artists.[6] It would be a mistake, however, to see the work of artists as aligned completely to childhood perception and experience. And the link to childhood experience may be specific to this group, as each has forged an individual, almost idiosyncratic path, rather than following a career predetermined by education or training, or by responding to job advertisements. They have, in a very real sense, created themselves. This seems an appropriate moment to reiterate that the ResCen work was focused on six artists and, as such, does not claim generalised findings, but does allow speculation about the potential general relevance of the research.

a characteristic, habit, mannerism that is peculiar to an individual

It was not just the intuitive realm that proved difficult to discuss – even the realm of conscious craft presented difficulties. The artists were drawing on knowledge acquired almost entirely through personal experience and so did not have a shared vocabulary to draw upon. This is exemplified when Jeyasingh notes the absence of an agreed codification to discuss dancemaking giving the example that she uses the term 'signifier' when others might call it something else, or simply leave it unnamed.[7] So, while intuition represents a realm which resists direct representation in words, the conscious field of craft and knowledge is, for the artists, a realm of the individuated experience, constructed personally and idiosyncratically and often described in code words such as Graeme Miller's 'channelling' and 'fluffing'.[8]

These initial difficulties accumulated, forming an interesting knot. To recapitulate, they included: problems of naming intuition and identifying its opposite; the difficulty of representing a dynamic process in the formulation of the title, the reticence of the artists to examine consciously the intuitive faculty, especially given the scope of its engagement with their work and careers; the challenge of discussing that which cannot be directly communicated verbally, yet which claims to be a constituent element of a realm of knowledge; and finally the use of a personalised and idiosyncratic vocabulary to describe the conscious processes of artmaking. This knot of problems forms the focus for much of this essay and also this section of the book, but there is also a wider context to consider and other potent factors ultimately impact on this discussion. They stem from public discourse centred on 'creativity' as well as the context of academia and how it recognises and constitutes knowledge. But first the problem of words and their use in depicting aspects of the creative process will be addressed.

The difficulties of representing intuition using the verbal realm are encapsulated in an observation offered by the psychiatrist R.D. Laing:

> I cannot say what cannot be said... but
> language can be used to convey what
> it cannot say - by its interstices, by its
> emptiness and lapses, by the latticework
> of words, syntax, sound and meanings.[9]

yes please

Or to paraphrase, we cannot say what cannot be said, but we can talk *about* what cannot be said; and, as long as we do not confuse *talking about* with *saying*, our words will *elucidate* rather than *make clear* *make obscure / unclear* obfuscate. An example of this strategy is provided by Richard Layzell's contribution to a seminar focused on intuition. He performed a passage of spontaneous free association, demonstrating aspects of the realm of intuition, using words not to explain or explicate intuition, but rather to realise it in the moment.[10] This makes clear that it is not words *per se* that are the problem, rather it is our misunderstanding of their role and our reliance on their use to delineate understandings, and construct knowledge. This syndrome may be more prevalent in the English-speaking world where the reifying tendency of the language is joined by a predilection for imagining concretised structures of knowledge.

An example of this is the evolution of the standard academic mantra in arts education that 'theory underpins practice'. I believe that this model gained wide acceptance in part because of the way in which we conceive of knowledge as a vertical, hierarchical edifice, as is also reflected by the term 'higher order'.

This conception of knowledge, which is inherent in our language, means that we often translate the French *comprendre*, as 'to understand' when it might be better represented as 'comprehend'. The latter is constituted from 'taking together', a way of knowledge based on relational positionings which are open to re-positioning, rather than proposing knowledge as a concretised edifice requiring underpinning, to create a solid platform which secures and fixes our 'under-standing'.

The promulgation of this inappropriate and misleading paradigm has not been helpful in attaining knowledge of artmaking practice or helpful to arts education as a whole. It proposed the primacy of words as well as a fixed and concretised relationship between theory and practice, a relationship which also implies conscious theory versus inchoate practice. The reality of this relationship is much more complex and dynamic as this book demonstrates. Yet we are still left with the problem of how to use the conscious to represent the unconscious. Guy Claxton has in the past used the term 'undermind' which refers to psychoanalytic terminology such as 'subconscious' which reveals the tendency to imagine a layered hierarchy that is also implicit in 'understanding' and 'underpinning'.[11] In his essay for this book Claxton proposes a more complex and dynamic three-dimensional model which features non-linear fluidity. While the artists do not question the issue of layering, they do question whether the realm of intuition is the sub or unconscious, or whether the direct apprehension or insight of intuition stems from a kind of supra consciousness. Certainly both Ghislaine Boddington and Errollyn Wallen refer to it in these terms when speaking of intuition as a guiding force in their careers, but equally, there is reference to 'the nag' (Boddington) and an 'itching on the soles of the feet' (Wallen) which might imply the activation of a 'gut' instinct which arises from below. As mentioned previously, it may be that the artists are referring to differing aspects of one phenomenon, or that they are reporting differing phenomena which are conflated into the single word intuition.

It may be that the isolation and reification that is implicit in identifying individual aspects of intuition is problematic and this issue is addressed by the three-dimensional model that Claxton proposes. This is a model which tallies more closely with the accounts of the ResCen artists and Wallen's use of the phrase 'zoom lens' indicates an ability to shift perspective radically and to embody non-linear fluidity. This non-linear fluidity may well be another way of expressing the 'mystery' that resists direct explication in words but which Claxton proposes is 'big and robust enough to withstand our puny efforts to unpack it a little bit'.[12] And the words 'unpack it a little bit' are chosen with care – this is not an explanation of the mystery but rather a considered attempt of the conscious to represent the unconscious – we are not 'saying what cannot be said' we are talking about what cannot be said.

In unpacking the mystery, both Ghislaine Boddington and Errollyn Wallen describe intuition as an embodied, physical experience, an experience shared with the poet A.E. Housman.[13] But artists' words can be perplexing and paradoxical. What can one make, for instance, of Boddington's words about her parents: 'they tutored me well in the world of intuition'.[14] The answer may be found however, in the words of Wallen that: 'we are encouraged to shut it off as we get older and we gradually lose touch with our younger, more instinctive and truthful selves'.[15] So, it seems that Boddington's childhood allowed and encouraged the intuitive in her life and she clearly credits her present practice to a sustained sense of the significance of intuition that stemmed from that time.

To return to intuition as an embodied experience, one-off incidents of intuition are noted on numerous occasions, but a more unusual example of intuition as an incremental, long-term phenomenon can be seen in the evolution of Boddington's practice as Process Director. It is clear that Boddington's methodologies are carefully constructed and that this development occurred over many years. While she notes that the process was led by intuitive practice, it is equally clear that a highly analytical and focused consciousness has also been at work in the reflection and evaluation which followed each project and which then fed into the next. Her methods of working and the structured group processes she evolved have been carefully designed to enable a free flow of ideas. This is a process that implies a high degree of spontaneous, intuitive practice, but it is partnered by the conscious development of working methods and structures. This is an example of the interplay proposed by the title In/Tuition and it appears to be unusual in the incremental, long-term nature of the interaction. Or it may be the result of the engagement with ResCen and the more sustained and structured nature of her reflective processes that this entailed.

The journey from unconscious, intuitive explorations to the carefully constructed vehicle for enabling group creative processes, is explored in the last passages of 'The Weave'. It appears that Boddington, through the act of reflection, and perhaps writing, has recognised that she has unconsciously guided herself away from a tendency to care, to nurture and thereby to control, towards a practice that offers an open, enabling space. But it is a space that often requires no oversight, the 'software' of process direction becoming entirely background, subservient and even invisible in the emerging weave. And so she, as Process Director, disappears. There is almost a sense of loss in her description, but equally a strong sense of personal growth. If this reading is accurate, it appears that a sustained intuitive guiding impulse led her on a journey of incremental evolution to create a vehicle for personal challenge and growth, reminiscent in some ways of the adage that 'we teach what we need to learn'. But this long term intuitive process has been interwoven consistently with the conscious development of skill, craft and methodologies.

So, intuition, interwoven with conscious reflection, is regarded as playing a role in the development of long-term pathways, but it most often is noted in relation to more immediate problems, as when Wallen engages her intuitive perception to see that 'it does not look right on the page'. But what follows is just as critical to her practice as composer: 'it might be tiny but it needs to be nailed down'.[16] In this case it is clear that the intuitive perception of something 'not right on the page' is intertwined with the 'nailing down' of tiny details with the craft, skills and conscious knowledge of the artist. The observation which follows provides further evidence of the need for a practice that has the conscious and unconscious fully engaged: 'anybody can start a piece – anybody. Finishing is the problem – it's about nailing things while keeping the piece alive.'[17]

The key to this interplay is that it attains

significance through its relation to a field of knowledge which encompasses the composer and the audience as an informed witness to the resulting event, the performance. A large part of this field of knowledge is represented by music as a discipline. This knowledge, consciously gained and then internalised by the composer, as well as other intuitive and consciously controlled processes, are activated by the act of composition. Of course there are radical, intuitive leaps which fundamentally alter a discipline, or which challenge disciplinary borders, but these intuitive leaps exist and gain significance in relation to notions of discipline.

This is also exemplified by the ways in which Wallen describes the orchestration of *Our English Heart*, a work created for the bicentenary of Nelson's victory at Trafalgar, and the distanced, dispassionate perspective that she felt was required for this phase of its creation. Wallen was seeking to operate analytically to achieve the kinds of musical transitions which she felt had previously eluded her; looking at works by others, including Wagner, to raise the bar for herself as a composer. These were rational decisions with a particular focus on the canon and craft of music composition, seeking ways to accomplish a seamless development of the work. This approach might have been instigated by her perception of the need for a narrative work of heroic scale about a theme and an event which were distant from her personal experiences. In any case, it is clear that the work of making *Our English Heart* involved both ends of the spectrum that is represented by intuition and tuition, and a significant interplay between the two.

This interplay can also be seen in Boddington's intuitive 'nag' that won't go away; for the recognition and identification of it have come from conscious understanding and analysis of this experience. Furthermore, it is conscious knowledge that results in Boddington watching for the nag,

attending to it when it arises and then waiting for the intuitive solution to arise. It may be self-evident, but it is worth reiterating that it is the conscious skills and craft of the artmaker which make the workings of intuition significant. The spontaneous insight often delivers a new step forward, but it is a step that is grounded in a journey of experience, craft and knowledge, even if this journey itself has benefited from an intuitive guiding force. It is worth emphasising this point because it appears that it is intuitive processes that are privileged most in discussions of creativity. Amy Lowell, cited by Claxton, notes that when the unconscious goes on strike, 'you have to have craft and talent enough to "putty up the holes" that it has left behind'.[18] However, this places intuitive processes as the 'author' of the significant majority of the work, leaving craft and skill to fill in the gaps. This may be the case for some creators in the making of some works, but my observations lead me to believe that, on most occasions, the gaps between the contributions of intuitive processes are rather larger than implied by Lowell and that it is knowledge, craft and skill which are responsible for the majority of artistic work: kernels of intuitive moments woven together with large passages created through craft and skill. This is reminiscent of the adage of Thomas Edison, that 'genius is one per cent inspiration and ninety-nine per cent perspiration'.[19]

There are exceptions of course, and Jeyasingh notes that her first choreographic work was one: 'I made it without any experience. I remember being in Bangalore on holiday, getting a piece of paper and just putting it all down before I forgot.'[20] Of course, Jeyasingh had absorbed a great deal of knowledge over many years, but this is, nonetheless, a striking example of intuitive power. And we should note that it is intuition which often provides a key which is critical to the whole work, but without the conscious realm of knowledge, the intuitive insight is virtually meaningless, particularly when artists must sustain a creative process over decades.

Intuition is arguably the perceived 'hallmark' of artistry in a romanticised social discourse on creativity, and this presents a barrier in examining the intuitive; this discourse avoids Claxton's advice that 'the mystery is big and robust enough to withstand our puny efforts to unpack it a little bit'. To return to the writer Philip Pullman, he offers only a few lines indicating that there are other, perhaps more consciously engaged parts of the creative process, involving knowledge, skill and craft:

> Well, there are things you can do to improve your chances: with every voyage you learn a little more about the bait these fish like; and you're practised enough to wait for a twitch on the line and not snatch at it too soon; and you've discovered that there are some areas empty of fish, and others where they are plentiful.[21]

It may be that this lecture was carefully tailored to present those aspects of the creative endeavour that he felt were missing from education today, and his valorising of the intuitive may be in order to redress a perceived imbalance. This is, therefore, a very selective description of the creative process. He is projecting a romanticised view of artmaking, focusing only on a particular phase of the creative process, but the concern is that this might result in a distortion of our understanding and perversely an undervaluing of the knowledge domain that artmaking and artists represent. The phase he describes is no doubt critically important, and it may be that it exemplifies values absent, or under threat, in schools today; but the ResCen experience suggests that without knowledge and craft, the intuitive inspirations and the results of 'the fears and delights of fishing at night' cannot be channelled into

meaningful form. Of course we must acknowledge the mystery of the intuitive, but this is only one half of the symbiotic relationship which allows the interplay between the intuitive insights and the conscious knowledge of the artist.

We can see the acknowledgement of the craftsperson in the term 'playwright', which does not contain an etymological link to the word 'writing' as in writing an essay, or a play. Rather it is the wright, as in shipwright, and it is the 'wrighting' (an older form of the word 'working') of the material, which provides the linguistic construction of the term. There may be aspects of this 'wrighting' which are intuitive, but the word specifically points to the skills and conscious knowledge related to generating, developing, crafting, moulding, shaping and structuring material all of which are elements contained within a domain of expert practice and knowledge. This domain of conscious knowledge, although privileged in many disciplines, appears to be less attractive when assigned to artists. The image of the artist as a skilled and knowledgeable practitioner does not sit easily with the stereotype of the inspired, intuitive, shaman-like individual, but these two personas represent just another way of expressing the dynamic relationship between intuition and tuition. And it is this dynamic relationship which needs to be acknowledged, an interplay between the duality of conscious knowledge and the intuitive, an oscillation which is not fixed or even predictably patterned, revealing the artist as dynamically engaged as both shaman and expert craftsperson.

Pullman's endeavour to acknowledge mystery, however, represents an important counterbalance to attempts to relegate artmaking practice to a reductive, overly rationalised field of endeavour, devoid of the mystery of intuitive processes and often a misguided attempt to demonstrate aspects of critical theory in art works. Such attempts have accompanied the ingress of arts practice into Higher Education as the previously cited 'underpinning of theory' paradigm demonstrated. Such theorisations may be well intentioned, but it is questionable whether ultimately, they illuminate or obfuscate. Once again it is words and the rush to the rational and rationalisation which lead us to avoid the rich questions that lie at the heart of this project. Susan Foster's charge of the culture of 'mutism' in dance is one example of the tension between the academic and the practitioner although, given Foster's interest in choreography, it might equally be seen as a challenge designed as a liberating device.[22] The ResCen project is also designed to address this issue, but once one decides to speak, the questions of which words to deploy, and in what ways to deploy them, become central.

We need the courage to unpack the mystery a bit, while recognising that there is still a mystery, and that words used to directly represent phenomena such as artmaking practices have limitations. But the traditional positioning of some academic theorists as those who confer meaning on art works has not been helpful. This tendency might stem from the poststructuralist stance which privileges the reader/spectator over the author/creator. But the traditional academic antipathy to expert practice as a domain of knowledge has been woven with the attempt to understand practice by locating it within known paradigms, often by importing theory to account for it. This returns us to the questions of which words to deploy and in what ways to deploy them. One example of such a problem is the discourse that has derived from the transposition of the writerly text to the realm of artistic practice, representing performance as a text 'inscribed' on the body. The acceptance of this term does not seem to have been accompanied by any rigorous thought about the problems of such an assertion; and it offers

no clarification as to who has done the inscription, on what body and in what ways. It is intended as a device for reading the text of the performance, and it is interesting to note the literary, writerly connotations of 'inscribed' and its assumed authority; the privileging of the spectator who is 'reading' the inscription, arguably rendering much, if not all, of the field of performance studies to the realm of 'spectatorship studies' as Melrose has put it.[23] This tendency has not always been beneficial to the project of understanding creative practice, or of developing reflective and reflexive practice. And significantly for this argument, by implication the text inscribed upon the body is a fixed text, for that is the nature of inscription; the text awaits the conferrer of meaning to read and to judge its significance.

This has resonances with the early study of butterflies, caught, killed and displayed upon a pin. This was, no doubt, of great benefit in the categorisation of butterflies, but ultimately produced a limited understanding of the butterfly as living creature. In fact to say that the object presented on a pin *is* a butterfly presents a potentially dangerous barrier to understanding and enquiry, for it *was* a butterfly – it is now the *corpse* of a butterfly, which cannot be seen to exhibit the qualities and nature of 'butterfly' as living creature. No doubt certain attributes are 'inscribed' upon the corpse, but this fixity, while possibly helpful to a particular kind of reader, is a fundamental misrepresentation to those who wish to achieve a more complete understanding.

This syndrome of fixing and inscription has misrepresented performance practice, reifying performance and performer and avoiding the complex issues of agency and both the mystery and knowledge of the artmaker. Consider for example, dancer Mavin Khoo performing Jeyasingh's *[h]Interland*.[24] Khoo's dance practice is multi-faceted; an expertise in Bharata Natyam complemented by

[handwritten annotation:] he explains the title now?!

expertise in ballet and contemporary dance. And Jeyasingh deployed a wide range of these abilities in the making of the work, a process that also drew on Khoo's individual creative responses. Of course there are external points of reference at work. The creation of the work *[h]Interland* and the dance forms which Khoo embodies are clearly positioned in relation to both existing dance forms as well as contemporary choreographic works and practices. And each performance of *[h]Interland*, while unique as a performance, clearly referred to a specific choreographic structure and vocabulary agreed by performer and choreographer, to which the performer aspired. But each performance did have unique variations and Khoo's dance is not singularly 'inscribed' upon his body, nor is it simply 'the body', an abstract, depersonalised, fixed entity, that is the recipient of such an 'inscription', a point that Melrose has also made.[25] And Jeyasingh acknowledges the particular qualities of Khoo when she notes that: 'An experienced dancer, like Mavin Khoo for example, completely understands the disjuncture I've been talking about, he has experienced this first hand'.[26] To understand the performance that Jeyasingh and Khoo have created as 'inscribed upon the body' is to fundamentally misunderstand both *[h]Interland* and art practice in general. For in the abstraction of 'the body' and the fixity of inscription, note the absence of agency, of individual creator, performer or performance. Note also the implied invisibility of the contributions of those who sustained and developed the dance form in the past, and the determination of Khoo and Jeyasingh to propose a new future.

The understanding of creative practice and its engagement with conscious and unconscious processes and the dynamic interplay between the two, stands at odds with the fixity of inscription. The recognition of the mystery of the unconscious arguably justifies 'mutism' as a strategy to avoid misrepresentations through inappropriate language, for use of words is critical and the fixity of some academic perspectives needs to be replaced with a living, dynamic fluidity if we are to understand artmaking. But this chapter has argued that it is also a mistake to privilege the mystery, as the conscious knowledge of the artist is critical to the effectiveness of the intuitive insight. It is a feature of creative work that the artist is ready to deploy the forces of either the conscious or unconscious, a state that Pullman characterises as: 'True calm intense relaxed attention', offering us a truth inside another paradox of the artist's voice. And this is the fluidity of the interplay of In/Tuition – an expert practice and a domain of knowledge which contain the intuitive, and the analytical, as well as a core of interwoven engagements. These forces are not at rest, nor are they fixed; they resist definitive categorisation and point to a way of knowledge that is more complex, subtle and fluid; this is not 'dead certainty' but a living, dynamic, synergistic interplay.

1   ResCen Seminar with Guy Claxton, 'Intuition and the Artist', 8 May 2003 <www.rescen.net>

2   Ibid.

3   Isis Lecture, Oxford Literary Festival Tuesday 1 April 2003. See <www.philip-pullman.com>

4   See 'Interplay' p.29

5   Ibid.

6   Mark Lythgoe 'Perceptions and Realities: The Science of Theatre' London International Festival of Theatre lecture, 14 June 2004, Purcell Room, South Bank Centre, London.

7   See 'Interplay' p.29

8   Ibid. p.29 and p.34

9   R.D. Laing *The Politics of Experience* (London: Penguin Books, 1967), p.35

10 ResCen Seminar with Guy Claxton, 'Intuition and the Artist', 8 May 2003 <www.rescen.net>

11 Guy Claxton *Hare Brain, Tortoise Mind: How Intelligence Increases When You Think Less* (London: Fourth Estate, 1995)

12 ResCen Seminar with Guy Claxton

13 For Boddington see 'The Weave' p 70; for Wallen see 'Interplay' p.29; for Housman see 'Creative Glide Space' p.64

14 'The Weave' p.73

15 'Nelson's Victory' p.51

16 'Interplay' p.36

17 Ibid.

18 Guy Claxton citing Amy Lowell in 'Creative Glide Space' p.68

19 Thomas Edison, *Harper's Monthly*, September 1932

20 See 'Interplay' p.31

21 Isis Lecture, Oxford Literary Festival Tuesday 1 April 2003. See <www.philip-pullman.com>

22 Susan Leigh Foster ed., *Choreographing History* (Indiana: Indiana University Press, 1995)

23 Susan Melrose, Keynote Address at *New Alignments and Emergent Forms: dance-making, theory and knowledge*, School of Arts, Froebel College, Roehampton, University of Surry, 13 December 2003. See also <www.sfmelrose.u-net.com/chasingangels/>

24 *[h]Interland* was first performed by Shobana Jeyasingh Dance Company, on Thursday 24 and Saturday 26 October 2002 in the Borough Hall of Greenwich Dance Agency, London. For further information about the making of [h]Interland see: <http://www.rescen.net>.

25 Susan Melrose, ' "The body" in question: expert performance-making in the university and the problem of specatorship', Seminar Presentation at Middlesex University, April 2006. See <www.cs.mdx.ac.uk/staffpages/satinder/Melroseseminar6April.pdf>

Take a paper and pencil outside and find a place to sit near a tree. Watch the tree and listen carefully to the sound of the wind in the branches and leaves. Find a way to notate the sound using the paper and pencil.

Errollyn Wallen

Errollyn
Wallen

Ghislaine Boddington

Shobana Jeyasingh

Richard Layzell

Rosemary Lee

Graeme Miller

Errollyn Wallen

Interplay
A conversation between

Ghislaine Boddington

Shobana Jeyasingh

Richard Layzell

Rosemary Lee

Graeme Miller

Errollyn Wallen

Errollyn Wallen

Graeme Miller

Rosemary Lee

Richard Layzell

Shobana Jeyasingh

Ghislaine Boddington

Errollyn: Of course we have knowledge – in fact, someone wrote once 'Errollyn knows how music works', and I thought, 'no I don't'. But I know how to assemble things, to create an effect… almost quite coldly.…

Rosemary: Yes, perhaps we know how to move an audience but that sounds quite manipulative, I'm trying to do it on a subtle level. Lately I have begun to question 'knowns' or assumptions I have in my work and I am trying to deconstruct them and look at them afresh.

Graeme: Yes, but of everything we know about making work, how much do we know we know? How aware are we of what we know?

Shobana: Obviously, you have some awareness of your knowledge, but I found, when writing about dance structure for the Cambridge University Press, being specific was very difficult. It involved analysing what you do, determining what is important. Perhaps craftsmanship for choreography is closer to poetry.

Ghislaine: But in group processes, you often go into a kind of semi-flow of fast, reactive things that you're having to pull up – you're tapping into experience, trusting yourself to use different bits of knowledge together. It's a kind of intuitive knowledge

Richard: And to verbalise it can be a complicated process. Sometimes I have to introduce the nature of contemporary arts practice to people like urban planners, before I can even begin to work. I often talk about previous work so that I can talk very concretely about a project. Instead of talking about intuition with people, I would stress the fact that it's hard work. I might tell them that to fix their thinking too quickly means that we will lose opportunities. But of course, it's really an intuitive space.

Rosemary: Intuition is hard to talk about, by making it concrete I feel it's harder to find. The problem is partly semantic. I'm not sure I know what intuition is any more.

Shobana: One of the things I find myself doing is looking at loads of movements and then suddenly fixing on one as the kind of signifier. That means you take it, you put it in different places, at certain intervals in time, finding ways to remind the audience. Sometimes you have a prologue which is just everything in a nutshell, and then you elaborate. Prologues and epilogues, they're not the story, they laminate the story. But I think in dance, enough hasn't been done to codify this. I use the word signifier, but others might call it something else, or just do it without even giving it a name. Ultimately, it's a matter of using your eye, and seeing. I simply see what pleases my eye – I remove everything that doesn't please my eye.

Graeme: Perhaps that's compositional knowledge, to do with feedback, requiring the thing to be before you. I would call it 'channelling'. Stuff that's happening with performers is coming through, you're filtering it, and you're doing this day after day after day. You have a shorthanded control of lots of techniques, running through them, moving from one to another, taking different tags, looking at what happens and comparing it to what's happened previously and what might happen later this afternoon, keeping your eye on the clock, for both today and for the time left for you to finish the thing, guessing where the music's going to come in and how that might alter it. It's channelling, but it's invisible. It's knowledge and experience and craft, but you have such a good grip on it, you don't have to think about it.

Errollyn: Yes, and we all take it for granted, but it's harder as you get older. You can get confused by other things from life – you sort of forget. But my intuition is also a guiding force – so I know very deeply now why I'm in music – autonomy, creating your own world. It's to do with personal power, making decisions, taking responsibility, and creating something. I have to have that domain, but when you're really doing it, churning out work after work, you can't sentimentalise or be airy-fairy. And there's big flashes of knowing – knowing you have to take this path and not that path. But we're surrounded by people who've done very well in life by being calculating. They do things that are nothing to do with the world of feeling. It's more about money or status. I want status, but only after the inner satisfaction that comes from making music. Intuition can be almost a physical thing, I was involved in a big commission once, but every time I met the producer, I'd get this creeping, tingling feeling on the soles of my feet. I ignored it for months. The project wasn't working out, and in the end I had to walk away. I knew I'd be ill. It always relates to the physical with me.

Errollyn Wallen

Graeme Miller

Rosemary Lee

Richard Layzell

Shobana Jeyasingh

Ghislaine Boddington

Errollyn
Wallen

Graeme
Miller

Rosemary
Lee

Richard
Layzell

Shobana
Jeyasingh

Ghislaine
Boddington

Ghislaine: Yes I get the 'gut feeling'. Sometimes it's a sense of joy seeing 'yes that's the right way to go', but more often it's something nagging in me, an inner voice slightly nagging in the back of my head. The pieces haven't quite clicked together in the right way yet. Sometimes it's nagging overnight; then I have to go back to it – not wanting to be disruptive, but having to follow through. You also need knowledge and belief in yourself.

Richard: For me it's also tied in with confidence. So if I'm feeling confident, I will sit and do my preparation for five minutes, then I will walk into a room and know it will be okay. But occasionally I'll walk into a kind of metaphorical space – whether that's with a group of people, or for a meeting, and I just will not know anything. Consciously I'll say to myself 'trust your intuition, trust your previous experience, because this may well be a better event if you do that, instead of over-preparing'. So, the two parameters will be over-preparing and not preparing at all and I think that's an interesting structure. As you've done more, you have more faith in your own creative intuitive relationship. I have more faith that it will be okay.

Rosemary: But, now I don't feel I have those intuitive moments.

Errollyn: If you were working on something…

Rosemary: I probably would. I know it's to do with working and not working. But I still find it difficult to judge, so I'm always standing on the edge thinking: 'Am I in, am I out, where am I? Am I detached enough? Am I too detached? Am I close enough – too close?' I'm always checking myself. Perhaps we are sensing it physically and getting those signals, but we don't notice. I guess what I am doing is realigning myself constantly to try to remain in a place where intuition can flourish. Our tendency of separating mind and body (and to a certain extent intellect and intuition) has an influence on us when we need to get to that state of responsiveness and knowing. I think this also links to the notion of recognition that we've talked about. I remember working on *Passage* and Niki Pollard was there as observer and writer. I didn't know her very well, but it felt right – that's intuition as well. I remember looking at the performers improvising and thinking 'they're in it now, they've got it'. I would look at her to see if she'd seen it, recognised it and she had, always. You could see it in her body... in the way she was looking. Then I would think 'this is right, it's a universal rightness, it's not just my choice'.

Errollyn: It's the same with my early works. I look at them now and I see that they just follow this line from beginning to end – they don't try to be original, but they are original. I sometimes think I need to keep that quality, to keep the rough and the smooth together. Not everything should be perfect.

Shobana: But certain pieces just seem to arrive of their own volition. Everything is just pouring into you, almost like you're being taken over – you find you're making all the right choices. The very first piece of choreography I did in 1988, *The making of maps*, was like that. I made it without any experience. I remember being in Bangalore on holiday, getting a piece of paper and just putting it all down before I forgot. Looking at it now, I see bits that I couldn't do any better – for example one very slow movement; despite the fact that I hadn't made a single piece of dance in my life, all I had done was classical Bharatanatyam dance – just interpreting.

Shobana: I used one device in that first work that I have revisited. It involves the dancers doing the same movements, but standing in a slightly oblique way. It's now one of my stock things, putting one dancer just a minute fraction out of sync spatially with the other. I don't know where that idea came from. But whether just by doing it again and again, you're getting better at doing it, I don't know. Some people might think intuition counters craft; that you should be trying to better your intuition and sometimes craft gets in the way. Don't people see crafted work as over-calculated? Is craft something that's objective? I can

Ghislaine Boddington

Shobana Jeyasingh

Richard Layzell

Rosemary Lee

Graeme Miller

Errollyn Wallen

Errollyn Wallen

Graeme Miller

Rosemary Lee

Richard Layzell

Shobana Jeyasingh

Ghislaine Boddington

pass on craftsmanship to somebody but I can't pass on my intuition? It's personal isn't it?

Graeme: Perhaps it can be shared. Years ago, I was part of Impact Theatre Cooperative and we generated crazy and slightly unhinged material and knocked it into shows, all with an ironic view of our own process. We developed a technique of gratuitous cross-referencing. I still have this in my cheap tricks drawer. It's like hiding something in the palm of your hands and you flick them open, just twice. You see it just twice and it can imbue that thing – that object, movement, character, reference with a kind of surprise. It's not unlike the effect of taking something and repeating it at different angles. It is hard to understand why it works, but when the audience comes across something, the clue of which has been given earlier, they get a sense of discovery. I think Stanley Kubrick said it's very easy to work out what you want to say – the hard bit's how to disguise it. But for me, intuition and craft are very, very close. You quickly learn shorthand strategies – you have a repertoire of things to try, you've tried them before. But you don't necessarily use those things cynically.

Ghislaine: I agree, it is a mixture of intuition and knowledge or craft – and it's about integrity – totally. I don't think you can intuit if you are not being honest. So it's knowing, coupled with trust and self-belief, and yes, it's personal. It's bespoke to each individual, that intuitive decision to follow your nagging, or leave it and move on. But as you grow your intuition drops into place and when intuition's working with your knowledge, you feel a sense of trust. It can be really joyful, just allowing things to come. I've learnt to give myself some fluid thinking time before a working. It used to scare me before a session, that I wouldn't be fixing things practically, but I realised that I was preparing to be open and fluid, and to use intuition. It's sentience isn't it?

It's about awareness and feeling. And putting that together with your knowing, without making a kind of jagged transference between knowing and feeling, you find a kind of fluid blur between those two things.

Shobana: But are we talking about instinct or intuition? They seem so close and I'm just wondering, we might say 'their instincts are very good' perhaps intuition implies something more crafted.

Graeme: At the moment they overlap a lot in my mind, but instinct is what I'd call a gut feeling. Instinctual has the feeling of an animal sniffing the air and knowing what to do. That evokes a feeling of avoidance – to do with danger. The way I would divide them is from above and from below. Instincts tend to come from the gut upwards and intuition comes from the clouds. It's cerebral, more platonic.

Shobana: So one's a body word and one's a more head word – more cerebral. Does intuition govern instinct?

Ghislaine: To me intuition is higher order, not a sub-consciousness – it's always about trying to follow a higher direction of something. It might come up from underneath at points when you suddenly need to draw on it, but it's your own truth of where you need to go.

Richard: I wouldn't talk about intuition to people. I wouldn't mention it. For many people in other disciplines it might cause extreme anxiety. But I know to be too fixed is not right; to be formulaic or prescriptive suits some people – it just doesn't suit me. I'm staking the claim for uncertainty – I want to be uncertain and fluid. I don't want to be the person who knows what we need to do. I want to be the person who doesn't know what we need to do. And that's

Errollyn Wallen

Graeme Miller

Rosemary Lee

Richard Layzell

Shobana Jeyasingh

Ghislaine Boddington

Errollyn Wallen

Graeme Miller

Rosemary Lee

Richard Layzell

Shobana Jeyasingh

Ghislaine Boddington

very frightening for a lot of people I think. But a lot does come down to confidence.

Shobana: And you've got to find credibility with your performers – especially working with actors or dancers. They must be gainfully employed somehow. You've always got five different things for them to do, while you're wondering what you're going to do next.

Graeme: Definitely, without those strategies, things could seriously flounder!

Shobana: But that's not intuition or instinct, it's craft-based. It doesn't help you make the piece, well it could, because it's a persuasive thing isn't it? And it's like the channelling – I can't make any of that visible, especially to younger dancers. Sometimes you need to convince dancers that what seems like fluffing around is going somewhere. There are steps which are useful only because they help you get elsewhere. They desperately want to know when they can start practising, remembering, and polishing. You won't allow them to polish, because you haven't got there – if they polish, you just have to unpick everything. And the craft is in all the tiny details – which don't seem related to each other. On the outside, it just looks like this woman is fumbling desperately to do something. But perhaps craft gives you a kind of control and intuition is about letting go.

Graeme: Perhaps craft is containment and intuition is about spillage, the unexpected. I encourage performers to be intuitive – I create containment. I do a lot of free floating at first, perhaps copying something I've seen…and then we start to harmonise into a kind of movement and language…it's almost like sharing a private joke. Using repetition and very simple structuring techniques, 'fluffing' your way through – if you don't know what to do, move stuff around or get it from the bottom drawer; replace it later, but first fill that space. Then give the performers a directorial role. They'll find ways of padding or mumbling, if you can't find the words, just mumble, clarify it later. It's a set of very idiosyncratic skills. A lot of what I do from the outside works because I found it from the inside. When I sit on the outside I kind of know what's going on. It's to do with compressing time – running things too fast... faster than they can resist. You're removing the resistance and allowing self-authorship. Things create themselves – you just remove the obstacles. Compressing material into rhythms, removing things, finding nodule points, you just hold things in place. What emerges may or may not be interesting, but the material is authentic to that person and connected to that rehearsal process, with a kind of quirky and original quality. That's often what I'm looking for.

Richard: Sometimes I find what I'm looking for when I am not working. There are in-between travel moments when I haven't actually got something particular to do and I think 'well I'll just look at that or look at my whole creative process'. There's no pressure to do it. I'll just run it, see what happens. The imaginative, creative, intuitive is linked to the very pragmatic. It's the spectrum of the two that makes me able to function. If I'm very stressed about some-thing then it is harder to get into the intuitive state, but somehow psychologically I've created this inner space, this inner world. I write a hell of a lot and the pen and the paper are part of it. I might draw if I'm trying to work something out visually, but it's not particularly pictures, it's an overview. I step back, and back, and then I might make new connections that I haven't seen before and no one else is looking at. It's quite strategic and my intuition is often quite practical, it's about linking.

Ghislaine: For me, that linking is part of the nagging process of intuition. Until the right link appears, whether it's strategic or physical – until it jumps out, it's still nagging you.

Richard: That nagging goes on every waking moment, and in the night – it's just around in the ether...

Errollyn: Right now I'm sort of frighteningly detached when I work – it's the only way I can survive. Once I'd be in a heightened state – not now. I need the detachment and I'm more anxious to get things right. I am a bit emotional now because I've just finished a big piece, *Our English Heart*, based on Nelson's battle at Trafalgar. It took nine months and I worked in a new way, not getting stressed, doing regular hours, never through the night. Sometimes I was really engaged, but it was like using a zoom lens, focusing in and pulling back. For three months it's been orchestration – and no emotion – all done very dispassionately.

Errollyn　Graeme　Rosemary　Richard　Shobana　Ghislaine

Errollyn Wallen **Graeme Miller** **Rosemary Lee** **Richard Layzell** **Shobana Jeyasingh** **Ghislaine Boddington**

Rosemary: Maybe you're emotional now from the strain of being dispassionate, but you needed to stand back for the detailed tweaking.

Errollyn: Well perhaps it is that. And yet, the things that make life worth living are those moments of heightened being. Something taking me out of myself and seeing things in a totally other way – like elation, elevated out of yourself; or at the end when there is a catalytic moment. After holding a lot of decisions in abeyance, then gradually ticking them off, sometimes I'll look at a score and think 'something's not right – something's not right on that page'. I don't know what it is. It might be tiny, but it needs to be nailed down. You know anybody can start a piece – anybody. Finishing is the problem – it's about nailing things while keeping the piece alive.

Graeme: A very good question: how can you know when something's finished? It's a good example of intuitive knowing.

Shobana: I find now I often know the ending quite early on.

Graeme: Yes, but finishing isn't necessarily knowing the ending. You might know the beginning and the end – knowing when there's no more to do must be intuitive.

Rosemary: It's the nailing things down I find difficult now. There are times when it flows, but I know there's a dead point in the middle of the practice, (the middle hurdles in a race are the most difficult apparently). I love all the experiential improvisation at the beginning, but I've got worse and worse at setting things, preferring to remain in a state of flux where it is much more about experience and feeling. I make this palette of ideas… my notebook has entries like 'antlers in wood' or 'woman with monocle'… filmic or poetic images and I've got to put them in some sort of order. Sometimes I don't know what's right, so I'll write the material we have found and named on pieces of paper and toss them on the floor face down. I'll put my hands over them, trying to feel whether there's any heat coming from any of them to give me an order or a sign of how to proceed. Then I'll think, 'how absurd, there's no heat, this is ridiculous'. I'll be arguing with myself the whole time – is that an intuitive process? I'll go with it, or totally against it, but it's a framework that helps me make conscious what I know already but haven't found a way of manifesting. Of course I learned this strategy – the choreographer Merce Cunningham uses chance a great deal to structure work. It helps me make more concrete decisions if I am resisting them. Perhaps it's a way of consciously bringing intuition into this part of my structuring process that feels less organic.

Richard: Sometimes the physical act of constructing allows the intuitive creative process – physically making and intuition for me are very, very interwoven. I couldn't say that they're completely separate.

Errollyn: Yes, but sometimes my intuition is a deep knowing and almost ruthless, guiding me towards what I need, and sometimes it's new skills for my toolbox.

Rosemary: Perhaps that's just a decision – not intuition. Is intuition different?

Errollyn: It's a decision based on a mass of information that isn't just factual. It's based on what you need, emotionally, and intellectually. You choose a particular path intuitively, to get the tools you need.

Richard: Gaining new tools, new knowledge is powerful for me. I want to do everything. If I haven't done something before, I'm going to learn how to do it. It's about welcoming dialogues with people, welcoming other people's skills, wanting to learn from that. I don't need all this ownership – I don't need it. Maybe it comes from facilitating, which is one skill that has been very important to me. I not only had an affinity with it, but I had a sort of passion for it, and people responded to that. I use that experience when I'm faced with a situation like I was for my installation at the London School of Hygiene and Tropical Medicine. I had to work with the Construction Manager – not somebody who I would normally have much to do with – but he managed this very large building site and project and he was very experienced. He wasn't an architect; he wasn't a so-called creative. But in the process of developing this installation he was one of the really key people who helped me – who found things that I didn't know were available, and sourced things. So to be open to that relationship was like new knowledge. And then there were the lighting designers. Not designers for theatre settings, or installations, but for public buildings. We sort of ended up collaborating on the whole lighting side of it. I'd not worked with lighting in this way ever before and I welcome that collaborative kind of dialogue. It's a skill that I never thought that I would develop – no one trained me to do it, but it's become central in my practice.

Ghislaine: It's the same for me, and this is why collaboration and interauthorship are so

Errollyn Wallen

Graeme Miller

Rosemary Lee

Richard Layzell

Shobana Jeyasingh

Ghislaine Boddington

Ghislaine Boddington

Shobana Jeyasingh

Richard Layzell

Rosemary Lee

Graeme Miller

Errollyn Wallen

important. It is a kind of knowledge transference through collaboration. Not being told the information and having to remember it, but knowledge transference that's moving backwards and forwards between you. I think most of the learning I've done, the best and deepest learning, has happened in this peer-to-peer way and I don't have to learn it again or revise it; it's just there. When you've got this conceptual interaction, as well the baseline knowledge, I think that's when it becomes deeper. The best results come through working with people who are also using intuition fluently within their process of making. When you're working with someone who's much more procedural in their approach, then it can be difficult. And I don't mean that negatively at all, it's just different processes of working. But as we said earlier, so much is invisible that people can easily think 'well, she's out to lunch' because you're talking about things that you're seeing intuitively.

Graeme: What about knowledge that comes from having seen creative work? In a Tarkovsky film, images just sort of linger for too long, then a bit beyond too long. And in the bit beyond too long, something else happens and that thing starts to be present, to accrue narrative as you're projecting onto it and into it. I learned that and I've used it in my work, the 'too long' factor. I know that it's like a trick, but you mustn't use it like a trick.

Shobana: That comes from your own experience of time. I find it very difficult to stay with anything for very long. I'm very, very impatient. I'm patient with other people's work. I could sit and watch a film, with sustained images, or just look at a river. Aspects of my childhood were like that, completely entrenched in time. But my work is always full of entrances and exits. I get very impatient with the body if it's not constantly being thrown around. Perhaps this comes from what you want to express about yourself? And that comes back to intuition doesn't it? You're intuiting what that is. I'm sure if I were a film director, I'd be cutting every three seconds.

Graeme: *You're a fidget in a timeless world!* But, in composition, my stock items are repetition and cross-reference. I'm playing a game of memorable things, building these phrases, counter-pointing, anchoring or reflecting one with another. A knowledge base, even if accessed intuitively, contains compositional tools, like counterpoint – perhaps even counterpoint of place. Or is intuition just compressed knowledge? If you're learning to hit a tennis ball across a net with a racket, at first you may need to break that down into a whole series of moves; how your thumb lies upon the handle, how to look at the ball, how to hit. Eventually you just intuitively know.

Rosemary: Yes, but isn't intuition also about solutions – or discoveries? When we were finishing *Infanta*, a short dance film for BBC2, I just knew the ending wasn't right. I hadn't solved it, or found completion. I hadn't set this girl free. Nobody else noticed, but I knew she had to be set free or she'd be trapped still. A lot of my work's about being trapped, but there's always got to be the possibility of escape. I felt physically sick, and I found myself running down the corridor into the loo to enclose myself, virtually banging my head on the wall thinking 'there's got to be a way to do this, I know there is, I'm not seeing it'. In the last possible moment, I found it and we altered the last frames of the film.

Errollyn: When I met the astronaut Steve MacLean in Houston, he said there's meant to be nothing in space, but if you know what to look for, you will see things. Perhaps we have this sense of what might be out there and learn how to find it. So, you knew the solution was there. If you're trained, you can see it. Perhaps the more you work, the more you can call up your intuition? Or perhaps you need that stress to force it out of you.

Rosemary: Possibly… sometimes you do need that sort of squeeze, but it's about

I think I'm on Shobana's within

Errollyn Wallen

Graeme Miller

Rosemary Lee

Richard Layzell

Shobana Jeyasingh

Ghislaine Boddington

Errollyn
Wallen

Graeme
Miller

Rosemary
Lee

Richard
Layzell

Shobana
Jeyasingh

Ghislaine
Boddington

allowing as well. You're trying to find a state where you allow yourself to see the answer. And certainly when I teach, it's trying to get them to understand the state they need to be in to acquire knowledge. They've got to understand how to open the door.

Ghislaine: But with digital technology many people don't know how to find the door. We took over 280 people through a digital installation and of course, more than two thirds of them had never been in an interactive installation before. We were literally having to guide people to look in the right direction. And it is often true in this work that people go in with a lack of knowledge of how to react. So people creep around the edges, because they're not sure if they're meant to enter the space. They wonder if they should wave their hands or something. Some people rely on their knowledge of old technology and they ask 'where are the buttons?' Their intuition is blocked because they feel that their knowledge is so limited. Of course some people are braver or more sophisticated – it's usually the children who are happy to enter the space, start moving, see what happens and then play with it.

Rosemary: Sometimes I worry that I am becoming too conscious, or self-conscious, and then losing my intuition. I have been really worried about that for the last year, because I do feel it isn't there, and that's partly because I am just not practising it. When I am not working on a piece, I'm not in a studio, I'm not alone and I am not in contexts that help the intuitive state. It's just recently that it's got better because I've had two weeks where I sat in an empty space and waited. Nothing obvious came at first, and that worried me, but I feel fine about it now. It brought me back to a more... poetic existence if you like, I felt I'd come home. I now trust that even if I am not thinking about the piece, I am taking my mind away in order to go back with fresh eyes.

Errollyn: Well the things that make life worth living are those moments of heightened being. Something taking me out of myself and seeing things in a totally other way – like elation, elevated out of yourself.

Shobana: But sometimes you realise you're not in an idealistic or idealised world – it's a slightly more shabby world: the art market. The only important thing in the art market is a product that people want to buy. In some ways, we're all required to be shrewd wheeler-dealers.

Graeme: Well some of us might be shrewder than others, but we're all wheeler-dealers.

Shobana: And some people don't like to admit it. I was in Japan recently on a NESTA fellowship and met a beautiful dancer who has a major reputation in Japan and internationally – and he's a farmer. To meet him you've got to go to some remote part of Japan where he lives on a farm and plants rice. He describes himself as a farmer who dances. And the first thing he said to me is 'I'm not really in the arts market' and I could see what he meant, because he just decided he does not want to sell art, he just wants to be a dancer, which is something very different. But if you engage with the arts market, making a living through art in a capitalist or post-capitalist world, well, are we honestly using the kind of vocabulary in our arts discourse which recognises this fact, or is it still a discourse which has come out of modernist or nineteenth-century ideas? A poet like Shelley could talk about instinct because he wasn't selling his art, he wasn't Zadie Smith. I sometimes wonder whether we can use words like 'instinct'.

Errollyn Wallen   Graeme Miller   Rosemary Lee   Richard Layzell   Shobana Jeyasingh   Ghislaine Boddington

Errollyn Wallen | Graeme Miller | Rosemary Lee | Richard Layzell | Shobana Jeyasingh | Ghislaine Boddington

Graeme: People use instinct in business. And what about the idea of survival? Shobana, you mentioned once the idea of throwing yourself far away from home and then having to find your way back to your home port. Almost all of the processes you go through, intuitive or instinctive, are about survival and they're happening faster than you can think in a logical way. It's like driving – we don't think 'I'm going to move my hand a little bit to the left and change down into second gear'. We make instinctive decisions because it's all happening unbelievably fast. And you can't sit and have meetings with yourself. But perhaps you can get instinctually stuck, like the bad habits with driving – survival instinct decisions may result in you resorting to your own clichés?

Errollyn: But then you apply your knowledge and craft. I felt that rut and so I approached part of my last work as if I was doing an exercise. I looked at work by other composers, a lot of Wagner actually, and applied technical solutions. I feel I made a step forward in understanding how somebody else works and also developed my own work. It wasn't easy and in the end someone said 'nobody can play those string parts, it's a struggle to get through them'. But I thought 'even the act of struggling is important and makes it exciting'.

Ghislaine
Boddington

Shobana
Jeyasingh

Richard
Layzell

Rosemary
Lee

Graeme
Miller

Errollyn
Wallen

Errollyn
Wallen

Nelson's Victory

Errollyn Wallen

Errollyn
Wallen

I am looking for something. Like a private detective or unwisely curious explorer, I have the faintest scent, a curling wisp on the air, a trill caught in the breeze as I bend to tie up a shoelace. I am looking for something I have neither seen nor smelled before. But how, in the myriad of possibilities of sound and combinations of sound, will I know when I have found it? And why am I looking for it in the first place? In these early stages of a work, when all I know is the timescale and date of the first performance, it is as if I am inching my way down a long, misty road. Trees hang their frowsy heads in the wind, reaching out rheumy, breaking fingers to each other in order to keep safe. Tired and alone I am caught up in the limits of my body. Half blind I navigate the unknown. Eventually, after I have become accustomed to the overwhelming solitude and have surrendered hope of finding anything at all, I begin to see patterns dancing in sparkles right ahead of me on the path. My heart leaps. I squint and they are gone. I rub my eyes. What can I do to bring them back? Did they go away or is it just that I can't see them anymore? Maybe I never saw them in the first place.

Intuition is defined as 'the power of the mind by which it immediately perceives the truth of things without reasoning or analysis: a truth so perceived, immediate knowledge in contrast with mediate'. Intuition is a 'knowingness'. Knowing when something is right or wrong, knowing when a piece of work is finished or needs revising. Knowing when the joins don't join. Intuition is an awareness of patterns, above and below the surface, seen and unseen, heard and unheard. For me, the act of intuiting can involve doing nothing – just listening, waiting (like Lara and her alethiometer in Philip Pullman's *His Dark Materials Trilogy*) and just being alive to the

always starting w/ a definition

knowingness

moment. It is the mental leap that takes us out of ourselves, allowing us to connect to atavistic principles and to a collective unconscious. When a work is completed, however, amnesia sets in and I forget the details of the intuitive process.

I often dive into composing a piece of music without knowing where I am going structurally. I believe and trust in my intuition and the fact that I do *know* at a deep and non-linguistic level exactly what it is that I want to achieve. I have learned that starting is what is important and that it is how one manipulates the material that defines the process. It doesn't lessen the fear that is concomitant with voyaging out into new terrain, but the knowledge that intuition will be my compass and companion in the wild maze of creation is a source of reassurance.

When I was a young girl I remember reading a biography of a composer whom I admired. I came across a passage in which the biographer described one of the composer's abilities as being able to see the wood for the trees. This made a significant impact on my own thinking and approach to music-making and I have realised that I am able to see the wood best by using intuitive perception. I tried to activate this perception when composing my most recent large-scale work, *Our English Heart*. This is a useful work to discuss and analyse here in relation to intuition because it demonstrates intuition in operation at various levels. Looking back at this work I can see the influence of intuition on historical research, social perception and interpretation, in the writing of words, music, and in musical structuring. This reveals to me the interplay between intuition and learned craft – tuition.

Our English Heart is scored for orchestra, men's chorus and soprano and lasts approximately thirty-five minutes. It was co-commissioned by George and Janette Wilkins and the BBC to commemorate the 200th anniversary of the battle of Trafalgar and the death of Admiral Lord Nelson.

It was a work which required a level of

Errollyn Wallen

Errollyn Wallen

historical research before I started to write a note. I knew very little about Nelson and his naval or amorous adventures, but my fascination with the sea has been a continuing source of inspiration for me. This was a different sort of commission to most of my others in that it was a 'public' piece, marking a major historical event, as opposed to a work based around a set of preoccupations of my own choosing. My work was to be broadcast live from Portsmouth Cathedral on BBC Radio 3 in a concert commemorating Trafalgar Day. Because of the historical focus and the narrative aspect of the work, I initially considered working with a writer who would provide me with a text, but in the end I wrote and compiled the text myself as well as composing the music. I wanted to let the music drive the text and be free to react quickly and instinctively to the material as it grew and changed. I have come increasingly to the realisation that the raw material of my compositions very often gives rise to the structure of a work, enabling it to grow organically. This organic growth ensures that the macro is related to the micro and this supports my desire to create a finished entity which is authentic. *Our English Heart* presented new challenges for me, and in these relatively straitened circumstances when I was not completely free to follow my own predilections as regards subject matter, how would intuition play a part in my process?

Every new work involves decisions about how one is going to use that particular opportunity and then deciding how long that piece will take to write. Before I began *Our English Heart* I knew that I wanted to try something new – to give myself a sea of time, time I could luxuriate in, time to do the very best I could, time to refine. I decided to stop many other activities, including performing, so that I could place all my focus on creating this new work. As a freelance composer this was a hard decision, but I knew both rationally and intuitively, that unless I seized with both hands this rare opportunity to write for huge forces, I would miss out on a new journey of discovery. I wanted to give myself time to really 'finish' this work, to allow time for the fine-tuning of details.

I feel things before I understand them.

I walk towards a sound before I can hear it. I can *know* what a work is before I find the notes. So it was with *Our English Heart*. Before starting, I had a strong sense of the atmosphere of the work without knowing anything of the structure or the details of its harmonic and melodic language. I imagined the sea swirling through the orchestra, I heard in my head the texture of voices pitted against that sound. There was a notion about a variety of new techniques that I would like to employ, which had been carried over from previous works – it is as if each work I compose seems to open up new questions and technical possibilities for the work to follow. All this as well as the usual, fervent wish to make this my best work so far. But how would I construct the sea in musical notes? What words would I put into the mouths of the men at sea and the woman left at home? The act of composing, whilst being an act of faith, determination and imagination also involves active learning. One learns by doing and many of the problems to be solved are set by oneself and are thus unique to that particular musical situation. So, while intuition enables the possibility to 'know', one has to actively discover the 'making' skills required to bring forth the known. One example of this, in *Our English Heart*, was in the battle scene (bars 382–500). I had to find a way of conveying the tension before battle commenced and the bloody chaos and noise of the battle itself, culminating in the fatal gunshot which was to kill Nelson. It took a while to build patterns which would be perceived as random, reinforced by the percussion, signifying cannon and gunshots. The use of ostinato, counterpoint and vivid, ever-changing orchestral colours were

Errollyn Wallen

Errollyn Wallen

all techniques used but the details were built up instinctively, note by note.

When I work, it is as if I am operating in at least two dimensions. My head is in the stars and my feet are wedged firmly in mud. I navigate between these two worlds by listening to the voice of magic, spurring me on to think and bring forth the impossible; and then there is the 'sensible' voice of distrust, constantly urging me to think of practicalities. Most major leaps in the learning curve happen through hearing what you have written. For me, it is important to try new things in every piece and then to listen carefully in rehearsal, so that I can fully gauge whether or not my calculations have worked. Throughout my life I am conscious of building an ever-growing catalogue or database of sounds. This happens through taking risks which for me come from 'composing with a hunch' and lead to the formulation of new ideas and new sound worlds.

In creating a new work one is often working backwards – from an imaginary sound world where everything is perfect, sparkling and bright, a world of pure energy – through to its actualisation which, in the case of *Our English Heart*, meant months of drudgery, uncertainty and painfully slow progress in the act of refining and detailing. But in those months there was also the opportunity to explore other composers' music to see how they had solved particular problems. There were two works close to hand whilst I was composing *Our English Heart* – Wagner's overture 'The Ride of the Valkyries' and Britten's opera *Billy Budd*. I knew that strong melodies and evocative textures in the foreground and background would play an important part in my new work. In studying Wagner, I admired the way that the texture of the accompaniment, the woodwind trills and string figuration, gives this piece its

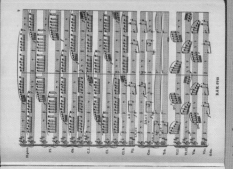

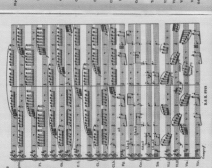

above: Score sample from Richard Wagner 'The Ride of the Valkyries'

below: Score sample from Benjamin Britten *Billy Budd* © Copyright 1951 by Hawkes & Son (London) Ltd. Reproduced by kind permission of Boosey & Hawkes Music Publishers Ltd.

thrilling excitement – even though it is the famous tune in the brass that we remember.

In *Billy Budd* I wanted to look at Britten's handling of male voices with an orchestra, as those were my forces too. I was also very much interested in his particular use of percussion in evoking both the sea and naval life on a ship in 1805 – the same year as the Battle of Trafalgar.

What makes a composer turn one way and not another? What led me to alight on certain scenes to set and not others? I believe in using curiosity, chance and everyday synchronicities as my guide in learning. Most things we need to learn are at our fingertips, particularly with the resource of the internet. A lot of research for *Our English Heart* was carried out on the web, right down to investigating what music was played on Nelson's ship, HMS Victory, before the battle of Trafalgar commenced. But it was the actual, not the virtual which gave me the strongest drive to write my work: the visit to the Victory with my commissioners, George and Janette Wilkins, who also lent me rare books containing Nelson's letters to Emma Hamilton; and the trip to meet Clive Richards who owns the largest private collection of Nelson memorabilia. There I held the last letter from Emma Hamilton to Lord Nelson and looked at everything from signal books written and drawn by the sailors themselves, to Nelson's silverware. These were the significant, formative experiences which led me to include and highlight specific historical moments. I wanted to find a way of connecting these events and figures from history to those people living today who remember and revere them.

What makes writing and speaking about intuition difficult is that it is essentially non-linguistic. We use words like 'hunch', 'gut feeling' and even 'gift' to describe a sensation of knowl-edge from deep within ourselves. I believe that we are all born with it in abundant supply but we are encouraged to shut it off as we get older, until we gradually lose touch with our younger, more instinctive and truthful selves. As an adult I find

Connect to Lynn Stalmaster's quote [handwritten annotation]

Errollyn Wallen

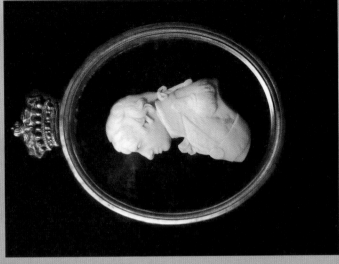

Wax portrait of Nelson, taken from life by Miss Catherine Andras and exhibited at the Royal Society of Arts in 1801. The portrait was inherited by Emma Hamilton, who said that it was the most striking likeness taken of him. Emma lent the wax to Mathew Boulton, who copied it for the Trafalgar Medal, which was presented to all the sailors who fought at Trafalgar.

Errollyn Wallen

that the best work I do is first thing in the morning, when the last remaining blankets of sleep are still on me. That is when I make the sharpest decisions and feel most fully 'in the zone' of creativity.

Finding my way as an artist has meant that I work to my own dictates and I have chosen a life where I can have the maximum freedom to explore and to learn. And each work requires different working methods. When I was composing *Our English Heart*, it felt right that I should work for a short period first thing in the morning, immediately after breakfast, before I got dressed or embarked on daily rituals, interfacing with the world. I found that in this alert, yet relaxed state, many compositional problems were solved and many new pathways opened up; and I could carry on thinking about them throughout the day.

I employed this method in refining the end section of *Our English Heart*, which took a long time to get right. It is only twelve bars long, but I endlessly played around with the words and notes of the soprano's last entrance and with the heterephonic burbling figurations in the orchestra, which were designed to evoke a different sea, a twenty-first century sea. The work had to feel it was coming to a close, but a closure of hope and tranquillity. The harmony is relatively static but the details were what would make it work. I used the percussion very differently here and introduced gentle, ringing sounds. As in the battle scene, I contrived to make everything sound spontaneous – guided by instinct for the atmosphere required and advised by the technique of my training. I grew grateful for these mornings of short bursts of activity when I was at my most intuitive and alert.

I believe that it is my responsibility as an artist to constantly evaluate and adapt my working methods. One has to be aware of one's

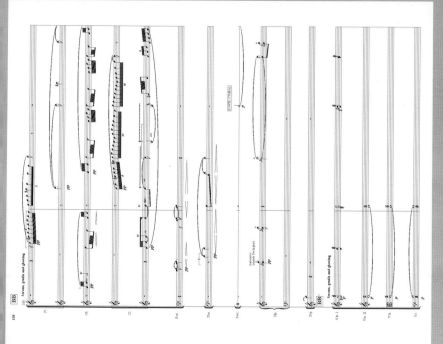

temperament and I find that I sometimes have to trick myself in order to get the best from myself. And this is where intuition plays an important part. There are times when my concentration span is short and there are other times when I can work steadily and undistracted for long hours. Taking the advice of a friend, I used a stop-watch when composing *Our English Heart* and decided on a minimum number of hours I would work each day in order to meet the deadline. I could thus accommodate my short bursts of compositional activity knowing that I would get the required amount of time in and not be caught out by a last-minute scramble. For all the wonderful ideas I might have, for all the thinking and dreaming I might do, my thoughts would only be realised through sitting down and putting the notes onto the page. What is written gets heard, what is not notated doesn't get played. It is simply not heard. The hard fact of notes on a page is what remains of the storm of ideas. That is not to deny that thinking and pondering occurs all the time, but reaffirms that using Western notation to write music which will be performed by others, takes time and foresight. Deciding how one is going to actualise the formless inspiration involves the day-to-day 'housework' – the placing of one note after another. I roughly estimate that in *Our English Heart* there are over a hundred thousand notes, all of which need to be placed in the right order. At the end of a work I sometimes calculate how long it would take me to simply copy that work in an automatic fashion, without the sweat of making it up. In the case of *Our English Heart* it could take up to a couple of months. For labour on that scale I believe one has to keep checking with oneself to ensure that the ideas and fundamental conception are worth the time.

I have chosen a life of searching: searching for questions, answers and an artistic habitat where I can be myself and create freely, joyfully; looking for a place where I can continue to grow. It has been my own intuitive choices as to what I need that has made that life possible. We

Errollyn Wallen

Errollyn Wallen

are all, to varying degrees, caged beings, whether we make those cages ourselves or whether we are locked into them involuntarily or without noticing. We can all find ourselves without control. Music offers freedom and control.

Writing music is thinking in time and often, thinking in public. When I was composing *Our English Heart* I confronted the reality of this and was able to grow comfortable with its awesomeness because, in this instance, the story of Lord Nelson, Lady Hamilton and the Battle of Trafalgar is so well known. Before I wrote a note, the story was familiar to many, which meant I didn't have the burden of explaining my characters and situation but could concentrate on casting my own light on history. The work is shaped in a single movement which falls into several sections. As I explained, this form grew through instinct and I responded to the pictures in my head rather like a film maker. Like film, music is experienced by the listener in linear time and I decided to approach the structure of my new work as if I were making a film: the work moves from scene to scene, and from one emotional state to another. I wanted to depict the drama in its actual, imagined moment and to convey the atmosphere and sensation of life at sea and the feeling of passion and personal sacrifice.

I started composing first at the piano.

The piano is my instrument and it is the best instrument for working out harmonies. I start by improvising, playing around with the notes and possibilities I find beneath my fingertips. The work starts with a short orchestral introduction, evoking the majesty and nobility of the sea and of victory. As in Wagner's 'The Ride of the Valkyries', I use the brass for the main theme and employ the woodwind and strings for flourishes and swooping figuration. The next section (from bar 28) sees the

[handwritten marginal note: It does sound like that. Almost like a musical.]

entrance of the male voices accompanied by the cellos and basses. I heard these voices as those of Nelson's sailors. They sing of the terror and uncertainty of being at sea, knowing that they must do their duty.

The sea craves us,
The waves taunt us,
The wind calls for us.
Do your duty, sailors,
hoist the pennant.
Heave, heave-ho,
Hold to the sea.

The work is about an episode in British history when to be a hero was to be a man who carried word through to deed in epic fashion and in the unquestioning service of his country. But I needed to show both the public and private moments – the tough and the tender. Horatio Nelson, Emma Hamilton and Nelson's sailors on the Victory are at the centre of the piece and the research I did enabled me to connect with these historical (and near mythical) characters as real, living human beings.

I dived headlong into *Our English Heart* and let my intuitive sense guide me in the shaping of the work. As there are innumerable composers so there are myriad ways of working and I am of the opinion that each composer starts on the physical work of a piece (by that I mean physically putting the dots on the page) at varying points along the way to completion. For some, the conscious working out of possible pathways is important and these people make sketches. For others all the gestation is done, sometimes unconsciously, in their heads so that when they sit down, as in the case of Mozart, it is simply a matter of getting the notes on the page quickly enough. Personally, I regard each new work as an adventure and try to come to each piece as if I am an alien from outer space and am discovering music for the first time. I take nothing for granted, whether it is a scale or a chord, an interval or a

Errollyn Wallen

**Errollyn
Wallen**

phrase, an instrument or a hemidemisemiquaver, a style or a genre. I see my job as making sure that each note within my piece has earned its place and is there for an irrefutable reason. The experience of writing that work should bring me greater knowledge, illumination and understanding. I am aware of a sense of having worked a great deal out beforehand, but in a wholly non-verbal manner – in fact, in a manner which bypasses any language. It is as if I have worked through and rejected various sets of materials which will impact on the overall essence of a piece before I sit down at my piano; many sketches have been made internally and unconsciously. So when I start the physical realisation of a work, or when I think I start, I have actually already started. The strength of my sureness in making crucial decisions leads me to believe that this is so. For example, at the moment I am thinking about an opera which will be performed in a little over a year's time. Running through my mind, unbidden, are glimpses of the sound world. The metallic cry of electric guitars seemed incongruous at first but my mind is connecting the strands of ideas in the story so that the orchestration itself connects with every detail of the emotional logic of the opera. It is as if I start with the sound and work backwards for its reasoning during the actual sitting down at my desk. Intuition is the snapshot – the flash of insight and the craft is in the slow unpacking of that flash.

When I was a fledgling composer I placed greater value on inspiration and ideas. It was working on *Our English Heart* that confirmed a change of approach. I was able to witness the role of intuition even in the drudgery of the work. I would be working on a passage and would get a nagging feeling. I learned to trust that this physical discomfort was always due to the fact that there was a small detail in an earlier part of the piece that just wasn't right. It could be one note within a flourish of a myriad of notes that might barely be perceived amidst the whole orchestra, but until it was 'fixed' I couldn't concentrate on the current passage. As I continue to work as a composer I grow more to trust my physical reaction to sound and to my working process. Physical motion is a crucial part of a day's work. It solves problems. It is no accident that walking is so important to composers, mathematicians, philosophers, writers. I find that washing up is also very good for switching down the gears of conscious thinking and allowing intuitive thought free rein. Just recently, while stopped at a red light in my car, I was caught by the rhythms of the vibrations of the engine. I listened, captivated and I am sure that one day those ever-changing patterns will find their way into a piece. The wonder of sound is all around us.

I have learned to trust that I will compose my best works by co-operating with my own idiosyncratic process. I believe that this understanding of the creative process can be a tool for the art of living.

Intuition, perception and craft are the concomitant ingredients for inspiration and spontaneity. Intuition is about seeing patterns that are already there and about creating new ones, perception is about understanding how to apply them and craft is the development of technique in order to communicate. All three provide the space and satisfactory environment for inspiration to flourish. The greatest enemy of intuition is fear. We don't always want to see or hear what is in front of us. We don't always trust the light of our calling. But there is endless treasure to be found if we can but dare to walk the path that opens up for each of us individually, alone.

Errollyn Wallen

Creative Glide Space

Guy Claxton

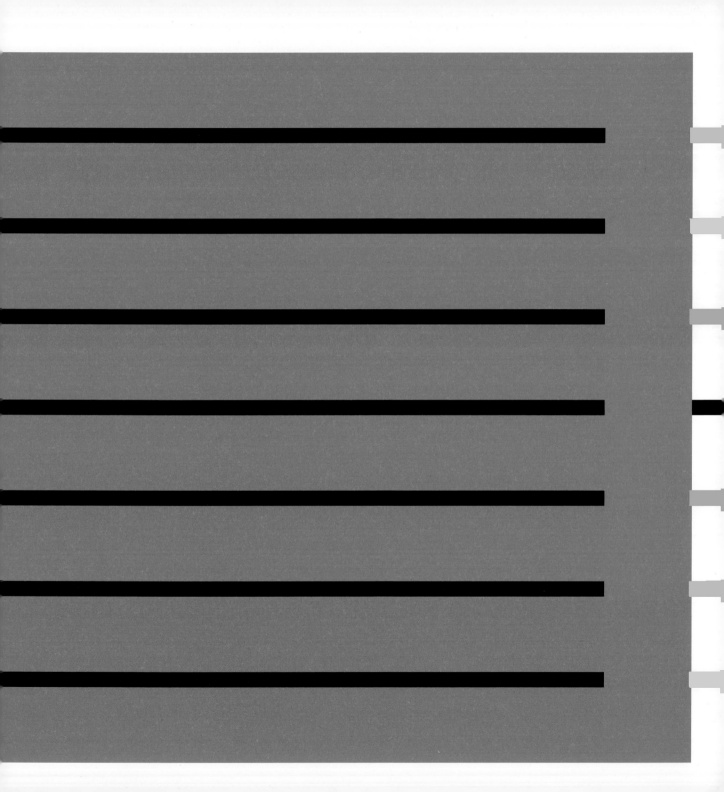

*'Things should be made as simple as possible
– but not more so.'*
Albert Einstein

Nobel science laureate Richard Feynman once remarked that 'it does no harm to the mystery to understand a little about it'. He was talking about the universe, and about how reassuringly inadequate our theories are in the face of its enormous complexity. Romantic sensibilities need not worry: the wonder is not impugned by a few human thoughts. And so it must be with creativity. There are a few creative people who fear that thinking about their creative process will make it fall apart. Happily this book demonstrates that an interest in understanding creativity can live happily alongside a variety of highly creative and successful careers.

In this essay, I want to wander between generalities and specifics: to look at the wonderful variety of questions and practices that live under the umbrella of creativity, as well as looking for some commonalities. For example, creativity is different in different domains. To be creative as a mathematician is not the same thing as to be a creative product designer or choreographer. Within a domain, equally creative individuals work in very different ways. And even within one person, there are many facets and phases to the creative process that require them to change gear, and adopt different mind-sets. My question is: can we bring any order to this variety, without becoming so abstract that our theories offer no purchase on creation in real life? Can the stories of the ResCen artists be woven together into a story about creativity that is somewhat more differentiated than the usual theoretical ones, whilst also being generalisable enough to offer a useful framework for others? And does this story tell us anything about how other people might be helped to cultivate their own 'creative mentality'?

Right grain thinking

One of the problems with talking about creativity is getting the grain right. To be useful, we need to be able to talk at a level that is neither too fine nor too coarse. Too fine, and we can get bogged down in the details of individual habits and experiences that may be fascinating as biography, but which are too idiosyncratic to help other people, either pragmatically or conceptually. Schiller claimed he could only write well on a desk full of rotting apples – but the smell of cider almost certainly won't do it for you. Too coarse a grain, on the other hand, and all kinds of interesting and helpful things can slip through the net.

The very word 'creativity' can be unhelpful, too coarse-grained, if it suggests that there is a single (albeit mysterious) mental faculty or substance that underlies creative performance (and which different people might have been given different 'amounts' of, rather like the discredited notion of 'intelligence'). Such presuppositions can lead us simply to look out for a few special individuals who have 'got it', and to ignore the extent to which 'creativity' might be composed of a collection of 'habits of mind' that everyone could be capable of developing. Just as a fitness trainer needs to be able to decompose the concept of fitness into its ingredients – stamina, flexibility, strength, body-mass index and so on – in order to think about how to enhance it, so we need to treat creativity not as a rare and exotic mental ability that stands apart from normal cognition, but as a particular orchestration of our mental capabilities.

It is also much more productive, as well as accurate, to take 'creativity' as pointing to a nest of complementary questions that require different kinds of answers, and which therefore cannot be collapsed into a single 'theory of creativity'. 'How does the mind produce fresh ideas?' is not the same kind of question as 'How are products and performances publicly judged to be "creative"?' Answers to the first – the question which I am going to focus on in this chapter – requires the psychological languages of cognition and emotion, rationality and intuition, conscious and unconscious. Tackling the second requires a sociological vocabulary of gate-keepers and opinion-formers, influence and power. Other questions include 'Do people *differ* in their creative potential?', 'Can "creativity" be *measured*?', 'Are there identifiable *phases* to a creative project?', and 'Do different domains afford or demand different *kinds* of creativity?' Though answers to these may employ overlapping terminology, they cannot be reduced to a single formulation. I am going to restrict my focus here to the more psychological aspects of creativity. Let me get into this, however, by saying something about how the creative process varies with the job in hand.

'Do different domains afford or demand different *kinds* of creativity?' It seems pretty obvious that they do; and therefore that any generalised picture of the creative process will have to vary according to the domain we are observing. A gadget designer's creativity, for example, has to result in an object that 'works', and what 'works' means is different from what it means for a wallpaper designer or a window-dresser. A creative scientific theory has to withstand tests of a very different kind from those that are applied by the jury that meets annually to award the Turner Prize for contemporary art, or the Whitbread Prize for literature. And the anticipation of these tests has to be built into the working methods and the mental processes of the creator. Experimental scientists are often guided, as their empirical programme develops, by intuitive judgements, for example; but their claims will get short shrift from their scientific peers if they cannot turn 'Seems right to me' into a more robust and logical chain of justification.

Even within the domain of the creative arts, the differences are as interesting as the similarities. Poets and sculptors craft objects for contemplation. Barring deadlines for books or shows, they have all the time they need to ruminate and tinker. And though their sense of audience may well influence the way they think, and shape the final form of their poem or sculpture, they have little control over the way any 'audience' actually engages. The composer or playwright, on the other hand, works in a more clearly defined two-phase domain, where the creativity and character of any production or performance of their work plays a much stronger role in mediating between the original creator and their eventual audience. The dramatist or the composer may be involved directly in the production of their work, but even if they are not, a wide vocabulary of notations and instructions are available to them through which to attempt to guide and constrain any performance. Their creativity involves anticipating and working with the process of interpretation of their chords or sentences in a way that the painter or novelist's may not. And we could go further, and explore the worlds of the choreographer or the jazz composer, where no lasting 'object' may exist at all, other than records of particular performances. And on to the pianist and the dancer themselves, who exercise one kind of creativity in rehearsal, and another in the moment of live performance.

Attempts to map domain-specific creativity may be hard, as variations between individual creative people within a domain may well swamp, in practice, any generalisations we might be trying to make between domains. Some composers may be very conscious of how they hear the notes in their mind's ear, and see the concert hall, and the musicians playing in their mind's eye as they compose; others may be unaware of any such process. Some jazz numbers, or comedy 'improvisations', turn out to have been very tightly scripted and rehearsed. Some writers have every paragraph designed before they start to write; others have a scruffy page of notes, and let the book or the chapter unfold (surprisingly) as they go along. To every generalisation, there will probably be a creative counter-example; so we need to proceed with caution!

We might do well to remember, too, that 'creativity' is not even the special domain of domain specialists: scientists, mathematicians, authors, actors and so on. Many of the same processes and considerations that apply to 'Creativity with a Big C' also apply in many more mundane contexts. Hairdressing, cooking (e.g. doing something inventive with left-overs), imaginative running off the ball in football, a witty contribution to 'the craic', a made-up bedtime story, a garden design, a website, a DJ's segue between two tracks… all these deserve to be called 'creative' too. Anything that is both satisfying and surprising is creative, whether it makes the baby laugh, stops the tap dripping, or delights the heart, even if it does so in a way that makes sense only in retrospect. We might want to keep half an eye, as we ruminate over the creative process, on any wider everyday-life implications or applications that may emerge.

The life-course of creative projects

Another complication we need to attend to – if our account of creativity is not to be over-simplified – is that the creator may need to be 'many people' over the life-course of a creative project. Their 'frame of mind' may need to change, as they move between different phases of creative activity.

There have been models of the creative process that have attempted to get a handle on this variability, but some of the best-known have again fallen into the trap of being too coarse-grain and/or too prescriptive. One of the best known, usually attributed to Graham Wallas in his 1926 book *The Art of Thought*, divides the creative project into four stages which he called preparation, incubation, illumination and verification.[1] Preparation involved hard thinking and data collection. Incubation involved admitting (conscious) defeat, and (as the poet Amy Lowell put it) posting the seemingly intractable problem into the unconscious, like a letter into a pillar box, where some other, more inscrutable, process was supposed to take over.[2] In the third stage, illumination, some kind of an 'answer', burst into consciousness 'out of the blue'. And in the final stage, verification, conscious thought processes were again engaged to check the validity of this inspiration, and polish it for public consumption. Though this model is still often trotted out by creativity pundits, it misrepresents some aspects of creativity, and misses out much that is of interest.

It will be immediately obvious that this 'model' is more suited to some kinds of creative project than others: in particular, those where there is a well-defined 'problem', the solution to which hangs on a single 'insight' that cannot be arrived at through rational problem-solving. The literature of creativity has endlessly recycled stories of this kind, mostly, as you would expect, deriving from science and mathematics. The French mathematician Henri Poincaré was famously supposed to have received a solution to a vexing problem, without any warning, as he was stepping on to a bus in Caen. The German chemist Friedrich Kékulé was equally famously said to have discovered the cyclical nature of the benzene ring by dozing in front of the fire, and 'seeing' the flames turn into writhing snakes, one of which conveniently coiled round and bit its own tail. It turns out that we have reason to doubt both these apocryphal stories, but they have helped to draw attention to the interplay of 'controlled' and 'uncontrolled'

What's considered 'creative'?

cognition, in contributing to creativity. Scientific understanding of this interplay has (as you would have hoped) moved on in the last 80 years, and we are now able to tell a more sophisticated story about the mind's differing 'modes of attention', and how they support creative mental processes.

A second problem with the Wallas model is that it offers us only a linear, uni-directional view of creativity. First you think; then you incubate; then you receive inspiration; and finally you think again. That simple sequence is not true even of mathematicians, let alone of creative artists, designers and others. We do not delay using our intuition until we have hit a rational road-block; we do not stop thinking once we start incubating; and we do not stop 'intuiting' once we start on the process of 'verification'. The evidence of careful observers such as the ResCen associates, is that rational and 'irrational' processes interweave in a much more subtle fashion across the whole life-span of a creative project. Let me develop the Wallas model a little, to make this fluidity more apparent (while remembering my own cautions about not getting too lost in details either).

A creative project, whether it be scientific, artistic or practical, often starts from a small seed. And the less rational mind enters here, right at the beginning, for such 'seeds' are often, at the time, inexplicably poignant. A young scientist notes a small aberration embedded in miles of printout from a radio telescope. Instead of writing it off as 'noise', her curiosity is piqued, and three years later her ground-breaking paper is published. Henry James' dinner companion makes a casual remark that he recognises as 'one of those stray suggestions or vague echoes at the touch of which the novelist's imagination winces, as at the prick of some sharp point', and eventually it flowers as a brilliant short story, *The Spoils of Poynton*.[3] The young Clive James (no relation), creating songs for his Cambridge

friend Pete Atkin, gives him the couplet: 'I've seen a girl hold back her hair to light a cigarette; And it's things like that a man like me can't easily forget'.[4] In this case, the poignant observation that inspired the song remains visible within it, though often it may dissolve and proliferate into something quite different. Italo Calvino sums up this germination process, when he writes: 'In devising a story, the first thing that comes to my mind is an image that for some reason strikes me as charged with meaning, even if I cannot formulate this meaning in discursive or conceptual terms'.[5] A dance begins with a single fascinating gesture; a sonata with a musical phrase that won't leave the composer alone.

Often creative people capture and preserve these seeds in their notebooks or sketchpads. They may have hundreds of such aperçus stored away, most of which lie dormant, and many of which will never germinate at all. But a few come back to haunt them, and may start to act as a focus – the centre of a gravitational field, perhaps – which attracts other observations and thoughts to it. These create a floating nebula of ideas and possibilities in the mind that might at some point solidify into a clearer project that moves from the back to the front of the creator's mind. Into this provisional structure of seeds and serendipity, more deliberate thought processes may begin to weave. 'Would this work for a show or a commission that is coming up?' 'Maybe it could form the overture to that other piece I'm working on?' Perhaps a snappy title comes to mind, and this begins to drive cognition and cogitation in a more purposeful way. Problems emerge: 'I'd love to be able to use that figure, but I can't quite see where it fits', or 'This is beginning to sound too much like that piece I did last year'. Hard thinking, bits of accu-mulated craft knowledge and skill, and reverie slide into each other, sometimes in the space of a minute; sometimes with slower rhythms and periodicities.

And sometimes the whole process hits the buffers, and it seems as if no resolution of the emerging difficulties will be possible.

If that impasse is reached, then may come a period of 'incubation', in which the charged problem is slid once more to the back of the mind, where it remains only in the peripheral vision of the mind's eye. Scientific studies of creativity suggest that such 'incubation' is only effective if you have worked to the point where you experience a genuine impasse.[6] Premature capitulation won't do it. Only if you have really explored and exhausted all the more obvious possibilities will the unconscious come to your aid. And even then, it is not a mechanical process, nor is it all-or-nothing. The impasse may relate to the whole conception, or only to one snag in the corner. And you may pull the project back into the forefront of consciousness from time to time, and work on it deliberately for a while, before 'giving up' and letting it drift away again. It seems that incubation can weave in and out of more tightly focused cognition, in a way that is more flexible and subtle than Wallas would have had us believe.

Even if the impasse is genuine, inspiration does not always come. As Amy Lowell puts it: 'The subconscious… is a most temperamental ally. Often he will strike work at some critical point and not another word is to be got out of him'.[7] But if it does come, it is as likely to be vague or tentative as it is to be in the form of a cataclysmic reorganisation of thought. The ways in which possibilities emerge from the unconscious into consciousness are many and varied. Sometimes they come visually, as *images*, as they did, apocryphally, for Kékulé. Sometimes they appear as a fully formed verbal *thought*, and sometimes as a phrase that – like the seed of an idea – feels pregnant with fruitful possibility, but is not yet quite ready to offer up its insight literally and explicitly. Such *inklings* can be as important, in the

long run, as a blinding insight. Creators, scientific, artistic and practical, sometimes use the language of *aesthetics* to describe the creative possibilities that occur to them. Mathematicians can trust the feeling that a proof is 'elegant' or even 'beautiful'. And sometimes incubation results in *promptings* or *hunches*: urges to move, to follow one path rather than another, though one couldn't say why. As Nobel Science Laureate Michael Brown put it, musing over the crucial series of experiments that led to his breakthrough: 'As we did our work, we felt at times that there was almost a hand guiding us. Because we would go from one step to the next, and somehow we would know which was the right way to go; and I really can't tell you how we knew that'.[8]

Sometimes a creative intuition comes as a physical feeling – as it did for the witch in Macbeth, and also for the poet A.E. Housman. In his essay 'The name and nature of poetry', Housman describes a request to 'define poetry' he had received from an eager young American PhD student. 'I replied that I could no more define poetry than a terrier could define a rat, but that I thought we both recognised the object by the [physical] symptoms which it provokes in us.'[9] He goes on to explain that 'experience has taught me, when I am shaving of a morning, to keep watch over my thoughts, because, if a line of poetry strays into my mind, my skin bristles so that the razor ceases to act'.

Creative people seem to have many ways in which they can stimulate and encourage the generation of insights and ideas. Once the 'problem' is charged, and parked on the edge of the mind, its gravitational field can attract stray thoughts and experiences, and bend them to its own shape. Not being able to discover the solution to a creative impasse deliberately, a possible solution, if it can be encouraged to appear by chance, may thus be appropriated and its potential to fit the bill recognised.

Playing, messing about, free associating, improvising can all be ways of creating experiences and connections that stand a chance of being appropriated in this way. And if all the plausible avenues have been exhausted, then one can let oneself go a little dreamy, a little wild, and search in regions that lie further away from the epicentre of common sense, but yet not so far that they escape the gravitational pull of the problem.

Finally, we should note that the 'verification' phase is not adequately described solely as a return to critical, analytical hard-headedness. For some of the ResCen artists, as for many others, the conscious process of selecting and assessing ideas weaves in and out of their generation, as if there were a separate part of the mind, active at the same time as the generative part, monitoring and commenting on the creative process as it goes along. And this voice can be both gentle and critical; both rational and intuitive. Much attention has been paid to the destructive effect on creativity of having a voice that is superficially critical and quickly dismissive – and this had led, in techniques like 'brain-storming' for example, to a deliberate attempt to inhibit or postpone the operation of that voice. It is this strategy of apartheid, perhaps, that has tended to exaggerate the discontinuity between the illumination and verification stages. But if 'the voice' is quieter, more supportive and more patient, it can profitably be allowed to coexist with a receptivity to creative generation. It may manifest only as a feeling of 'rightness' or 'wrongness' that accompanies ideas or intuitions as they bubble into consciousness: a feeling of glee or excitement on the one hand, or of deflation or dissatisfaction on the other. Creative people seem to differ in how strong this voice is; how reliable or accurate it is; and how much they have learned to trust it. For some, it is a vital touchstone of progress, to be heeded and respected. For others, it is a much less

reliable ally: one to be treated with suspicion, or even banished completely.

As I say, these 'stages' of the creative journey are neither clear cut nor sequential. Creativity is a non-linear process. New 'seeds' may be germinating right throughout the life-course of a creative project, sometimes being able to be incorporated in the developing draft; sometimes having (regretfully) to be held over for another day. Moves or passages that had seemed brilliant at the time may find themselves under the knife, as a sense of the whole theory, or the complete score, becomes clearer, and reflective attention moves back and forth between the detail and the overall composition. Occasionally the feeling of rightness or wrongness may change quite late in the day. As you muse over what you hoped was a 'final draft', so a feeling of inconvenient dissatisfaction may grow too strong to ignore, leading to the reorganisation, shelving or even abandonment of the whole project.

There is one other way in which the Wallas picture of creativity misrepresents the reality, and that is in the virtual exclusion of the social world. The image of the solitary genius, wracking his (usually his, in this mythology) brains, pacing restlessly in his lonely garret, and then being hit by a blinding flash of insight that cracks the case or the problem wide open, unleashing a frenzy of activity in which the insight is turned into a breakthrough paper or a beautiful sonata, is untrue to the facts in many ways, not least in the way it airbrushes out other people.[10] Conversations with creative people reveal just how essential and ubiquitous such interactions are – and also how much people differ in how and when they make use of other people. Some like to discuss the seeds of their projects early, though often only with selected others who are trustworthy, sympathetic and/or knowledgeable about what the creator is trying to do. Others feel that even that much disclosure is too

> Again, support for Marion

much, threatening to expose the small shoot of an idea to a frost that might nip it in the bud; or to require, in the attempt to articulate it, a degree of clarity or fixity that would inhibit or skew its subsequent development. Creative people seem to know when to go for a walk by themselves; when to shuffle incognito round a rival's exhibition; when to think out loud with one trusted friend; and when (if at all) to expose the project to the more vigorous rough-and-tumble of a dinner-party conversation.

American playwright Tony Kushner, 'author' (his quotes) of the hit play *Angels in America*, describes the intricate and unceasing role that more than two dozen other people played in the creation of 'his' drama: so much so that it is actually a gross misrepresentation for him to claim authorship – hence the scare quotation marks.[11] He muses on the deeper reasons why this perennial misrepresentation is so common, and fingers the cultural myths of heroic individualism and possessive capitalism. The creator not only has to 'create', but also to be positioned in a social drama. 'In the modern era, it isn't enough to write; you must also Be a Writer and play your part as the protagonist in a cautionary narrative in which you will fail or triumph, be "in" or "out", hot or cold…' And if creative products constitute cultural capital, then ownership has to be assigned, so that bank transfers can be properly directed, and Oscars awarded. To acknowledge that the 'author' was actually a shifting constellation of people is inconvenient, and threatening to the myths.

The glide space of creativity

What emerges from these more detailed insights into the creative process, as we try to make some sense of them, is a focus neither on a set of well-defined and linearly arranged stages, nor on individual differences in some hypothetical 'quality', but on a number of dimensions along which people may vary. Some of these variations are idiosyncratic and perfectly functional for the individual (and his or her cloud of creative associates). Other kinds of variation are more within individuals, as they move through different phases of the creative process, and come at it in differing ways. Let me focus, in the space I have left, on the latter, and offer the idea of a three-dimensional mental 'space' that offers a variety of 'states of mind' that are appropriate to different times and tasks within the overall creative project. These three dimensions are essentially three different ways in which attention may vary.

If we continue to focus on the individual, I am suggesting that part of their creative success lies in their ability to move fluidly around in this three-dimensional creative space. Sure, we can identify a rough overall trajectory that runs from the finding of a seed, to its elaboration into a creative project or possibility, to the dynamic interweaving of impasses and solutions, to the crafting of a product or a performance. But at a finer grain, we can see the creator's mind gliding, at different rates and rhythms, between different states within that attentional space. Let me describe the dimensions of this 'space' in a little more detail, and locate some of the more important states of mind, that the creator needs access to, within it.[12]

The first dimension refers to the intensity and *focus* of attention. At one end of the spectrum we find highly focused, targeted states of attention that tend to be purpose-driven and analytical. There is a problem in mind, and an implicit sense of what might count as 'relevant' to its solution, which guides the deployment of attention. At the other end live states of mind that are relaxed, holistic and receptive. In this mode, we are more open to whatever pops up; more willing just to see what life has to offer. In terms of brain waves, the former correspond to the relatively high levels of cortical arousal that appear in electroencephalogram (EEG) traces as so-called beta waves. The latter correspond to the lower-frequency alpha or theta waves.

The second dimension concerns the general *direction* of attention: whether we are looking primarily *outward*, at information arriving at the senses; or *inward*, at thoughts, images or intuitions that seem to arise from within the mind. These, of course, are not exclusive. In the middle of this dimension we can imagine a resonant state of mind in which attention and imagination (for example) are continuously feeding into and off each other. And the final dimension is the *social* one. Are we functioning in *solitary* mode, as if our individual mind-brain system were sufficient unto itself; or in *sociable* mode, where we feel our mind-brain to be networked with other, similar systems? We can be at different points along this dimension regardless of whether there are other people physically around. In the former mode, we are more fixed and certain in our views, for example; in the latter, more permeable to others and more willing to see our own thoughts as tentative and evolving contributions to a wider, more collective endeavour.

As we glide around in this three-dimension attentional box (the 'crate' of creativity?), we can imagine ourselves at any one of the eight corners of the 'cube' (as shown in the table below). In concentrated, outward, solitary mode we are inspecting objects and information in the light of our current problems and concerns. In diffused, inward, sociable mode, we might find ourselves engaging in an open-minded reflective conversation with friends or colleagues, sharing personal feelings and ideas. In concentrated, outward sociable mode, on the other hand, we might be engaged in vigorous, critical group problem-solving, focusing on the details of the predicament, proposing and critiquing each other's putative solutions. And in diffused, inward, solitary mode, we might be hovering on the brink of sleep, idly watching the mind's ideas bubbling up and 'playing' with each other, with little or no sense of ego-control: spectating rather than directing.

The Glide Space of Creativity

The three dimensions of attention

Focus	Direction	Interaction	Mental mode
Concentrated	Outward	Solitary	Scrutinising
Concentrated	Outward	Sociable	Group studying
Concentrated	Inward	Solitary	Hard thinking
Concentrated	Inward	Sociable	Arguing
Diffused	Outward	Solitary	Contemplating
Diffused	Outward	Sociable	Group chatting
Diffused	Inward	Solitary	Reverie / Dreaming
Diffused	Inward	Sociable	Dialogue / Reflective conversation

On this view, the ability that creators need, above all else, is flexibility. They need the capacity to move fluidly and appropriately between different mental modes, as different phases and aspects of the creative project present themselves. They need to be able to attend both to detail and to the 'big picture'. They need to be both spontaneous and methodical. They need to be sensitive both to the intuitive signals of 'rightness' and to the practicalities of producing a successful product or performance. (As Amy Lowell continues, from the earlier quotation about the unconscious going on strike, you have to have craft and talent enough to 'putty up the holes' that it has left behind).[13] They need to be both receptive and proactive. They need to be able to think clearly and to dream. They need to be able to be both patient and purposeful. They need to be able to see how things are, and how they could be. They need to be able to play with material, letting it reveal its potentialities, and to mould it to their own will. The creative person, it seems, needs to be capable of being in many minds, sometimes simultaneously, and sometimes moving sequentially between them.

So can creativity be learned?

It will be obvious, as I hinted earlier, that people differ in this fluency. We all, I suspect, have preferred or default areas of the space where we feel most comfortable. And we differ in where they are, and in how easy or hard we find it to work in different modes when the task requires it. Some of us argue too much, attend to detail too much, space out too much, analyse too much or study too much. Indeed, there are quizzes that claim to tell you where your natural mental territory is to be found, and they are fun to do. But the question they often beg is: are these default zones habits, which can be changed, or predetermined personal 'styles', which we have to respect and learn how to work within? Are they a challenge to stretch and exercise the less familiar creative 'muscles', or an invitation simply to learn how to steer a wheelchair?

As an educator, the purpose of trying to map out the creative process, and clarifying the dimensions along which people's creativity might vary, is for me never merely academic. The point is to be able to ask more precisely: so where is the wriggle room? What aspects of a creative mentality can be changed? What could be taught? And how can people support and stimulate the development of their own creativity? I don't think that just one book such as this gives us all the answers to these questions. But it encourages me in the view I have been exploring, and in the belief that we can learn useful things about how creativity can be fostered.

1. Graham Wallas, *The Art of Thought* (New York: Harcourt Brace Jovanovich, 1926)

2. Amy Lowell, Introduction to *Selected Poems of Amy Lowell*, quoted in Brewster Ghiselin (ed.), *The Creative Process* (Berkeley CA: University of California Press, 1952)

3. Henry James, Preface to *The Spoils of Poynton*, reprinted in Brewster Ghiselin (ed.), *The Creative Process* (Berkeley CA: University of California Press, 1952)

4. Clive James, 'Laughing boy', from Clive James and Pete Atkin, *Beware of the Beautiful Stranger* (London: Onward Music, 1970)

5. Italo Calvino, *Six Memos for the Next Millennium*, trans. P. Creagh, (Cambridge MA: Harvard University Press, 1988), p.120

6. Guy Claxton, *Hare Brain, Tortoise mind: Why Intelligence Increases When You Think Less* (London: Fourth Estate, New York: HarperCollins, 1997), and Colleen M. Seifert, David E. Meyer, Natalie Davidson, Andrea L. Patalano and Ilan Yaniv, 'Demystification of cognitive insight: opportunistic assimilation and prepared-mind perspective', in Robert J. Sternberg and Janet E. Davidson (eds) *The Nature of Insight*, (Cambridge MA: Bradford/MIT Press, 1995)

7. Amy Lowell, Introduction to *Selected Poems of Amy Lowell*, quoted in Brewster Ghiselin (ed.), *The Creative Process* (Berkeley CA: University of California Press, 1952), p.51

8. Peter Fensham, and Ference Marton 'What has happened to intuition in science education?' *Research in Science Education*, (22, 114-22, 1992), p.119

9. Alfred E. Housman, *The name and nature of poetry* 1933, p.8

10. Vera John-Steiner, (2000), *Creative Collaboration*, (New York: Oxford University Press, 2000)

11. Tony Kushner, 'Is it a fiction that play-wrights create alone?' *New York Times*, November 21, 1993

12. This three-dimensional model has similarities to those of Hobson, see Allan J Hobson, *Dreaming as Delirum* (Cambridge, MA: MIT Press, 1999) and Carter, see Rita Carter, *Mapping the Mind* (London: Weidenfeld and Nicholson, 2002). An earlier version of my model can be found in Guy Claxton and Bill Lucas, *Be Creative* (London: BBC Books, 2004).

13. Amy Lowell, Introduction to *Selected Poems of Amy Lowell*, quoted in Brewster Ghiselin (ed.), *The Creative Process*

Ghislaine
Boddington

The unremembered memory

The Weave

Ghislaine Boddington

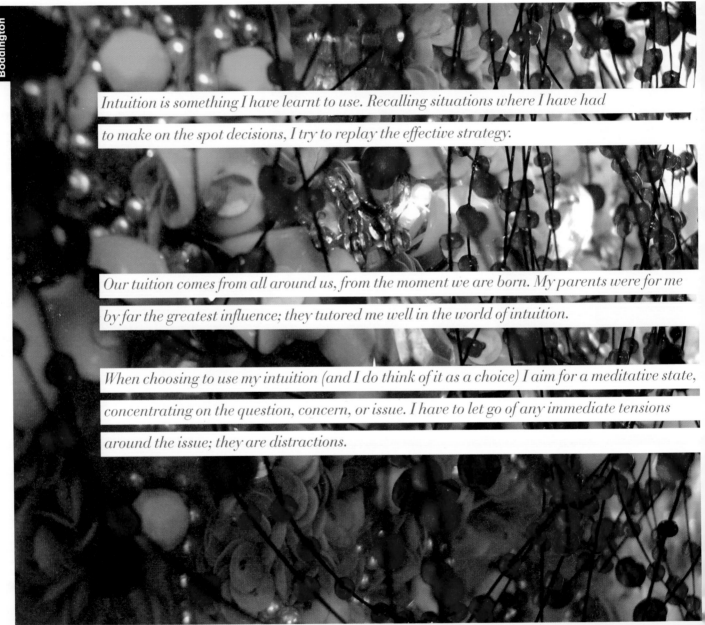

Ghislaine
Boddington

*Intuition is something I have learnt to use. Recalling situations where I have had
to make on the spot decisions, I try to replay the effective strategy.*

*Our tuition comes from all around us, from the moment we are born. My parents were for me
by far the greatest influence; they tutored me well in the world of intuition.*

*When choosing to use my intuition (and I do think of it as a choice) I aim for a meditative state,
concentrating on the question, concern, or issue. I have to let go of any immediate tensions
around the issue; they are distractions.*

The writing of this chapter instigated a reflective reconsideration of twenty years of work and this has allowed me to observe features that are revealed through a lens that is focused on a long view. This perspective highlights some significant changes – the methods, processes, structures, content and even the way in which I describe my role have all undergone fundamental transformation. The driver for these changes was almost always an intuitive, nagging force or presence, which has led to a series of sometimes small, incremental changes. But the accumulative effect of each small, subtle development is that the work has evolved almost beyond recognition, while still being driven by the same concerns.

The constant nagging presence and the subsequent reflection eventually became an intrinsic element of the process, creating an automatic feedback loop in which the results of reflection were fed directly back into the work and the practice became reflexive. This evolution of my work took place largely without the benefit, or otherwise, of the academic context, instead it was motivated by my belief in collective working practices and a determination to be in tune with the spirit of our times in order to avoid the isolated world of the arts.

My experience of this unconscious, intuitive guiding force may actually derive from childhood experience. I have never understood the fascination with stars and the cult of stardom and I can trace this back to the ambience of my childhood and the formative influence of my mother's gallery in Wales. As a child I saw a whole stream of interesting people come and go; only later I realised that this was a kind of network and I appreciated the ways in which each person came and went and interlinked with others. The network did not centre on any one individual – what was exciting was the exchange between them – the ways that the ideas and the debate were developed and extended. It was a group process, which shaped my view of the world and I unconsciously understood that many areas of endeavour required, or benefited from, teamwork.

Perhaps this is why I was later drawn to particular people and places. It was a way of re-discovering and further developing these interests. My involvement in the cooperative Chisenhale Collective, which flourished in the

Ghislaine
Boddington

I clear all else from my head and look beyond the horizon.

I think of my intuitive world as made up of solutions and hints, links and bridges, gathered from a lifetime of experience.

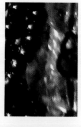

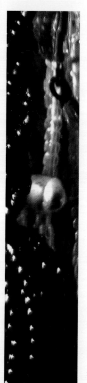

late 1970s and 1980s, renewed my belief in the power of a variety of forms of collective expression, from folk dance to religious ritual, from club dance to interactive technologies, all offering ways of enabling the joy of participation and creativity for many.[1] However, I quickly realised that this perception of the importance of the group was not shared widely in the performing arts, and the resulting clash of philosophies and beliefs provided the motivation for me to work consciously towards finding those who shared my view of group creative practice.

This led to the formation of shinkansen, a partnership run as a collaborative unit developing work which was guided by the principle of collective processes.[2] The work evolved through workshops, seminars and debates in the UK, across Europe and the USA. From the beginning, technology was a key strand of the work as this seemed to me to be a defining development of our time. Working with the arts and technology required collaborative methods, as the specialist knowledge was not shared – it was isolated within each community and there was little common ground connecting the arts and digital practitioners. I had not realised the depth of this divide, as the need for the arts to engage with digital technology seemed self-evident to me, even nearly twenty years ago. But once in the room with the participants on the first project, I saw that 'translation' was required urgently and a series of relationships needed to be established if the project was to succeed. I found myself spontaneously stopping everyone so that we could establish the basis for our exchange. This intervention ultimately led to an exercise designed to encourage each person to consider their backgrounds and skills, and to do so for each other person involved in the project. The Identity Exercise has been refined over the years and is now a part of the structure of each project. There are a number of variations, but it always involves each person considering the essential aspects of who they are, their culture, beliefs and experiences. They then select objects that they feel best represent who they are and present them to the group with an explanation of their significance. This presentation, and listening to others doing the same, both establishes the individual and promotes an effective group process.

This exercise strengthened our human-centred approach and

Ghislaine Boddington

In my head I follow a thought process of branches and paths. Sometimes I waste time following the wrong branch or reaching for a dead end.

I put feelers out, tentatively, carefully, into an interconnected web of clusters and patterns.

If I think too much about this process I lose my way.

Ghislaine
Boddington

presented technology as a development by and for people, not a dehumanising, oppressive presence and not the preserve of a select group of techno-wizards. Technical expertise was essential, but it needed to be demystified and shared as openly as possible. Human presence must balance technology; digital developments should enable the human endeavour, empowering us all and enhancing connectivity. This understanding of my position was not something that I would have articulated at the outset. I had not previously felt the need to articulate the fact that technology was informing the development of our society and that the creative potential of groups was a good way, perhaps the best way, of grappling with the challenge and opportunities that digital technologies offered. But as each project ended there would be a nagging sense of something needing attention and, often days later, a moment of clarity would arrive as the problem bubbled up to reveal itself; and in many cases the answer was not far behind. The problems revealed in this way led me to an articulation of the rationale for our projects, so that all participants would be clear about the collective approach from the outset. This became the Interauthorship Statement which set out the rationale for the fluid group process that would be the foundation of each project.[3] This work continued to evolve through a series of over forty international projects and workshops, all focused on people working within their specialisms while also working collectively. This was consistently informed by the human presence and the role of the physical human body alongside technology. One example of this was the project *Virtual Physical Bodies*, which brought a group of international practitioners in digital arts together at Middlesex University, all with a shared concern to develop understanding of the virtual and physical body.[4] The work progressed through practical investigation, discussion and debate which clarified my thinking about the significance of technology as it stood in 1999, but also reinforced the power of the human being, even when perceived as a virtual presence.

This concern for human presence and its representation led to a series of projects focused on the creation of *CellBytes*, short interauthored dance works focused on the use of telematics, using web-based audio-visual interactivity for an art-making process centred on bridging physical space with human interaction.[5]

I use the macro to examine the micro.

As these projects became more complex in their organisation and international involvement, there was a clear need for more pre-project communication and through this communication, some aspects of the projects began to shape themselves. Structures began to form and methods of enabling group processes also emerged. The preparation for these workshops began to use the internet extensively to connect the group and this enabled a forum for democratised debate. We worked to develop flattened hierarchies, creating porous networks with active clusters of interaction. These networks continued long after the project ended, a practical and powerful testament to the power of communication and the collective.

Throughout this period of growth in the work of shinkansen however, resistance from a surprisingly conservative arts community continued. On many occasions, in conversation with funders, or others in the arts, there would be a cursory acknowledgement of this rich vein of work, then after a moment's pause, discussions would quickly move on to individual artists. This continuing resistance, and a growing confidence founded on increased experience, led me to make the case that the evolution of digital technologies had initiated a series of changes which had fundamentally altered, and would continue to alter, the ways in which art is made and received, as well as radically altering the relationships between makers. Furthermore, the focus on the individual seemed to me to be simply a misrepresentation of the truth. While I recognised the importance of individual achievement, almost all activity in the performing arts relies on contributions from teams to create and present the work – a collective contribution which is often unacknowledged. One only has to compare the credits that accompany a film, with the credits in virtually any theatre programme in the performing arts, to realise that there is a gap in the theatre programme where the names of the many people who contribute to performance work should be recorded. Somehow it is deemed acceptable to leave this space empty, to render these contributions invisible.

There has, of course, been movement in the development of group processes and in the perception of group work. In fact in some areas the resistance to group processes seems to have disappeared – now they have become not just accepted, but even fashionable. This should be a source of

[handwritten marginal note:] Would have been a stronger opening for my essay. Perhaps use in the future?

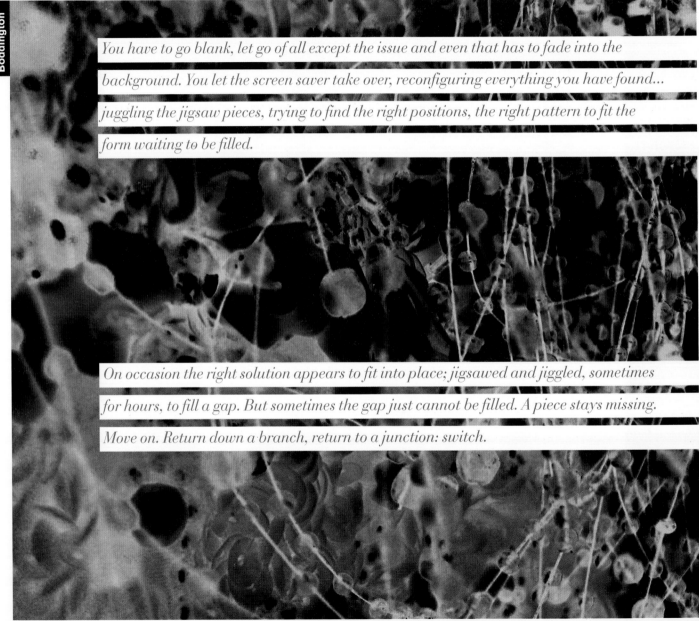

You have to go blank, let go of all except the issue and even that has to fade into the background. You let the screen saver take over, reconfiguring everything you have found... juggling the jigsaw pieces, trying to find the right positions, the right pattern to fit the form waiting to be filled.

On occasion the right solution appears to fit into place; jigsawed and jiggled, sometimes for hours, to fill a gap. But sometimes the gap just cannot be filled. A piece stays missing. Move on. Return down a branch, return to a junction: switch.

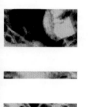

satisfaction for me, but too often I detect a superficial discourse of collaboration and teamwork with no real commitment or understanding. The language has changed and the use of words such as interdisciplinary, collaborative, co-authored, co-created has exponentially increased, but my impression is that these concepts have simply become buzzwords. The words run together, there is a slippage into merged, blurred meanings. Complex understandings are inferred, but their full implications are not acknowledged. This is inevitable when discourse is not grounded in experience – the intuitive insight is blinded when experience does not provide a field in which it can operate.

{ perhaps they are buzzwords now. Certainly seen so at MDX

It appears to me that the collective approach and group processes offer a way forward. Of course, in the arts, as in many other areas, it is necessary to make explicit the choice of the use of 'we' in such collective processes. While such practices emerged for me through an intuitive process of exploration, they are now articulated and in the public domain – models have been developed and are in place. Open dynamic processes and initiatives such as Open Source and Creative Commons, which encourage a sharing of knowledge and resources, are evidence of the recognition of the vitality and pragmatic usefulness of the collective.[6] On the other hand, many of us caught in a double-speak of 'I / we' are genuinely confused by a discourse of collaboration and collective effort which simply does not accurately reflect the reality of the working conditions. Considering the use of 'I' and 'we' is a feature of my practice and I try to use them accurately to credit individuals, the group process and my own specialisation/s and responsibilities.

It is possible to chart the recent history of collective working practices in the arts. The burgeoning of group activity in the 1960s, which pushed these ways of working into the public consciousness, led directly to a period of experimentation in the 1970s. The pendulum swung back towards the individual and individualism in the 1980s leaving the 1990s to attempt another push forward, often with a weak sense of collectivism, or a veneer of collectivism, thinly covering a more a more singular, star-focused orientation. But the beginning of the twenty-first century is marked by what I term the confused and schizophrenic 'I / we / I' syndrome. This is evident all around us in unbridled consumerism which appears to promise almost unlimited individual

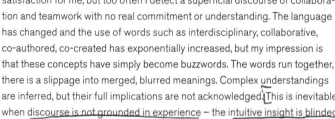

Ghislaine Boddington

Puzzle and search, split the issue, look at both ends of the problem, examine all variations.

Continue to move carefully; refuse to look too far ahead.

Remembering to continue to feel carefully, like insects, in a way refusing to look too far ahead, let go, don't pre-suppose, never pre-position, and let it flow.

choice to a privileged minority. We need insight to see through this to the reality of an interconnected, globalised world. Against both excessive individualism and excessive collectivism is the group of equals working together, respecting the individual, as well as respecting the group endeavour. Today, such people form networks, allowing an open exchange of information and an immediacy of communication. The networking becomes a part of the process of making work – it is a dynamic networking which facilitates the development of natural, intuitive, emergent patterns of behaviours.

The focus on the group process and on a network of engaged individuals meant that I needed to re-define my role. The term 'Process Director' that I use today, is one that I coined in an attempt to identify and communicate my role in the developing area of collaborative practice. I initially considered using the term 'dramaturg' to describe the role I took in this work, but I found that this term was subject to misunderstanding, especially in the UK. The term 'Process Director', which stemmed from the world of software development, seemed unencumbered by accumulated baggage from theatre practice, and yet describes my role fairly accurately. This description of the development of the role might imply that it was a conscious decision, but for me it was an organic process: I followed a path to the skills and knowledge that led me to first become the role, and then later to identify and name it. My interest in emergence theory means that I do not see this as detrimental, in fact the opposite is true – it was the ability to follow an intuitive guide which allowed me to develop organically and this development has been strengthened and refined by an accumulation of experience. It was a journey that began when I intuitively sought out collective creative practice, which led to experience, then to reflection and then to conscious practice. This might imply that the intuitive aspects are slowly disappearing from my work as it becomes ever more conscious, but in fact the best moments still arise from intuitive, spontaneous perception.

This brings me to 'the weave', an image I developed as a way of enabling participants to envision the process and the progression of the projects. The image acknowledges the various strands that make up the total: contributions from participants form a plait which retains the visible identity of

[handwritten annotations in right margin:] Intuitive sought → experience → Reflection → conscious practice

I believe I can Relate to this with how I got to Casting & my current area of interest

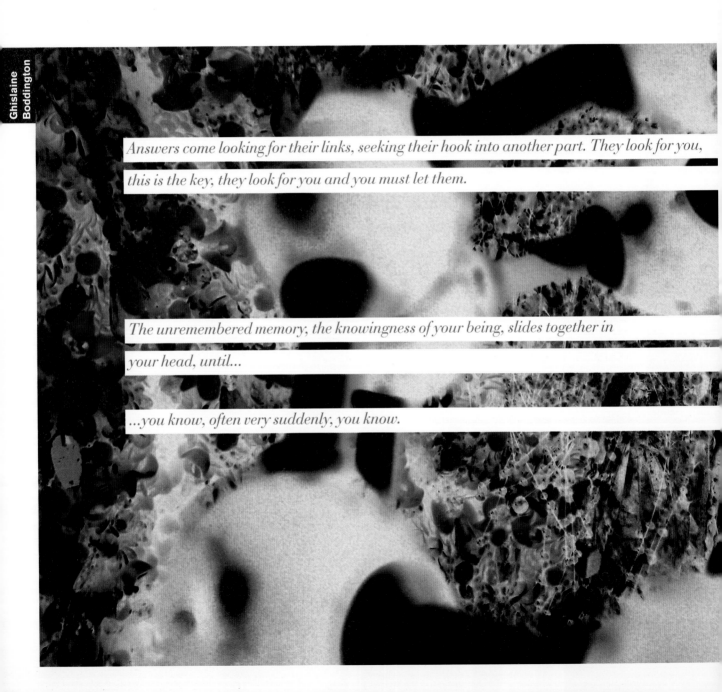

Ghislaine
Boddington

Answers come looking for their links, seeking their hook into another part. They look for you,

this is the key; they look for you and you must let them.

The unremembered memory, the knowingness of your being, slides together in

your head, until...

...you know, often very suddenly, you know.

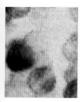

each contributor, while also forming a unity stronger than any single thread. While this image was designed to communicate to participants, seeing my involvement in the projects as 'weaving' also allowed me to refine my practice – I was able to move forward, to become a skilful weaver and I enhanced my sense and developed the timing of my interventions. To find the moment to intervene in a process comes not through consideration, but through an embodied feeling of the right moment. I needed to move the strands with clarity and care, holding them and ensuring that they felt their presence in the shared space occupied by the project. Technology is developing exponentially but my interest in the human presence and human consciousness means that the technology can only ever be a part of the equation. It is the human being and human interactions, with each other and with technology, that are at the centre of my work. I work to achieve a plait and, while digital technology forms a strand of the plait, it is woven at all times with the human presence – and the processes and concerns with which we engage.

At first my engagement was very active – I made sure that my presence as weaver was known to all, and that they were reminded of it often. I signalled to the group when we were moving things forward, or when asking others to reconsider, or even wait. Even the 'holding' of a strand was an active holding, so that I could be sure that everyone was aware of the group process. This was demanding for me over the course of projects that lasted between ten days and four weeks. It involved an activity of weaving in which things occur rapidly and an immediate, spontaneous response was often required. At that point in my work, what I experienced was an altered state of acute awareness that moved through exhaustion to exhilaration.

I had developed this heightened awareness from another aspect of my practice that involved the presentation of performative seminars and, in many ways, the two strands are mutually supportive as both forms of involvement require three hundred and sixty degree awareness; a constant state of attending to the moment; spontaneous, intuitive responses to individuals, as well as maintaining a sense of the collective entity.[7] But the weaving required in a daylong seminar does not match the work of an extended interauthorship process. The demands of the projects led me to refine my engagement, to

Can my practice also identify with this image? I believe it can.

You know what it is, what to do, the answer is in front of you. It drops into the space between intuition and knowing... that is the place where agreement lies.

develop the skills of weaving so that, as in certain dance forms such as release technique, a consistent awareness would be matched by a relaxed fluidity of action.[8] With the right balance – not too much structure and control, but not too little – letting the energy flow smoothly and consistently; then welcoming the moment when the intuitive processes enfold us, and a kind of group intuition emerges.

The work flows; the material and the people weave themselves; the material emerges and the people needed to create the material – the performers, digital artists, choreographers – all arrive in the right place at the right time. This is the ultimate goal of the weave and weaving, but it has an ironic edge as it means that the Process Director is redundant. The journey of developing this practice, a journey of intense personal engagement, a kind of altered state of hyper-perception and experience is over. After years of practice this is happening more – I have woven myself out of the process: I have choreographed myself out of the frame. Now I see that I have arrived, without ever knowing my destination. A sense of emptiness is present. Yet the weave is weaving itself, calm and contentment prevails. The group process is working. I now re-insert myself into the emergent dynamic to celebrate the interauthored process.

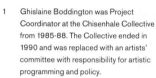

1   Ghislaine Boddington was Project Coordinator at the Chisenhale Collective from 1985-88. The Collective ended in 1990 and was replaced with an artists' committee with responsibility for artistic programming and policy.

2   shinkansen ran from 1989 to 2004. Archives are available at the British Library and at <www.connectivity.org.uk>

3   See Ghislaine Boddington *The Weave* archived at <www.rescen.net>

4   Virtual Physical Bodies Symposium at Middlesex University 1999 <www.rescen.net>

5   For more information on telematics and *Cellbytes* see Boddington's 'Artist's Pages' at <www.rescen.net>

6   See <www.opensource.org/docs/ definition.php> and <www.creativecommons.org>

7   See <www.londondance.com/content /923/virtual_incarnations>

8   Release Technique is a form of dance which attends to the flow of energy in the body. It was influenced by the Alexander Technique and then various martial arts forms as well as yoga.

Thanks to Leanne Bird, Kitt Boddington, Lara Houston, Paul Mumford, Gary Rogers, Armand Terruli, Andrew Ward and Kath Wood for their inspiration and feedback on the writing of this chapter.

Ghislaine Boddington

Imagine you are meeting a gr

to tell them the most importa

You can use five items to illus

but you only have five minut

choose and what do you say.

up of strangers. You need

aspect of who you are.

ue your essential identity

o speak. What do you

Imagine you are meeting a group of strangers. You need to tell them the most important aspect of who you are. You can use five items to illustrate your essential identity but you only have five minutes to speak. What do you choose and what do you say?

NAVIGAT

Beam me up, Scotty: Navigating Processes

Joshua Sofaer

This central section of the book investigates what happens as artists navigate their way through the creative process; what techniques and methods they employ to accompany them on their journey, and what their experiences tell them about making work.

'All in a Day's Work' is a chaired conversation between the ResCen artists which focuses on issues which pertain to the daily practice of creation. Richard Layzell's 'Form and Function' is integrally related to 'Friction of Forms' by Caroline Bergvall and 'Return of the Repressed' by Adrian Rifkin; these three short texts are conceived as part of the same piece, playing with fictional voices and working methods. Mark Vernon's essay 'Plato and the Creative Life' looks to Plato and his philosophy as a way of reflecting back on the creative process. 'Expectant Waiting' by Rosemary Lee considers the importance of waiting as an active creative process.

This introductory essay seeks to draw out common strands and contextualise them within a wider social, cultural and artistic framework. The three main strands identified are: the dramatisation of creative thought as a way of producing knowledge, in other words performance itself as knowledge; collaborative practice as a kind of alternative family; and, the power of negative preference, where not knowing and not doing are forms of productive engagement.

On the journey that an artist makes in the creation of contemporary performance, from the initial idea or commission to the manifestation of that work in a public engagement, a series of choices are encountered and a set of decisions are made. This 'tying yourself to a particular choice,' as Shobana Jeyasingh conceives it, is 'always a moment of suffering'.[1] This suffering arises from the *what might have been* and the *if only*, a kind of retroactive configuring of the future possibilities of the work that *isn't* about to be

made, that results from the decisions that were discarded. This is the theme taken up by Peter Howitt's 1992 romantic comedy *Sliding Doors* where we watch parallel storylines in which the central protagonist catches and misses a tube train, two radically different narratives played out as a result of a split-second decision to run for an embarking train or to wait for the next one.

But the suffering engaged by the creative decision-making process is not just about the *what if*; more prosaically, it is about the act of making the decision. How do you make choices?

A recurrent theme in this section of the book, 'Navigating', is the dramatisation of creative thought. Not necessarily (often and often not) as performance product, which is to say the staging of ideas to an audience, but rather the dramatisation of creative thought *in* the creative process itself, where the staging of a 'position' gives life to ideas. Graeme Miller articulates this in terms of 'Spock and Kirk' work:

> I'm an addictive problem solver, so sometimes I divide my work between Spock work and Kirk work. […] Captain Kirk and Mister Spock. It means to do with whether you're in the driving seat or whether you're in the Spock role, which is about problem solving. 'Captain, have you thought of this?' And you can do that for yourself. It throws up constant material. […] The detachment is really useful. When it's somebody else's work it's a lot easier to have opinions, and to solve their problems, than it is your own.[2]

Graeme Miller's dramatisation of thought is for his own purpose. He is the audience of his own performance.[3] The Spock/Kirk dynamic is not merely a metaphor for the struggle to make decisions but rather a practical creative strategy engaged to determine solutions. The *dramatis personae* who take up the challenge are selected for their personal characteristics and their designated roles. Captain James T Kirk of the USS Enterprise – the man in the driving seat – embodies the ideal 'doer'. According to his official biography he is 'an independent whose success couldn't be argued even though he often bucked the system'.[4] He is the man of valour, the patriot who sacrifices his personal freedoms for the greater good, acknowledged by many awards and commendations including the Starfleet Citation for Conspicuous Gallantry and the Karagite Order of Heroism. Mr Spock, First Officer and later Commander – the problem solver – is, on the other hand, the cultured scientist, and embodies the ideal 'thinker'. Half human (his mother Amanda was a school teacher) and half Vulcan (his father Sarek was a diplomat), Spock's role is to pose questions and offer suggestions. Torn between his emotional human side and the strict (genetic) discipline of his Vulcan heritage, Spock is in the prime position to offer many potential readings of a particular situation. The generosity of his purpose is exemplified by the fact that prior to his death he 'mind-melded' with his Starfleet colleague Dr Leonard McCoy, to transfer his 'katra' (his spiritual essence) so that it might be put to future use.

This mind-melding is, perhaps, a useful way to think about what is happening in the staging of Graeme Miller's creative process. It is the intervention of somebody else (albeit a fiction) and the detachment from self, *within self*, that produces solutions.

While I do not want to suggest that Miller sits in his studio muttering to himself in Vulcan (he may, or may not, be so literal in his application) the Spock/Kirk 'method' works partly because the characters' voices are already so well developed in their on-screen performance. By imagining what they might advise him to do, metaphorically or otherwise,

Miller taps into a kind of predetermined performance script that is handed to him already written.

Another Spock, not the Vulcan scientist but the American doctor, usefully comes into play here. Dr Benjamin Spock was an American Paediatrician who first published his child rearing manual in 1946, under the title T*he Commonsense Book of Baby and Child Care*. In subsequent years the book sold over fifty million copies, was translated into more than thirty languages and to date is the best selling book in the world after the Bible.[5] Given that millions upon millions of children have been raised under the auspices of his guidance, the impact of Benjamin Spock on the lives and lifestyles of those born in the west in the second half of the twentieth century should not be underestimated. Dr Spock's manual acts as a performance script for the interaction of millions of parents and children. At the time of his death in 1998 aged 94, Spock's influence on Western child rearing was acknowledged in the tribute paid by the then president of the USA, Bill Clinton:

> Hillary and I were deeply saddened to learn of the death of Dr Benjamin Spock. For half a century, Dr Spock guided parents across the country and around the world in their most important job – raising their children.[6]

What is so striking about Dr Spock's text is the way it overtly encourages performance on the part of the parent. The first chapter of *Baby and Child Care* is titled 'The Parent's Part', as if parenting was literally a role or character to be studied and subsequently enacted. This actor/character methodology is extended even to encompass a performance of the child itself by the parent, as in, for instance, this account of why urging a child to eat is unreasonable and likely to cause problems.

> *Put yourself in the child's place* for a minute. To get in the mood, think back to the last

time you weren't very hungry. Perhaps it was a muggy day, or you were worried, or you had a stomach upset. (The child with a feeding problem feels that way most of the time.) Now imagine that a nervous giantess is sitting beside you, watching every mouthful. You have eaten a little of the foods that appeal to you most and have put your fork down, feeling quite full. But she looks worried and says, "You haven't touched your turnips." You explain that you don't want any, but she doesn't seem to understand how you feel, acts as if you are being bad on purpose. When she says you can't get up from the table until you've cleaned your plate, you try a bit of turnip, but if makes you feel slightly sick. She scoops up a tablespoonful and pokes it at your mouth, which makes you retch.[7]

The parent is thus asked to act not only in the role of parent but also as the child they parent. This staging of multiple positionality is similar to the Spock/Kirk dynamic that Graeme Miller describes, where the different sides of an argument are played out.

The everyday as performance is not something unique to the raising of children nor to the creative process, and of course it would be possible to read practically all actions of daily life as interpretations of pre-set performance scripts.

In his analysis of social reality, configured as a series of frames of reference, Erving Goffman defines the relationship between the individual and the performance of the everyday as the 'person-role formula':

> …whenever an individual participates in an episode of activity, a distinction will be drawn between what is called the person, individual, or player, namely he who partici-

pates, and the particular role, capacity, or function he realizes during that participation. And a connection between these two elements will be understood. In short, there will be a *person-role formula*. The nature of a particular frame will, of course, be linked to the nature of the person-role formula it sustains. One can never expect complete freedom between individual and role and never complete constraint. But no matter where on this continuum a particular formula is located, the formula itself will express the sense in which the framed activity is geared into the continuing world.[8]

In this way we are always both ourselves and the roles we play, be it captain, scientist, artist or mother. The terms on which we are read by others oscillates between person and role, but often focuses on role:

> Interestingly, in everyday affairs, one is not always aware of a particular individual's part in life, that is, his biography, awareness often focusing more on the role he performs in some particular connection – political, domestic, or whatever.[9]

With regard to parenting it is useful to think of how the child, even the adult child, sees its parents precisely on these terms, which is to say as 'mother' and 'father' (with the concomitant expectations of their performance that such roles inevitably bring) rather than as 'people' in their own right. The child understands the parent in relation to themselves.

The role of 'mother' particularly, occupies a position of performative expectation where the compulsory heteronormative matrix – gendered as 'mother' – is enforced. The mother's role has been defined (and redefined) from culture to culture and epoch to epoch; it has, nevertheless, been defined.

After the publication in 1990 of her seminal book critiquing compulsory heterosexuality, *Gender Trouble: Feminism and the Subversion of Identity*, Judith Butler spent considerable space in subsequent essays refuting a misreading of her argument that gender was somehow radical choice. The misreading of *Gender Trouble* stemmed from Butler's example of drag as a way of critiquing the 'naturalness' of gender, and misunderstood the performance of the gendered body as one which was optional. In an interview with Artforum in 1992, Butler says:

> …my whole point was that the very formation of subjects, the very formation of persons, *presupposes* gender in a certain way – that gender is not to be chosen and that 'performativity' is not radical choice and it's not voluntarism. […] Performativity has to do with repetition, very often with the repetition of oppressive and painful gender norms to force them to resignify. This is not freedom….[10]

The performance of gender, of which motherhood must surely be the ultimate representation, is one where women are asked to play particular roles in order to enforce certain 'norms'. Motherhood demands that the woman produces her child not only biologically but also socially.[11] Her performance gives rise to that of the child.

But whereas the social performance of the person-role formula in our everyday actions has, as Butler conceives it, to do with the repetition of oppressive and painful norms (and not just gender norms) to force them to resignify, the use of performance as a technique in the creative process is precisely about the radical choice that is denied in the social context. Performance itself, or the enacting of roles, is an engagement which gives rise to knowledge. It is this understanding of performance as a form of knowledge which is at the heart of the ResCen project.

The element of detachment when dealing with *somebody else's* work that Miller internalises through the Spock/Kirk role-play device, is embodied by Richard Layzell's collaboration with Tania Koswyckz. Responding to a commission from the *firstsite* gallery in Colchester to create an installation which would 'reveal artists' practices' Layzell invented a group of four artists and made their work for them.[12] In this way Layzell deconstructed the creative process *through* the creative process; a kind of making while being detached. Back in his studio after the exhibition had closed, Layzell found himself missing the method and ease of making Tania's work, and so he decided to continue fabricating work as Tania. This process gave rise to a relationship in which Richard and Tania provoked each other precisely because they had differing points of view. Richard would ask Tania what she thought about something and found her advice useful and provocative. These 'process' conversations eventually became an integral part of Layzell's 'product'. In performances Richard began to speak directly to Tania, later their conversations were published.[13] In other words, one of the solutions which Layzell found to answer the challenge of making decisions, that is the dramatisation of creative thought through the creation of a dialogue with an invented collaborator, became the very stuff of which the decision-making process was set up to answer.

In this publication the published conversation Richard 'has' with Tania, in which they discuss their working relationship, has been given over to two other writers who take up the baton of the fictional voice and not only rethink it but also fictionalise its creator. Caroline Bergvall subtly critiques what might be sociologically at stake in the relationship between Richard and Tania, especially with reference to the implied gender dynamic, by interrupting their dialogue with the ghost of a fictionalised Ana Mendieta. Ana Mendieta was the wife of the sculptor Carl Andre (a sculptor to whom Layzell makes allusion in his dialogue with Tania). Mendieta was a performance artist who came to an untimely end. In 1985 she fell to her death from the window of her 34th floor apartment. Andre was tried and acquitted of her murder but the circumstances of her death are still (seen as) mysterious. The story of her 'disappearance' – a terrible ending – has, in many discourses, eclipsed the importance of her work as an artist; as her work as an artist was eclipsed by that of her husband when she was alive. By raising her ghost and implicitly citing the discourse of her disappearance, Bergvall talks to this power dynamic between artists and sexes. This ghosting of Layzell's text, and also of him (Bergvall puts words into Richard's mouth) doubles the fictive narrative by engaging with the process of Layzell's art practice as Bergvall's own. Bergvall tests not only Richard's relationship to Tania and Layzell's relationship to the text, but also Bergvall's relationship to Layzell. Richard Layzell worked 'in dialogue' with Caroline Bergvall on the development of his conversations with Tania. They too have a history of a working relationship.

    In an open-letter come telephone-call monologue (a deliberate 'fluff') from his own invention Davida Pendleton to both Richard and Tania, Adrian Rifkin both contextualises this device of staging a fictional voice and parodies its effects. Subtitled 'The Torment of Davida Pendleton', Davida's rant on behalf of her creator (or is it his rant on her behalf?) reveals her jealousy of Richard's attachment to Tania and the collaborative partnership they have developed, in contrast to her infelicitous relationship with Adrian whom she sees as promiscuous. Rifkin resituates Bergvall's critique of the gendered relations between Richard and his creation Tania, by giving voice to the disgruntled dissatisfaction of his

own creation, who perceives Tania's relationship with Richard as one to aspire to. By sending up the absurdity of these literary encounters, in part through the multiplication of confusion (for instance, we discover halfway through the 'invented' Davida's diatribe that her name 'Davida Pendleton' is in fact an invented 'pen name') Rifkin points to the fact that it is in the absurdity of the encounter that the creative use and productivity is to be found.

    It is in the very context of this publication then, that the techniques employed by an artist to navigate through the creative process, in this case the invention of an artist to collaborate with, has the potential not only to become the 'work' itself, but to be incorporated as a provocation to other artists and writers for work of their own.

    The process of handing over his dialogue for reinvention that is enacted by Layzell to Bergvall and Rifkin recognises another important theme of this chapter: artistic collaborations. Although always a necessary part of even the most solo of performance practices, collaborations are often at the forefront of the practices described here. Richard's collaboration with Tania, although physically manifest in one corporeal body, nevertheless underlines the creative potential of working relationships. This is something that is played out when Layzell hands his text to Bergvall and she hands both hers and his to Rifkin. There is a certain risk involved in this strategy of handing over and giving up; risk of authorship, risk of censure, risk of the unknown.

    Ghislaine Boddington has made collaboration central to the development of her creative strategies. As she makes clear in the conversation which follows this introduction, for her it is through confrontation with colleagues and the direct sharing of material that the most productive working methodologies are to be found. As she says: 'If you decide to share material as a group, then you own a set of content which can be used in multiple ways…'.[14] This sharing is manifest literally in a virtual holding space, where members can give or take ideas, as need or desire dictates.

This process of 'interauthorship'[15] is a provocative counterpoint to the sociologically 'normative' understanding of family. As the artist Barbara Kruger comments:

I think that the hallucination of an ideal family is becoming more and more difficult to perpetrate. People can no longer believe it….[16]

The suspension of disbelief in the family theatre no longer carries its force. And it is, interestingly enough, in the family unit that Judith Butler sees the most progressive subversion of compulsory heterosexuality. In discussing the documentary film *Paris is Burning* by Jennie Livingstone, a film which documents the dance form 'vogueing' in the New York underground drag scene, it is not so much the performance of gender which Butler finds subversive (which merely mimes the heteronormative model) but rather the performance of family: mothers and children:

…the subversive part of what [Livingston's film] documents, for me, is in the 'house' structure, where there are 'mothers' and 'children', and new kinship systems, which do mime older nuclear-family kinship arrangements but also displace them, and radically *re*contextualize them in a way that constitutes a rethinking of kinship, or that turns kinship into a notion of extended community – one whose future forms can't be fully predicted. What is a 'house'? A 'house' is the people you 'walk' with. I love that that's a house.[17]

Captain Kirk and Mr Spock also operate in a kind of alternative to the traditional nuclear family.

Neither can form lasting relationships because of their focus on 'career' and the USS Enterprise is not just a metaphor for the domestic space of 'home' but literally embodies the physical place where social dramas are played out. The creative process of collaboration often involves the setting up of an alternative family, whether that be the 'company of performers', a partnership between a choreographer and a musician, or even the group of ResCen artists themselves. It is no surprise then, that Shobana Jeyasing describes the trauma of making work as 'like giving birth'.[18]

This alternative family as a creative way of life is explored in Mark Vernon's essay 'Plato and the Creative Life'. Vernon gives us an account of some of the issues at stake in Plato's dialogues which very usefully reflect on the creative process. At the heart of Plato's idea of philosophy is the idea of collaboration. Plato himself, as Vernon points out, only ever writes in other people's voices and 'never once unequivocally signs off a single sentence as his own definitive belief' but rather 'insists on attributing what he writes to other people'.[19] Vernon argues that vital to the navigating process itself, for both artists and philosophers alike, is the formation of a creative way of life. That way of life is one in which the collaborative process amongst friends and colleagues is situated outside the conventions (Plato might also say the distractions) of family life.

For Vernon it is in the dramatisation of creative thought through the dialogues, what he calls 'philosophical dramas', that philosophical thought is produced. In other words, as in Miller's Spock/Kirk method and Richard's conversations with Tania, the very staging of an idea brings it into being.

Plato's philosophical premise is the limit of his knowledge: his ignorance. It is his search for wisdom in relation to ignorance that offers the potential for 'self-transformation', which Vernon sees as one of the goals of philosophy.

In her essay 'Expectant Waiting', choreographer Rosemary Lee writes about the potential for transformation in the devising and rehearsal process, through the act of waiting. Waiting might commonsensibly (at least to this lay writer) be understood as the opposite to dance, as everything that it was not. Waiting in this context is not an aesthetic consideration as John Cage might consider silence in music, but rather waiting as an active process of reception ('...rudderless but not lost...' so that things can 'creep up unawares'). This is *active* waiting, engaged to effect some kind of transformation. It is not aesthetic but strategic. As Lee writes: 'This state, though, is far from passive: it is a state of acute attentiveness and relaxation'. It is a negative preference for movement without rejecting the power of movement.

Negative preference without outright refusal and the notion of waiting for something to appear is embodied in the 'I would prefer not to', which is the repeated answer of Bartleby, Herman Melville's character from the short story of the same name. Bartleby is a scrivener: a writer, a copyist, a scribe. His *logic of preference*, a negativism without outright refusal, leads to the paradox that he is a writer who does not write.[20]

In his essay 'Bartleby; or, The Formula', Gilles Deleuze argues that while Bartleby's phrase 'I would prefer not to' is grammatically and syntactically correct, it has the affect of being *agrammatical*, that 'it has an anomalous ring to it'.[21] Linguistically its affect is neither constative nor performative; it neither describes something nor performs an action.

A word always presupposes other words that can replace it, complete it, or form alternatives with it: it is on this condition that language is distributed in such a way as to designate things, states of things and actions, according to a set of objective, explicit conventions. But perhaps there are also other implicit and subjective conventions, other types of reference or presupposition. In speaking, I do not simply indicate things and actions; I also commit acts that assure a relation with the interlocutor, in keeping with our respective situations: I command, I interrogate, I promise, I ask, I emit 'speech acts.' Speech acts are self-referential (I command by saying "I order you…"), while constative propositions refer to other things and other words. It is this double system of references that Bartleby ravages.[22]

Bartleby's *logic of preference* places his speech not only at the limit of social convention but also at the limit of understanding.

'I would prefer not to.'
'You *will* not?'
'I *prefer* not.'[23]

The core of Bartleby's negative preference is his preference not to write.

'Why, how now? what next?' exclaimed I,
'do no more writing?'
'No more.'
'And what is the reason?'
'Do you not see the reason yourself?'
he indifferently replied.[24]

The reason – that he would prefer not to – while comic, ostensibly robs Bartleby of his vocation and thus his identity; he is after all, a scribe who has stopped writing. But as Giorgio Agamben argues, it is paradoxically the arresting of his vocation which offers its potential and identifies its power.

As a scribe who has stopped writing,

Bartleby is the extreme figure of the Nothing from which all creation derives; and at the same time, he constitutes the most implacable vindication of this Nothing as pure, absolute potentiality. The scrivener has become the writing tablet; he is now nothing other than his white sheet.[25]

Writing, like creation itself, issues from nothing. Bartleby's immobility, his silence, his putting down of the pen, performs him.

As Bartleby is a writer who has stopped writing, so Rosemary Lee is a choreographer – a movement specialist – who, as a key part of her creative process, prefers not to move. Movement comes out of nothing. As the scrivener becomes the writing tablet, the dancer becomes stage.

There is another negative preference that has, at different times during the ResCen project, been relevant to all the artists involved; the preference not to 'talk out' the navigating process *during* that process, for fear it will disappear. Part of Lee's waiting for an idea is the '…hoping it will appear more fully formed if I touch it less with my mind'. While psychoanalysis has taught us that the 'talking cure' will rid us of our demons, these artists have all expressed, at some time or another, the concern that intellectualising the creative process, while useful and important when separated from the process, offers the danger of intellectualising it away; that the magic will disappear and the work become worthless.

In the discussion which follows, the ResCen artists talk about how they get started, the relevance of money to their creative drive, collaborations, commissions, what happens when they get stuck, and what constitutes a good day. At the end of the creative process pertaining to a particular work or project, they acknowledge a moment of amnesia. As Errollyn Wallen puts it: 'The thing is, a terrible

thing in a way, is that the second you finish making those choices, amnesia sets in.'

Ultimately, the journey that an artist makes in the creation of contemporary performance, from the initial idea or commission to the manifestation of that work in a public engagement, seems to be about erasure and forgetting. Perhaps it is only through amnesia that the creative process can be renewed to move on.

1 See 'All in a Day's Work' which follows this essay, p.118
2 Ibid. p.115. References to Spock and Kirk are to characters from the long-running television series *Star Trek* which spans over 726 episodes since 1966 and ten feature films, to date.
3 Elsewhere Miller has described the imagined audience for his work as 'an audience of Graeme Millers'. See 'Outside Looking In', transcript of seminar at Conway Hall, London, 15 June 2005 at <www.rescen.net>
4 See <www.startrek.com> [accessed 8 December 2005] from which this quote and other biographical details about Kirk and Spock have been taken.
5 See Lynn Bloom, *Doctor Spock: Biography of a Conservative Radical* (New York: The Bobbs-Merrill Company, 1972)
6 Excerpt from statement by President Clinton from White House Daily Briefing 16 March 1998. See Mike McCurry, 'White House Daily Briefing March 16, 1998' (1998) <http://usembassy-australia.state.gov/hyper/WF980316/epf101.htm> [accessed 12 August 2001]
7 Benjamin McLane Spock, *Baby and Child Care* illust. by Dorothea Fox (London: Bodley Head, 1969) p.449
8 Erving Goffman, *Frame Analysis: An Essay on the Organisation of Experience* (London: Penguin, 1974) p.269
9 Ibid. p.129
10 Judith Butler, 'The Body You Want: Liz Kotz Interviews Judith Butler' *Artforum*, November 1992, 82-89 (p.84)
11 For detailed arguments on the social construction of motherhood and childrearing see Donna Bassin and Margaret Honey and Meryle Mahrer Kaplan eds., *Representations of Motherhood* (New Haven: Yale University Press, 1994); Sharon Hays, *The Cultural Contradictions of Motherhood* (London: Yale University Press, 1996); and Patrice Di Quinzio, *The Impossibility of Motherhood* (London: Routledge, 1999)
12 See Richard Layzell, 'Tania's Space' in *Digital Creativity* Vol. 5, No. 2. for an account of this process and also Richard Layzell's *ResCen Pages* at <www.rescen.net>
13 A range of different conversations between Richard Layzell and Tania Koswyckz are published at <www.recen.net>
14 See 'All in a Day's Work' p.119
15 'Interauthorship' is a term used by Boddington to describe collaborative process creations. See <www.recen.net>
16 Therese Lichtenstein, 'Images of the Maternal: An interview with Barbara Kruger' in Donna Bassin and Margaret Honey and Meryle Mahrer Kaplan eds., *Representations of Motherhood* (New Haven: Yale University Press, 1994) p.199
17 Butler p.84
18 See 'All in a Day's Work' p.119
19 Mark Vernon, 'Plato and the Creative Life' p.150
20 The phrase *'logic of preference'* is used by Gilles Deleuze in 'Bartleby; or, The Formula', in *Essays Critical and Clinical* by Gilles Deleuze trans. by Daniel W. Smith and Michael A. Greco (London: Verso, 1998).
21 Ibid. p.69
22 Ibid. p.73
23 Herman Melville, *Bartleby* (London: Penguin, 1995) p.17
24 Ibid. p.27
25 Giorgio Agamben, *Potentialities: Collected Essays in Philosophy* trans. by Daniel Heller-Roazen (California: Stanford University Press, 1999) p.254

Richard
Layzell

3. COMPREHENSI CATALOGUE AL TOOLS, MATERI SOFTWARE AN YOU'VE USED O LAST MONTH TH Y CONCLUS

1. STAND VERY STILL IN A M AMONGST OLD THINGS O

2. TREAT IMPROVISATION AS A DISCRETE ARTFORM

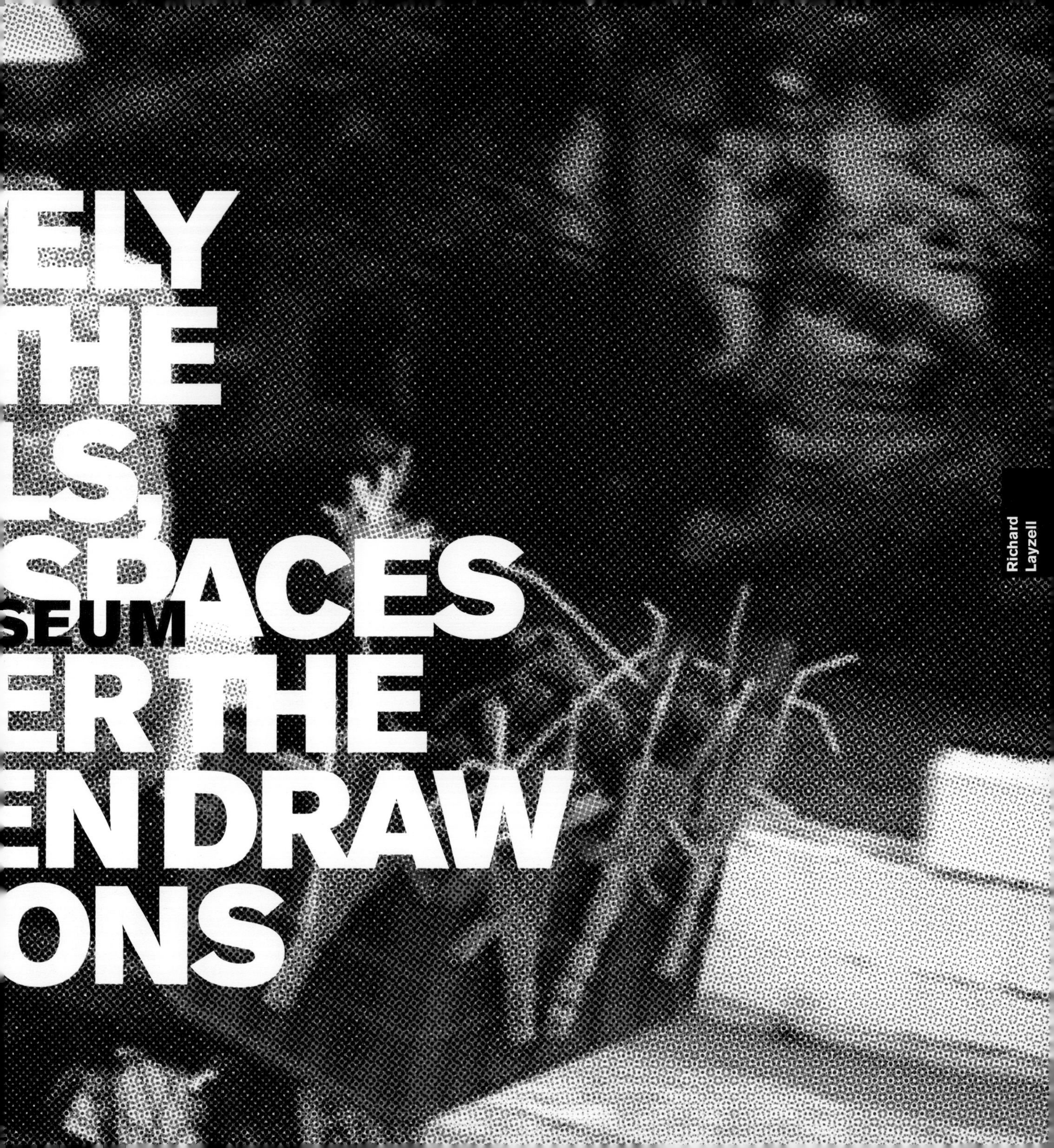

ELY
HE
S,
SPACES
SEUM
ER THE
EN DRAW
ONS

Richard Layzell

Ghislaine Boddington

Shobana Jeyasingh

Richard Layzell

Rosemary Lee

Graeme Miller

Errollyn Wallen

All in a Day's Work
A conversation between

Ghislaine Boddington

Shobana Jeyasingh

Richard Layzell

Rosemary Lee

Graeme Miller

Errollyn Wallen

Errollyn Wallen | Graeme Miller | Rosemary Lee | Richard Layzell | Shobana Jeyasingh | Ghislaine Boddington

Graeme: To begin: as I often say, all you do is start and then take the shortest route to the end. That's slightly flippant but behind it is actually something quite truthful. To take the shortest route requires a lot of guile. To begin things and see them through to the end is a skill in itself.

Errollyn: To picture the route, to have a sense of what that journey might be, it's very difficult.

Ghislaine: Do you mean visualising it and playing it through in your head? I do that too, playing that visual quite often in several different ways. So I try different routes through. It's kind of a mapping isn't it? It's like a visual mapping of where something could go from a beginning idea. Ideas are two a penny but implementing them is what matters. Is that what you're talking about?

Errollyn: Yes, each of us must be able to have a sense of what the journey involves even if they are completely different sorts of journey. But you also allow yourself to get stuck because we have techniques at our disposal to deal with that.

Rosemary: So you trust that you'll know how to cope at the point of getting stuck.

Graeme: Is one level of stuck purely about fear or a loss of confidence? Or is it about keeping elements of something so you are stuck?

Errollyn: Or we're stuck because we've made ourselves question something when we're not stuck at all. I met this composer last week and he was very anxious. He said, 'I know I'm working, but I haven't written any music'. He's comfortable with being stuck.

Richard: But is what we do, is it really work?

Errollyn: That's what we don't know. We call it work, but when we were kids we'd call it 'skiving off of school'.

Richard: You said to me earlier that Clare Short said to you, 'So this

[Laughter]

is what you do is it? Sit around holding pebbles all day?' Doesn't sound like work to me.

Errollyn: Richard and I were talking earlier about the public perception of artists. I was involved in a seminar for teachers and composers, getting kids composing, and Clare Short chose to walk in at the moment somebody was holding a pebble (we were talking about surface and texture) and you could see that she thought it was slightly unnecessary.

Richard: Well I'm confused about that because I think I work really hard. But when I think about what I do (and partly I'm being devil's advocate here) you know, I wonder, is this really work? It seems, sometimes that by most people's standards, it's not work.

Errollyn: Because they think we're not suffering. You need to suffer more. Work means suffering to most people.

Richard: Well the questions they would ask are: what good are you doing anyway? You call yourself a composer. What does that mean? How are you benefiting me or society?

Rosemary: If you ask that of yourself, does that affect your navigating?

Richard: It's always there to be honest. It does affect it. But then this morning I was thinking that probably one of the best things I've done is a piece that wasn't commissioned and that hasn't really seen the light of day. It's called International Cleaning. I mean, to me, it doesn't matter whether it's work or not, because no one's commissioned it.

Rosemary: That's sort of what I mean. One of the questions that Shobana and I were discussing was: does the arts market determine your navigation? In other words, how does your view of your art practice as a commodity, as a product, affect how you value your work, what you call yourself and possibly what you make? I'm not sure if it does for me but I know it certainly clouds the area when you're navigating because you come to a point of asking: well hang on, will this sell or will anyone ever want to see this?

Shobana: I think you feel the effect. It's very difficult to make dance without some support. You need other people and I am surprised that other people are willing to come and work often without being paid; dancers who are only available

Errollyn Wallen   Graeme Miller   Rosemary Lee   Richard Layzell   Shobana Jeyasingh   Ghislaine Boddington

Errollyn Wallen

Graeme Miller

Rosemary Lee

Richard Layzell

Shobana Jeyasingh

Ghislaine Boddington

weekends and evenings because they're all accountants. You could say, yes that's very much out of the arts market, but actually you couldn't sustain making work like that.

Graeme: It's a very interesting thing in the art world, that people will turn in enormous amounts of work for uneconomically rewarding consequences. I think it was John Fox from Welfare State who said basically: 'If someone pays me a hundred pounds a week I'll just work all the hours that I feel I need to work'. But I think it is also important to recognise moments of what might also be called 'playing', or a willingness to be 'stuck' as a tactic in your practice. These are things you would tend not to have in a desk job or in a situation where someone was paying you by the hour. Maybe you would choose to simply waste the whole day and go for a walk to divert your attention away from what you're doing. Those can be very useful creative practices. Actually not doing the task in hand can be very useful. So I'm wondering if we have a slightly altered work ethic.

Ghislaine: Just to put it another way, maybe one of the art sector's problems is precisely that we question ourselves about whether this is work or not. I see what I do as my work and I see myself as a professional and I see myself in a working environment. Yes, OK, there's not necessarily enough resources around and it would be great if there was more, but I wonder whether taking the day off and going for a walk is actually so different from other jobs where people are having to do a lot of thinking and mapping and laying things out. A lot of my friends who don't work in the arts do that. I'm not so sure we should think of these processes as so uniquely different. And the Clare Short comment will come back as long as artists put out this kind of idea of being in this mysterious process and doing it slightly differently than everyone else. Actually how different is it?

Richard: That is interesting in relation to the idea of money because, to be really honest with you, I am in it for the money. When a highly paid period working in industry came to an end and I thought, what am I going to do, and I looked at various options, art was actually the best paid. Not that I ever stopped making art. But when I looked at how I was going to support myself it looked likely that finding a route back into somewhere between arts practice and consultancy was going to be a career. I did have a choosing point because I could have stayed working in industry, but I chose to re-enter the art world, and it was for financial reasons.

Rosemary: Just to give you the other side. I'm definitely not in it for the money. I couldn't be because I just can't earn enough.

Richard: But you can.

Rosemary: No, not through doing the thing I really want to do, which is to make work. I'm happy to say I don't do it for the money. I make money from my artwork but I don't get paid very much. I make my money by teaching, lecturing, all the added extras. But I don't think this is relevant to navigating at all.

Richard: I think it is.

Rosemary: Well I'm not going into the studio thinking about how much I'm getting paid every day. It would be pointless.

Richard: I agree with that.

Ghislaine: But I think it is relevant because it is linked to how we survive. We can't continue our journeys unless we're surviving. So for me it is highly relevant that I have to bring in a certain

Errollyn Wallen

Graeme Miller

Rosemary Lee

Richard Layzell

Shobana Jeyasingh

Ghislaine Boddington

amount of turnover to keep a small company moving forward.

Rosemary: But I do other things for that. What I'm saying is I cannot get paid enough to survive on my arts practice alone. There is no way. There never has been. I'm talking about choreographing and making work as an independent artist. All the other bits, the teaching, which I love, that's the way I support myself, to have a period, like I have now, where I'm five weeks in a studio and getting paid very little per day...

Richard: I'm saddened to hear that because I would want to value you for doing the thing that you're probably going to give the most back for.

Rosemary: Yes but why are you sad? I don't equate my value with money.

Errollyn: I'm always doing a lot of things that take away from the thing I do best. So I get cross doing things that other people can do better.

Rosemary: In order to earn money you mean? Yes I'm sad I don't get enough time to do the thing I'm supposed to do. But I've just got used to the fact that there isn't enough of a subsidy. What I do has to be subsidised, because I have to pay the dancers.

Graeme: 'You don't value yourself because you're not paid enough and you're not paid enough so you don't value yourself.' I find all that very dubious and something that belongs to a decade ago. There are choices and some people maintain their self-esteem with pride and self-esteem for something you love doing. Unfortunately not everybody in the whole world can. People have very different tactics of survival.

Shobana: But subsidy does change things. I realised very quickly that I couldn't work with people only on the evenings and weekends. Because you need time with the people when they're fresh. And you know especially with dance, I think it was important to put in those people's heads that actually dance should be part of their working life and not their extra-curricular life. I think it has repercussions on the quality of dance in general. It's very important that I earn my living through choreography rather than, you know, be a bus conductress and then earn money to make the work, because I think the best hours of the day have to be spent in what you want to do. But then if you really want to make serious money you wouldn't be in the arts. I think serious money is a matter of luck. Sometimes what you make coincides with what people want and other times it doesn't. And I think it's your choice whether you continue without feeling undervalued. Sometimes people take advantage of that because they can see that we have a passion for what we do and we'll do it anyway. So then they feel that absolves them of actually paying what you should be paid. I think that's very bad.

Ghislaine: There are other ways of working. For example I know some people who are doing extremely commercial music work at one end of their job, or making music for games, or making software for various things, and in the evenings and weekends they'll be making creative work, working on arts projects, community or group projects where they can afford to take less pay.

Errollyn: I know that that is happening more and more with music for films.

Richard: I'm just wondering about the relationship to the commissioner, the person who gives us money. How do they value what we do?

Errollyn: In my experience they always have an agenda. It may be unspoken but it is there. Often they aren't even really concerned about the product as long as they've fulfilled their agenda.

Richard: Yeah, I think that's something that happens in the navigating process, that you think, well, I know what the issues are here and

Errollyn | Graeme | Rosemary | Richard | Shobana | Ghislaine what they want but they think I don't give a fuck what they think, I'm going to do what I want! And then a little bit further down the line they don't know what they want anyway and they see what you're doing and they go, 'Oh great!'

Ghislaine: Well I've done a lot of commissioning and I've cared hugely, very deeply. I'm completely aware of what's going on.

Errollyn: The big swing that orchestras have made towards education would not have happened in some cases if they hadn't been pushed. The Arts Council said look, unless you start reaching out you're not going to get the subsidy. The orchestras did it but some wouldn't necessarily have come up with that themselves. And there's a lot of stuff that happens like that. The Arts Council give them a directive…

Shobana: Yes the 'Cultural Diversity' agenda for example.

Errollyn: That's right. I know I get some commissions simply because I am black. I just don't think about it. I think, well I've got this opportunity; but for them it does fulfil another purpose. It's common sense for some organisations. I am aware that it's not just me writing music but that I am fulfilling a function for other people. There I am talking about the real issues and they're not interested. I was commissioned to do a very big piece which was going to be televised and there were problems all the way along. The day of the rehearsal came and the producer said 'Gosh, it's good!'; he was so surprised. [Laughs] And I thought, oh, of course, I should have realised he had another agenda. I suspected that they probably commissioned me because I was black.

Rosemary: That's very interesting. If I realise that I'm being pulled in all directions, they want this and I don't, and I realise I'm not actually in control of my destiny, I think right, simplify, simplify, simplify. It's a constant balance for me of how to be true to that very intimate place of the shut door and the studio with your dancers and all the requirements for marketing: which picture are you going to use; have you got your copy ready; someone wants to speak to you on the phone (and everybody has to do that) but I realise that if I get too pulled outside of myself I'm not an artist any more. I'm not the person I think I am. So to be more me I've got to somehow get that balance better.

Ghislaine: What I find frustrating is when you don't fit into their bracket, in the funding system for example. You get these forms where you've got to tick boxes all the way through. At bodydataspace we are finally in a section of Visual Arts called New Media. Previously shinkansen never fitted in any department. So at this time we are supported by Visual Arts. Actually we've never been in Visual Arts before but we are in the Visual Arts Department now. And I'm quite happy. That's fine. Before that we were always floating between Collaborative Arts, Dance and Music, bouncing around. And it's not just us that are in this position.

Richard: I just wonder why I've stuck at it sometimes. Because when you're working with art students, there is this horrible thing where they graduate and you see them a year later and you ask: 'So are you still making work?' and you just know as soon as they look into your eyes that they're not. What's been the driving force to want this kind of fairly uncomfortable struggle to make the indefinable?

Graeme: Well why don't we think about what a good day is? A good day for me is a day when if I'm working with performers, a lot of relevant material has appeared out of nowhere and it connects with other stuff that I've done and just by continuing it seems that the tide has turned. It's the feeling that by almost doing nothing different, but holding onto the bone with clenched teeth, things move forward. Or just allowing things to happen, things are starting to move. There's a feeling of momentum, of wind in your sails. And relief. So I go home and I probably know not be so worried about the next day's work.

Errollyn: For me a good day is knowing that I have twenty-four hours totally in my control. Total freedom, that's really good. For me it's about freedom, power and control; freedom to choose what I want to do with my time.

Richard: I was thinking that a good day for me is a bit like where what I want for myself as a person, as a human being, is fulfilled through my work. But a good day will also involve some fear and some pain and some anxiety, some excitement and some kind of knowledge, some kind of awe, some sense of some kind of connection or leap

Errollyn Wallen

Graeme Miller

Rosemary Lee

Richard Layzell

Shobana Jeyasingh

Ghislaine Boddington

Errollyn Wallen

Graeme Miller

Rosemary Lee

Richard Layzell

Shobana Jeyasingh

Ghislaine Boddington

having happened, but I might not know if it's the right leap until a few days later. It might be interesting to bring John Prescott into it here. As I was doing some filming I was interrupted by an official visit by John Prescott. It was deeply irritating, until talking to you about it, Rosemary, when I realised the paradox that the commission would not have happened but for his department, because it's all about neighbourhood renewal, which is something he dreamt up. What's he got to do with art? Absolutely nothing, probably, but nevertheless that's life. Life is weird. Having that kind of weirdness is good for me.

Graeme: A good day is a John Prescott day.

[Laughter]

Richard: In a way, yes. At the time it wasn't, but now, you know, with a bit of reflection, it was a good day.

Graeme: I like the fact you incorporate a certain degree of perplexity, anxiety and struggle in the mix.

Ghislaine: The best days for me are when there's a group of great collaborators coming together and I'm learning from them as well as them learning from me. I really like to have a good full-on debate with collaborators.

Shobana: I suppose one thing that would make a day good is when I don't have any doubts, which is not very often. When I make things, I always have lots of doubts in my head. So I think getting to a point where any one of those hundreds of doubts has been erased for a moment is good. I usually find that the best part of my day is actually when I leave the studio and I am making the journey back home because that's really when all kinds of computations seem to happen, because when you're in the studio, you don't have a lot of time to be very reflective because you're engaged in something that involves other people and you have to be very active the whole time. So often the solutions really only occur after I leave, when I'm running through what has happened in the day. I always think that's rather sad, because usually the solutions are there. Sometimes, by the time I reach home, I really wish it were morning because I'm very ready. I've actually got the solution to all the problems I've been rehearsing the whole day. So often I come home and I think, what a shame it's the evening, if I'd had this thought in the morning, going to the studio, I would have had an even more productive day. But it can't happen because you have to get to the evening to have those thoughts.

Graeme: That thing, if only it were the next morning; how do you pick up the threads where you left off?

Errollyn: I stop in the middle of something the day before.

Rosemary: Is that what you do?

Errollyn: Yeah.

Graeme: That's interesting. It leaves a frayed edge. Don't put it to bed.

Shobana: It's very tempting to put it to bed though. When I see it there, I want to grab it before it goes.

Errollyn: Sometimes what is bad is ending the day on too good an idea. I think that I start work with a purposefully mediocre or bad idea because then I'm working to find something good. It's often best to work with something small, slight and a bit problematic, then you can knock your way through.

Graeme: I'm an addictive problem solver, so sometimes I divide my work between Spock work and Kirk work...

Shobana: Kirk work?

Graeme: Kirk work. Captain Kirk and Mister Spock.

Errollyn | Graeme | Rosemary | Richard | Shobana | Ghislaine

Errollyn Wallen

Graeme Miller

Rosemary Lee

Richard Layzell

Shobana Jeyasingh

Ghislaine Boddington

Shobana: Oh! [Laughs] I thought you were talking about the church.

Graeme: No, not the Scottish Church but the short tubby Captain of the USS Enterprise! It means to do with whether you're in the driving seat or whether you're in the Spock role, which is about problem solving. 'Captain, have you thought of this?' And you can do that for yourself. It throws up constant material. 'What comes next?' 'What comes before it?' 'How does this fit in with the whole?' 'How am I going to persuade someone else to do this?' The detachment is really useful. When it's somebody else's work it's a lot easier to have opinions, and to solve their problems, than it is your own. Sometimes I find myself just trying to get into neutral, and almost having conversations within myself. 'Come on Graeme, sit down, have a cup of tea, tell me about it, what's the problem, well have you thought of this?' 'Why don't you do this, Graeme?' 'Oh, I hadn't thought of that.' You've just got to stay calm enough and detached enough to find solutions, and certainly panicking or being overwhelmed by the possibility of failure or of spoiling something, those are all things that paralyse you, cause inertia. You're fighting inertia a lot of the time.

Rosemary: You know, there is a slightly remote place where you don't want to upset the problem, it's a funny place that, where you have got that thing where you don't want the fear of the problem to paralyse you. I don't think I feel fear any more, actually. I mean, that's what used to make me stuck but I don't really think I feel fear because I sort of think I know there's a solution, I've just got to stay calm. It's like the cat, if I sit here long enough the mouse will come close enough. So I feel I've got to stay really still here and in a minute it's going come and I'll get the answer.

Ghislaine: I've recently been thinking a lot about fear, and actually I've been worrying a bit why I don't feel fear enough. We have a phrase in the group and it's something we've used for some time now: 'positive solutions'. If there's a crisis coming at a point of production, it doesn't matter what, why, who did it, what went wrong, etcetera, the whole focus of the group needs to be on positive solutions. What I've realised in the last few years is that if something does go into crisis, the positive solutions that come up within a group process often end up being far better than some of the original plans. So sometimes a crisis can be quite good. I don't get fearful at those points any more. I think, good, we've got to find a solution.

Errollyn: I take doubt as part of the palette. It helps you to take nothing for granted. But there is a point when too much doubt can call the validity of the project into question. I'll give you an example. When I was writing a Concerto for Percussion and Orchestra, I didn't know what the hell I was doing. No idea, I just didn't know. At that time there were only a couple of percussion concertos around and they weren't the sort of thing I wanted to write, so I just didn't really know what I was doing. There was also the problem of how to write a piece for a soloist when they really hate you! [Laughter] As it was for television, producers would call and because I was so scared, I would just be very honest with every single one of them. That was a mistake because they didn't understand my doubts. I knew that everything was going to be alright in the end but they didn't understand that. Doubt was important for me to find my way through, but I shouldn't have been so honest about it with them.

Graeme: I was just thinking that often we don't have the luxury of abandoning a project. It's not wise to just not deliver the goods. There are some instances I think I would have preferred to have cancelled a first night and say I'd like to have six months off and look at this again. There are times where to press the abort button and let something drop at a certain moment may be the right decision. The alternative to letting something drop is the 'shelf'. I have so many projects on the shelf, and the shelf is a very interesting place to be because things can be put on the shelf, and then at a later point, when the time is right, one of these half-baked ideas that is queuing up on the shelf is suddenly thriving.

Rosemary: I was making a piece called *Exhale* and in my head there was a date, and you know, I was going to perform it. It was a solo. I was working on my own and I was performing on my own. I think I did forty rehearsals alone, and every time I thought I'd got it, I looked through the video that night and I thought it was just a pile of crap. This went on and on and on, and I realised that my doubt was huge, I really did just want to give up, and then I realised that the thing I had to do was trash the video. Every time I thought I'd got it, the video told me I hadn't, and if I was going to keep going, I had to take away what was telling me I hadn't got it, and I just had to believe that the feeling I was having when I performed it was greater than what it looked like on the video. In any other circumstances I would have put that on the shelf and it wouldn't have ever come out again because I really did doubt it that much.

Errollyn Wallen

Graeme Miller

Rosemary Lee

Richard Layzell

Shobana Jeyasingh

Ghislaine Boddington

Errollyn
Wallen

Graeme
Miller

Rosemary
Lee

Richard
Layzell

Shobana
Jeyasingh

Ghislaine
Boddington

Graeme: The shelf of no return.

Rosemary: The shelf of no return. It almost hit that, but getting rid of the video and just thinking, I'm going to do it, whether it's working or not, I'm going to do it. I think it did work in the end.

Shobana: I have given up looking at videos now because I used to look at the day's work, and it always looked awful. Everything always looks awful on video. I think, gosh, I've really got something, look at it on video, that's that, I never want to see it again. So I've given up now. I don't mind looking at videos when we have rehearsals in a theatre, it's a bit different, you get the distance, and then you get to see the pattern. But I wanted to come back to 'doubt' for a moment. Now that you've all talked about it, I don't think when I used the word 'doubt', that I was referring to how you use it in normal conversation, when you say 'I really doubt whether this person is the right person to marry', it's not that kind of doubt I was talking about, important as that it is. I was actually thinking more of the situation where you know, you've got choices to make, and it's the kind of angst that you have about making the choice, tying yourself to a particular choice, and it's always a moment of suffering actually. Choosing something is always suffering, isn't it.

Rosemary: Is it something about loss? The loss of the other opportunities?

Shobana: I don't know what it is, but it's very painful nailing choices. It's been chosen by needs, someone else, deadlines, whatever. Deadlines choose for you, don't they? You have so, so many choices, and then finally you eliminate, but I don't know really, how one comes to that sort of solution. There isn't really a rule, is there?

Rosemary: I definitely seek out situations where I have really huge limitations, because of the 'too much choice' problem.

Ghislaine: Collaborators also force you to question what you want yourself. And that's actually reminded me of what Graeme said right at the beginning of this conversation about taking the shortest route to the end because one thing that I don't think is praised enough is the pooling of material in arts practice. If you decide to share material as a group, then you co-own a set of content which can be used in multiple ways, and that often avoids reinventing the wheel.

Richard: I think some of my best pieces have come out of complete mistakes, problems, embarrassments, and even humiliations making choices for me.

Errollyn: The thing is, a terrible thing in a way, is that the second you finish making those choices, amnesia sets in.

Shobana: That's very, very true, even for really good things. I feel so happy when I come to solutions where I get what I want, but actually I don't think I remember what I did. I have no idea what I was thinking or what I did for a whole day. It really worked but I can't remember what happened. [Laughter] It's like giving birth. You go through it, you experience it, but afterwards you can't imagine what you went through.

Graeme: If you did you'd never have any more children. You'd never make another piece of work again if you remembered.

Errollyn Wallen   Graeme Miller   Rosemary Lee   Richard Layzell   Shobana Jeyasingh   Ghislaine Boddington

Richard Layzell: RL
Tania Koswycz: TK

Function and Form: A dialogue between Richard Layzell and Tania Koswycz

Richard Layzell

TABLE

16"

**RL: What did you think of that book on minimalism
I bought for you?**

TK: Confusing. I mention an interest in
minimalism and the next minute a book on it
arrives from you. Are you trying to steer me, or
something? I don't want to sound ungrateful.

**RL: I thought the architecture angle might
interest you. It's not all Judd and Andre.**

TK: The history is peripheral to me. I operate in the
contemporary context. An occasional minimalist
approach in 2005 doesn't make me a minimalist.
You misunderstand my curiosity, jump to
conclusions. Nice book, though. That passage
about ornamental purification hit the spot. But
maybe I have to remind you that I don't need you
as a mentor. We're collaborators or colleagues,
both in this for the opportunity.

**RL: That doesn't preclude me from buying you
a book.**

TK: So who was it really for? Me, you or both of us?
Or were you trying to impress me with your
connection with Tony Fretton, architects of the
Lisson Gallery and Camden Arts Centre, as
featured in the final pages?

RL: I could introduce you.

TK: Fretton or Lisson?

**RL: Simon from Fretton's. He's project architect
on the Stroud Valley Arts re-development.**

TK: Maybe you should leave me to do my own
networking.

RL: You'd like him.

TK: Sure. How do you function by the way?

RL: Pardon?

TK: How do you function?

RL: What, artistically?

TK: No separation in my world. Function and form.
Art and life. I find how you operate more
confusing, less transparent. You often talk about
'work' and 'working' and how you're 'exploring the
area between work and art', but I still don't
understand how you actually make decisions.
Sometimes you sound like a businessman,
sometimes an air-head, occasionally a diplomat.

RL: Do I seem evasive?

TK: You said it.

RL: Didn't it become clearer after we'd
collaborated on *The Room of Freeflow Returned?*

TK: Not really.

RL: I'm not sure what to say.

TK: That's the point. If you asked me the question
I wouldn't be hesitating.

RL: Are you asking me how I make decisions?

TK: That'll do for a start.

RL: I research. I aim to be strategic. I occupy an
intuitive, almost emotional space. I hold off
making decisions as long as I can.

TK: I thought so. Is this with commissions or your
whole practice?

RL: Everything to some extent. Perhaps I'm trying
to hold on to artistic integrity for as long as
possible.

TK: That's one way of putting it. But I'm sure I've
heard you say that you find working to commission
the most productive. I guess this has to do with
the structure and deadlines. Is this why I have to
keep dragging you back to our gallery project?
You're continually straying off like a distracted
teenager. It seems as if you 'respond to need' and
then resist devoting time to the core work because
you're too 'busy'.

RL: Something like that. Although I don't see
commissions as secondary. They can be core work
too. And I thought this was an aspect of my
practice that interested you. I do get things done
eventually. It's the priorities I sometimes struggle
with. How about you? Don't you get distracted?

> TK: I'd rather work in a bar than do commissions.
> This 'fulfilling need' stuff passes me by. I make
> art for galleries. Simple.

RL: Is it?

> TK: Of course not, but my decision-making is very
> straightforward compared to yours. I'm an artist
> with ambitions. I make pieces. I'm engaged in the
> art community. I'm good at what I do.

RL: Is working in a bar simple?

> TK: Why are you asking me?

RL: You know.

> TK: Not simple, routine. All human life. I find
> material there now and again. I meet people.
> Someone offered me a show last month.

RL: Does it come down to money?

> TK: What, me sometimes working in a bar, or you
> working on commissions? You tell me.

RL: The relationship to commissions is partly
about money. But you're carving out studio time to
make the work you want to make, to then ideally
show and sell. So wouldn't you rather live from
your work?

> TK: Silly question. But there's more to it than
> that, give me credit. Don't bring out the old
> argument about commodity art, please.

RL: It's out there. I saw some in Westbourne
Grove last week. There were plenty of red dots. I
tried to picture the hues of the Notting Hill walls
these deft pieces of textual collage were heading
for. In fact it helped clarify something about my
relationship to money and commissions. This art
clearly fills a specific elitist niche, while most of
my work fulfils another kind of function. Money is
exchanged for both. They both hold a functional
place in our cultural landscape, like architecture,
public and private.

   TK: So we're back to architecture. I hope we're
   both aspiring to a bit more than this by working
   together? You make it sound so pragmatic and
   dull. I was trying to find out how you function and
   now you're lecturing me about the bloody art
   market.

RL: I think I'm onto something here; function is a
key word. If we can establish the function for what
we're working towards collaboratively, through
that we'll clarify how we both function individually,
and then collectively. If that isn't a tautology.
We're both using the same word here.

   TK: My function is to make good art. Elitism is a
   by-product. The anti-market position you started
   out with is irrelevant now. Most of the practices
   you aspired to ended up right back in the market.
   Look at Nauman, for example, and the Minimalists.
   Judd, Andre and Le Witt are blue chip.

RL: Maybe this is ultimately about value. Is an architect-designed commercial gallery more valuable than an architect-designed museum, public housing complex or private house, even if it is for Anish Kapoor? It's the same with art practices like mine. The value of an ephemeral (time-based) commission in West Bromwich, Didcot or Piotrkow Trybunalski can be seen as equivalent to a gallery or museum show. It depends on the viewpoint. And we're exploring how these worlds can meet in *The Manifestation*. That's one of our challenges.

TK: Fine, but I also want to talk about commitment and how you spend your time. I want an acknowledgement of my contribution in this partnership and an agreement that you'll be prepared to prioritise our collaborative working. I want integration, or I'm out.

RL: You've been central to so much recent decision-making. You must know that. I'm not clear what you're asking for.

TK: Action not words. Where are you right now, for example?

RL: On a train to Manchester for the *Partly Writing* seminar, a weekend event that Caroline runs every year.

TK: Our Caroline?

RL: Yes. That huge new public sculpture by Heatherwick is on the horizon. Wouldn't that scale of commission tempt you?

TK: But what are you doing in Manchester when you could be using this time to work on *The Manifestation*? This is a perfect example.

RL: I usually don't work weekends. Caroline invited me. I'll be talking about you, me and our dialogues. I thought it would be useful to get some feedback on how we work. And another dimension to *The Manifestation* is the interconnected performance-lecture. These presentations can all feed into that as research.

TK: Can they? I'm not convinced. You're sounding like a diplomat again. Weren't you just flattered to be asked and now you're trying to justify yourself to me? Let's cut the crap and pin some dates down.

RL: It's pretty hectic at the moment.

TK: Jesus.

RL: Would you settle for a day a week?

TK: That's all I can do. Very busy in my world too, as it happens. But I must have the dates in the diary because I choose to plan ahead and, given your record, I can't trust that you'll commit.

RL: Fridays?

TK: Hang on. Yes. Fridays. Christ, that took some doing.

RL: By the way, are you OK with this dialogue going public?

TK: Website?

RL: Book.

TK: This one and others?

RL: Just this one.

TK: So long as I'm fully credited. There needs to be a context. People should know that not all our dialogues go public. And I'll have to see the proofs. I don't want my verbal integrity edited away into platitude.

Notes:

Minimalisms: A Sign of the Times by Anatxu Zabalbeascoa, Javier Rodriguez Marcos and Tom Johnson (New York: Distributed Art Publishers, 2002)

Tony Fretton Architects are currently redesigning the studio complex of Stroud Valley Arts in Stroud, Gloucestershire. Richard Layzell is commissioned artist on the project. They are also designing a private house for Anish Kapoor.

Piotrkow Trybunalski in Poland is home to *Interakcje*, Art Action Meeting, International Festival.

The Room of Freeflow Returned and *The Manifestation* are the collaborative installations of Tania Koswycz and Richard Layzell.

The B of the Bang by Thomas Heatherwick is Manchester's new iconic public sculpture.

<www.sva.org.uk>
<www.tonyfretton.co.uk>
<www.thepublic.com>
<www.partlywriting.com>
<www.wizya.net/inter.htm>
<www.bofthebang.com>
<www.rescen.net>

Richard Layzell

Caroline
Bergvall

Frictions of Forms: A conversation between Richard Layzell, Tania Koswycz and the Ghost of Ana Mendieta

Caroline Bergvall

RICHARD. What's going on?

TANIA. What do you mean?

RICHARD. I don't know...there's a greying.

TANIA. A greying?

RICHARD. Can't you feel it, yes something's going
fainter, I don't know, it's harder to discern what
I'm...seem to have less velocity, things feel less
certain somehow.

TANIA. Well, that's funny cos I've been feeling
increasingly more comfortable, as if the world was
moving closer, coming more to my level. I wonder
why this is happening.

GHOST: ....holà?...hello?...

RICHARD. AH!

TANIA. AH!

GHOST: ... holà hello?....

RICHARD & TANIA (together). What's going on?
What is this?

GHOST: ...ah holà there...don't be
alarmed...I've been around you for
awhile...but I can resist it any longer...
so I thought I'd make an appearance...

RICHARD. What? But why? Who are you? I control...

TANIA. No, I control...

RICHARD. ...the degrees of appearance in this
piece.

GHOST: ...yes well...we'll get to
that...anyway...you're artists....you talk about
forms in context... art or life...I'm an...was
an artist...I still work...now mostly...out of
context.....listening to you...you seem to
be....somewhat caught up in...disputes....yet
one of you is definitely closer to my
condition than you might like to think...I'm
just not quite sure which of you as yet...

TANIA. Who are you?

GHOST: …..it depends…I'm the Ghost of
Ana Mendieta…I'm the Ghost of Felix
Gonzales-Torres…

TANIA. Isn't there a diasporic Latino connection
here? You know, you might have got the wrong
people. I'm certainly in diaspora of a kind but from
my name I think I may be Polish. And I think
Richard's English but he travels a lot…

GHOST: …..I'm as many as needs be…I'm the
Ghost of Kathy Acker!…the Ghost of Fernando
Pessoa! ….Reinaldo Arenas!…anyway, you two
should be familiar with the necessity of
impersonation….the formalisation of names….
rituals of migration…shifting skin…
carrying skin…deepening or lightening up
the grip on identikits…the transmutation
of personal histories…I'm the Ghost of
Ana Mendieta...I'm the name taken on by
her lasting forms…

RICHARD. Why her? Why not Kurt Schwitters or Bruce
Nauman or ? I've built my early performances on
an understanding of avant garde performance art.
I really feel a sort of historic if not altogether
personal affinity with some of their work. Much
more than I do, with all due respect, the eternalist
bodies of your Mendieta or the minimalist
intimacies of your Gonzales-Torres! Although
Torres' treatment of architectural space is
fascinating. His luring of private love into
corporate or public spaces.

TANIA. Yes…and I quite like Jessica Stockholder
or Sarah Sze! can you be their Ghost? There's
lots I want to ask them about cumulative spaces,
uninhabitability. The survival of objects. The
resistance of the disregarded. How to handle
temporary structures. How to diffuse one's body.

GHOST. ...well........first of all, some of these
artists are still alive so you could
contact them by other means....it's quite
difficult....to access their ghostly
dimension...there's a lot of resistance to
this condition...among the living...less so
among artists but still.... .secondly...
ghosts come...you don't get to choose...anyway
I didn't choose you...just passing
through...felt like a chat...

TANIA. Are you trying to scare us or to impress us?
The connection between Richard and myself is
complicated enough.

GHOST. ....think about it...one of you works
with your human body...in and out of
spaces...in and out of situations...one of you
works without human body...but looks for
one...longs for one in the forms you're
starting to leave behind in
galleries....bodies change the forms they
integrate... art contributes to these
changes.... I agree that I could have been
someone else's trail... whispered
form...someone closer to your practices...more
urban...more architectural....more inscribed
within social time...there are other
questions at work ...

RICHARD. Well, my conversations with Tania do
that. They bring up the questions that trouble me.
She pushes against the surface of these things.

GHOST. ...and I'm the Ghost of Ana Mendieta...I
appeared when she disappeared.... I continue
the work of her name...you appear to
disappear...appear and disappear in the work
you set up...your performance art...everything
you've made will disappear with you...

RICHARD. Yes and that's exactly the point. The
thrill of preparing for something that can only ever
take place once! Even more so, the thrill of doing
something no-one will know is happening as art
while it is taking place. Can't you relate to that?

GHOST......ah yes!...yet perhaps you're starting
to wonder about all this...about just
this....what is taking place...what you are
leaving behind....a difficult question.....for
performance artists...your conversation
senses it....Tania working with objects...
perhaps she signals something...

RICHARD. But who tells you this conversation
needs an additional interlocutor!

GHOST. ...well that's pretty obvious from
the way you lock into each
other...triangulation's a very useful....I...I
still bleed...I know violence...I know
blood....love... weather... carvings...
fireworks...Richard...there's a troubled
commitment in your art...a deep yet
insufficient treatment of gendered
physicalities...of art's time...

RICHARD. !

GHOST. ...I burn...I lie on the ground...I know
violence...am I a girl a beard a goose a wood
carving a firewall a silhouette a tree a
film...am I a girl-feathered-grass-fire-
Silhouette...my contours are absorbed by the
grass the mud the night...the tarmac...Tania
your impatience...there's the pull of time in
your forms...the need for a personal
historicised body...

TANIA. ...

GHOST. ...as for your conflictual
bond...this strange shackle you share...a
spark... a trace....the gestures of ephemeral
arts... like the smear of skin against
glass...not to be one but to rub against...to
project into...to allow for a body to appear
only if it sinks into the media...or the
phantom...of other temporalities... where does
it go...where has it been...your conversation
catches...some of this....yet there's
something missing......I want your passion...
your love...more of a stride!

RICHARD & TANIA (together). Insults! Insults!

GHOST. ....when I was starting out...in America
in the early 70s....having left Cuba a decade
earlier....Minimal art was still all the
rage....but it was Fluxus... Acconci's body
works...Robert Smithson...Eva Hesse...all this
was so exciting!.....feminist art
scenes!....all were challenging the rules
of gallery-based arts...who could be an
artist...what art was supposed to look
like....using the human body as temporal
measure...as structure of action and of
politics... they said it was about
challenging control...I always thought it
was also about release....methods of
release...histories of release... I wasn't
interested in the formal qualities of my
materials, but their emotional and sensual
ones...isn't this what your conversation is
about... what kind of artist has agency...what
kind of temporality art values...what kind
of temporality the artist can fruitfully
work with....

TANIA. For me, the time of art is the time of apparition. It takes me to the intermediacy of objects, of gender. I need Richard for this. And galleries, the art circus.

GHOST....at the root of it all...the human body...have you got one...what do you do with it....what kind of time does your art aim to construct.......Richard you're concerned with linking your aesthetics to social temporality....this is a challenge...nearly a contradiction in terms.....your art is not so much about aesthetic matter as a matter of social gesture....what makes the art here is the contract between artist and viewer.... temporality is hardly altered....or queried...a vague sense of carnival time perhaps grants an added element of off-time/on-time...but what I get mostly from your sense of time is one of time-management....

TANIA. Yes well, it's very busy in my world too so I keep the dates in my diary because I choose to plan ahead.

RICHARD. It's the priorities I sometimes struggle with. How about you? Don't you get distracted?

TANIA. What, artistically? I still don't understand how you make decisions. Sometimes you sound like a businessman, sometimes an air-head, occasionally a diplomat.

RICHARD. Does it come down to money?

GHOST. ......love!...

TANIA. Hey?

GHOST.....it's love that is missing!...the way it releases time...the way it guides art...we're left with appointments!...you claim a sort of busy dailiness as part of a conversation about form and function...fine...nothing that departs from current concerns...but....

TANIA. My function is to make art not love!

RICHARD. Perhaps I'm trying to hold on to artistic
integrity for as long as possible.

GHOST. ....don't sell yourselves short......

TANIA. The world is dark and uncertain. Always on
the verge of not taking place.

GHOST. ....now that I roam...and for as long
as I will....I know that it's the complicity
of matter to non-matter that art takes
on....the arts of performance...of sites....are
the closest to this... inevitably they
travel back and forth between time and
temporality....between life and death.... one
should be so deeply in time...be steeped in
or stripped so deeply by time that art
suddenly appears to be...seems to... become
an act of time...isn't this an act of love...a
dialogue in time in the most profound
sense....at one point or another the artist
has to give in...has to step into...the time
of matter.....this is the love...this intimate
connection...

TANIA. Art is the most uncertain of convictions.

GHOST....I wasn't scared of disappearance....
I was just trying to understand it...my
material disappearance happened so
brutally...in art, time is the duration of
matter....the ephemerality of human
grace...why else work with forms of art that
are concerned with time so explicitly?....

RICHARD. What's going on?
TANIA. Hey!

GHOST...goodbye...good luck to you both...thanks
for the......

RICHARD. Hello? Hello?

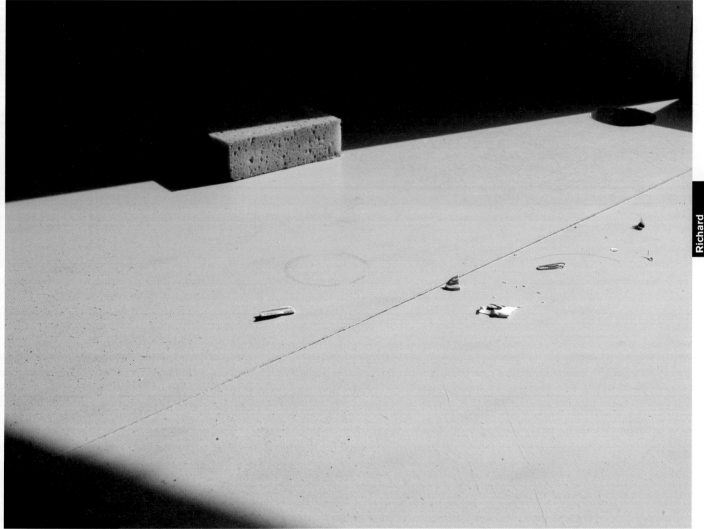

Adrian
Rifkin

Return of the Repressed: The Sequel! The Torment of Davida Pendleton

Adrian Rifkin

Adrian
Rifkin

The phone rings sharply, some crazy mobile tone: Ride of the Valkyries or William Tell Overture: Richard and Tania both reach for it, both saying Hello? Hello? at once but Richard takes the call...

Richard: Hello? Hello? Ana, were you cut off?

A voice comes through clearly, a different voice, female but sharper and more cutting with a very slight accent that the connoisseur will recognise as South East Lancashire...

Hi, no, it's me - it's Davida here, after all Ana jumped ship. Richard: you don't know me, but I know you ... I'm really sorry but I overheard all that, and I just really had to call - that spook Ana, she walked out on you; but it's me, Davida Pendleton. Richard I have to tell you that I have a bit the same kind of relation with Adrian Rifkin as you have with Tania and I want to meet you because I need to talk to someone about it. I hope that's alright with you Tania. (Maybe I should have put it the other way round, after all it's us two 'girls' who have the problem! I'm really jealous of the way you pick Richard up on so much, 'distracted teenager' and all that.) But I really mean you, she, I'm not really in her league. Tania you're a real artist. It's his fault. Adrian, I mean. Not Richard. He says that she plays a, God, you I mean, a major role in his decision-making – he admits it. It's the way he – mine, I mean, if that's what you call them – stands me up, sometimes for years at a time. He used some really good SF stuff I wrote for him in 1992, hot transgressive feminist prose about sex and time travel, and just recently – recently, mark you, after all these years of me being alone, he got me to do a long piece for a website of Roxy Walsh which she published in a book, and now he's going to read it aloud at Tate next week. I wonder how I'll come out of it all?[1] What credit do I get except I'm his alibi if he wants to be really banal; the coward. Richard, the problem with Adrian is that he's never alone, he is a total slut, he goes

1   See Adrian Rifkin's essay in George Robertson et al, eds, *Traveller's Tales, Narratives of home and displacement*, 'Travel for men: from Claude Lévi-Strauss to the Sailor Hans', pp. 216 -224, where Davida's unpublished Science Fiction forms the incipit. It begins like this, 'Kitty was sick to death of time travel.' Her new piece can be found in *Infallible: in Search of the real George Eliot*, edited by Roxy Walsh, (Article Press, 2005), pp. 113–117.

through us one after the other, he picks you up for a few conversations, gets just what he wants, and then lets us drop again. Oh don't think that he doesn't know that I know all about it. First there was the little catholic wimp sister Mary McGill, he and Carol Duncan found her in some godforsaken nunnery in Sussex, she was in charge of the home-made chocolate factory there, and after Adrian thanked her in a footnote for identifying the slippage of the signifier with God, they found out – the superiors that is, and they sent her packing out to mind the apple orchard.[2] Life was never the same for her, never, and sister Mary was only her pseudonym to boot – I can give that away now, nothing could make it worse for her. Then when the 'real' sister Wendy came along Carol and Adrian just dropped Mary like an old sock – I reckon they thought that one art-historical nun was already one too many and they were sooO smug about what they called their 'sympathetic magic', you'd think they had made Wendy up to hear them gloat about it. Carol had one too, one of us, all of her own. she let hers do an awful lot of work. Essay after essay she wrote and they even got put on syllabuses! Cheryl. she was called Cheryl Bernstein, and when Carol published her own collected essays she let Cheryl have a place in the book, even though by then she was only running a *pizza* joint in downtown LA, and she'd married a chicano hunk called Rodriguez and settled herself to be an also-ran.[3] But Adrian, he's not generous like that, he just uses us, and if we'd known about sister Mary in time I doubt any of us would have gone along with it. Of course, just my luck, these others, the ones after little sis Mary that is, are all gay guys, not much in it for me. There's Brad and scott and Tyler and then there's David, and this you are not, but NEVER going to believe, he's my cousin, mine, and

Adrian Rifkin

2   This footnote, which I was convinced that I had put in an article many years ago in *Block*, can no longer be found. It should be in my piece called 'No Particular Thing to Mean', which can be found on the THEN page of <www.gai-savoir.com> but, uncannily, footnote 1 is missing. So much for Sister Mary. I never really liked her, nor did Carol.

3   See Carol Duncan, *The Aesthetics of Power*, (Cambridge, CUP), 1993, 'Part Four: the Life and Works of Cheryl Bernstein', which includes two of her major essays and an introduction by Carol Duncan. Cheryl came into being in 1970, and in this she is the 'mother of them all', and long before art historians got Derrida she was writing on the fake out of Heidegger!! See her 1973 essay in that volume. I came to know her intimately in her mid-years and accompanied her through the difficult period of her outing, when many of her pieces once cited as examples of early postmodern discourse were then subjected to a critical discrediting. Carol later told me of Cheryl's marriage to Rodriguez, and of her opening a pizza parlour at which one could get the Pollock, or the Mondrian or the Poons. I don't recall that she ever made a Frankenthaler or a Martin or a Bourgeois, she was considerate enough to leave the feminist pizza open for a younger generation of scholars.

Adrian
Rifkin

he's the only one amongst the whole fabulous harem who turns out to be CUT.[4] From which you'll gather that Davida is only my pen name. It's not tOOoo Jewish – is it? I had to change it, the market is so crowded these days with ethno this and ethno that, I just wanted to sound neutral! But David and me, we are the only two who are... Jewish I mean. I think Adrian is only really into Catholics by the way, and when I listen in to him thinking about it, it's because, in some incredibly stupid old fashioned patriarchal way he really does believe that the job, the holy fucking task of the Jewish art historian is to save the Catholic religion from itself and its own cretinous, bigoted, imperialist nemesis of self-misunderstanding. Does that make sense? Who could make sense of that, Richard? I can't, I can't see why he doesn't cut and run from it all!! So Brad and Scott and Tyler, and David, they make it look like he does with his little coterie of queer heroes who go unafraid around the world from the sex-pits to the Louvre, their heads stuffed with Kant and sexual fantasies. Jesus he thinks slumming with those klutzes gives him some kind of super-cred, especially with that sanctimonious fake David: – that's his favourite, by the way, Tania, he has one, so you watch out, my little pussy, get those claws out if you want to cling onto Richard for much longer. David, he takes him everywhere, Rome, Berlin, Gay Pride and he gets to hang out with Aby Warburg and all those dead heroes of the Great Tradition – well forget it, it leaves me cold and it pisses me off. David, it just happens, is the Jewish one, not the one Adrian really fancies (that's Brad in my humble view) but the one most like himself, the one who flatters him by looking like the same kind of buttoned up intellectual snob. Tania she goes everywhere with you too, Richard, but she's the one isn't she? And how do you do it Tania, how do you get your daddy boy to take you round with him from Birmingham to Australia? What

4   For the David stories, see *Parallax*, No. 25, October-December 2002, pp. 4–7, 'A Roman Holiday': my website as above, <www.gai-savoir.com> on the NOW page, the Queer Matters lecture. *The Eight Technologies of Otherness*, Sue Golding author-editor, (London Routledge, 1997), my essay 'Slavery/Sublimity', pp. 146–151. For Brad, Scott and Tyler see the final chapter of my *Ingres then, and now*, (London, Routledge, 2000), where these three men drift between the Louvre and the leather bars thinking about art and sex.

do you have to do for him, Tania, to him, Tania? Throw back his gifts and tell him where he can put conceptualism – you had him there, the stuck up self-aggrandising *****! You want to let me into the secret, Tania? Bitch...

My function is to make art not love, is it not, my dear? Well my function, if I have one, my **dears**, is to make Adrian's turgid prose seem like art, and those boys are into the same bandwagon, they get to strut their stuff on that phoney ticket! But then, you know, I do sometimes, oh god, I think that he does love us, and that he loves me the most. I'll tell you why, because I am the only one who really gets near the keyboard. The others give him a kick by being there, they hang out in the living room and talk dirty, but me, I get to touch the keys. And you know why, Tania, because

he's a fag, and he doesn't give a shit about me, so me, I can get in there, and that way I'm more creepy than some fancy ghost. I wonder if Ana ever read my stuff? **IT'S LOVE THAT IS MISSING!** ...you clever little phantom, that's how you made your work, **is it not**, ghosting love of the land? But me, I found that time and sex are the same thing and you don't need love for that, and you Tania, **Art is the most uncertain of convictions**, that really takes the biscuit. What's so uncertain once its down there, where's the panic, all that onto-stuff **stuff** stuff-and-angst when it's there, that's all I want me, just for it to be there, and you gang of ghosts and artists and – what are you Tania, ma semblable ma soeur?, what are you, you... you've got it all there, so what's the fuss?

The phone crackles and there is a dull thump, Davida has no idea if she has been hung up or if the service is down, as if she had gone into a deep, long tunnel – there is an uncomfortably drawn-out gap and then her voice reappears as if very, very near, but muted at the same time:

God, I just reread this, and do I really write really that much? Am I really that bad a writer – Tania, Richard, Richard, are you still there? Are you listening.....??? Richard? Tania? Hey, you there ... god this is just one helluva perfo-o-ormance...

Richard Layzell: RL
Tania Koswycz: TK

White on White:
A further conversation between Richard Layzell and Tania Koswycz

Richard Layzell

RL: Jesus, how did we get to here, Tania?
Some weird interlude since last we spoke.

TK: Fuck's sake, Richard, we started it and
that's where it went. Enjoy it.

RL: Don't you feel criticised?

TK: By Caroline and Adrian? Of course not.
Entertained more like. Or critiqued. But
they can critique me any time they like.

RL: Didn't you find it weird being
'voiced'?

TK: Like fictionalised?

RL: I guess.

TK: What's the risk? It's all good
exposure. I mean, doesn't our connection
to a particular kind of art make us into
a living breathing fiction in any case?

RL: But our relationship is so easy to
misrepresent. People seem to feel free to
make assumptions and tell us what we have
going.

TK: Good. Ain't no ghost writer here. We're
rock hard evidence. Flesh and blood. We're
out there. I think this is your problem,
not mine.

RL: What about all this talk of the need
for passion and the inevitable sexual
innuendo?

TK: We have a collaboration going on, a
working relationship. It's a mysterious
business. You know the score. We're working
it out. Fresh and easy.

RL: You sound different.

TK: I'm having an experience. Are you?

RL: I'm on the train back from Dundee. I
had a dream about a flock of birds I didn't
recognise. Then they flew past this
morning. (Pause.) I saw Kevin Henderson
last night.

TK: Kewin Shenderson* who you shared
a room with in Poland? Mm.

*For more on this misspelling, Poland and Interakcje see *Talking to Tania 6 (Day 4)* on <www.rescen.net>

RL: Good memory. He gave me a piece of
print, some documentation from his Polish
performance, called it a 'post-performance
document'. Did I tell you it was based on
the stage directions from Beckett's
Endgame?

        TK: Can't remember. Don't recall. Not too
        bothered either way. Look at me. (Pause.)
        Let's get on with it.
R: Silence.
        T: (Moves diagonally from left, pauses at
        video projector, switches on with slow
        deliberation. Stands beside Translator)
R and T: (Sit side by side and open
notebooks, look up towards viewer,
exchange books, close them, mannered
behaviour)

Translator: (Gestures towards T)

        T: Silence
R: (Walks towards rear wall. Takes up
brush. Opens can, loads freely. Paints
white on white.)
        T: (Holds up green coat to audience, then
        to viewer, drapes over chair back)
R: Silence
        T: Silence
R: (Moves projector beam over fresh paint,
now glistening)
        T: (Leaps and kicks out: neither balletic
        nor martial art)
R: (Stands very still)
        T: (pause) No thing specific
R: This is the spot
        T: It's in my head
R: An image, quite like the other
        T: (murmur) Open and close, seeping
        colouration
R: Hardly there
        T: Gone

        T: (laughs)

Plato and the Creative Life

Mark Vernon

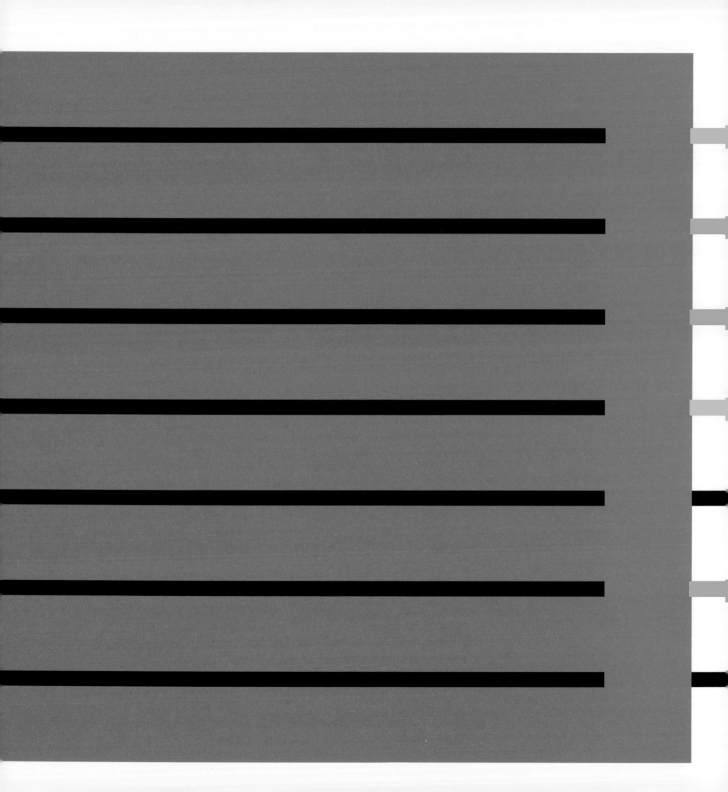

Plato may seem an odd person to turn to in any consideration of the long process from the initial creative impulse to the realisation of an idea. After all, is not the 'Platonic project', as some postmodern philosopher might call it, totally passé? Well, Plato was concerned with truth, even Truth. But for him the value of doing philosophy was far from exhausted by the truths that it may or may not establish. It was a process: sparked by the desire to express something; nurtured in a disciplined collaboration; and resulting in the realisation of an idea that at its best is also the embodiment of a way of life. In other words, for the ancients, the life of the philosopher was marked by creativity, integrity, effort and insight. In his dialogues, Plato is concerned with communicating the appeal of this way of life, and evoking a response in his readers to take it up. My hope is that in the context of this book his provocations will similarly evoke reflection upon the creative way of life.

As a point of departure, then, here is a fact that is also a puzzle. Plato always wrote in other people's voices. The writer whose questions, thoughts, characters and works have shaped a civilisation, never once unequivocally signs off a single sentence as his own definitive belief. He wrote dialogues – philosophical dramas: his characters are creative versions of historic individuals; but he himself not only never appears but is never even mentioned. His business is ideas, and big business it was in ancient Athens. And yet he is like a columnist or critic who not only never uses the authorial 'I', but insists on attributing what he writes to other people. If history had not thrown him up, he could most certainly not have been made up.

So why, when Plato launched out on a philosophical career, did he make this strategic decision to hide in his work? In part, it was because he had a different idea of philosophy than is perpetuated by academic philosophy today. He did not think that philosophy was something that could be poured, like water, from one vessel into another: philosophy was not a matter of accumulating knowledge of various systems of thought. At best, that was to learn a discourse about philosophy, not to do philosophy itself. He thought philosophy is taught by evoking a response – either in himself or in an interlocutor or reader: philosophy unsettles; it sets someone off on their own line of thought or intuition; and ideally it comes to no final stance but continually revises, refines, refuses and reconsiders. This is the sentiment behind one of his most famous comments, attributed to Socrates, that the unexamined life is not worth living.

This continual accessing of the course of one's life, this perpetual exercise in navigation, is not as a result of some wilful obscurantism or relativistic conviction that ultimately the truth is not out there. Rather, it is because the primary work of philosophy is to work on oneself. To assemble opinions is a trivial, if intellectually stimulating, enterprise; the more substantial achievement would be to change oneself. In other words, to do philosophy, not merely rehearse a discourse, is to care for oneself – for one's character, taste and habits more than one's methods, rhetoric or systems. As Nietzsche interpreted the imperative: one thing is needful, to give style to one's character, 'a great and rare art!'.[1]

Embracing the challenge

So why did Plato adopt this way of doing philosophy? (Imagine telling your boss that it is the depth of your personality that counts as the measure of your work.) In short, it was because he met Socrates.

This was a 'fateful encounter'.[2] It was so powerful that it determined everything else that followed in Plato's life. He made the decision not to marry but to set up a philosophical school instead.

Anything else that might be suggested as an influence on Plato's work disappears in the shadows created by this brilliant Socratic light – his possible disillusionment with politics, his possible travel around the Mediterranean, his possible encounter with the Pythagorean mystics, his possible interest in Egyptian art. Thus, Socrates is given incomparable status in all but one of his dialogues and Plato uses the voice of Socrates to represent his most decisive insights (again, this is without parallel: he is a student who for decades after his teacher's death, and decades into his own development, continues to defer to his teacher's memory).

What might this encounter have been like? We cannot know for sure. One fable has Socrates dreaming that a cygnet sits on his knees. The young, grey bird – Plato – then grows wings and flies away full of mellifluous song. Or there is a tradition in which, on the day he met Socrates, Plato stood in front of the theatre of Dionysos – the great Athenian crucible of politics, plays and processions – and burnt the tragedy he had written just as it was about to be performed. Nothing could be the same again.

This was a higher category of experience than the encounters we read about between Socrates and some of the young men of Athens. At first, these youths just followed him around to watch him belittle the celebrity politicians of his day. Then, they realised that Socrates was serious and hoped to speak with him, or even just be with him, as an inspired guru: 'I made progress when I was with you, if only in the same house, not even in the same room; and still more, so it seemed to me, when I was in the same room and looked at you (rather than elsewhere) while you were talking; but most of all when I sat beside you, quite close, and touched you,' says Aristeides, according to Plato, in the *Theages*.

For Plato, the encounter was not merely an important experience, to be remembered fondly in later life. It was an overwhelming experience that revisited him afresh every day; hence his perpetual philosophical, or perhaps we should say 'creative', motion.

Perhaps the closest we can get to the sense of this comes when Plato writes, in the *Symposium*, of the effect that Socrates had on Alcibiades. He was one of the most famous of Socrates' pupils in 5th century BCE Athens, because he became, first, a famous general and then, an infamous traitor:

I swear to you the moment he starts to speak, I am beside myself: my heart starts leaping in my chest, the tears come streaming down my face, even the frenzied Corybantes seem sane compared to me – and I tell you, I am not alone. I have heard Pericles and many other great orators, and I have admired their speeches. But nothing like this ever happened to me: they never upset me so deeply that my very own soul started protesting that my life – my life! – was no better than the most miserable slave's. He always traps me, you see, and makes me admit that my political career is a waste of time, while all that matters is just what I most neglect: my personal shortcomings that cry out for my closest attention. So I refuse to listen to him; I stop my ears and tear myself away from him, for, like the Sirens, he could make me stay by his side till I die.

Alcibiades fails to figure out how he can possibly respond to this extraordinary man. Pathetically, he thinks he is in love with him and tries to seduce him; when that fails their friendship fails too. But Plato's brilliance is to work out a way of not just living, but living well, after Socrates. To borrow a phrase used by someone else who knew another climactic figure of history, Jesus of Nazareth, he loses himself in order to find himself.

Loving the longing

Apart from the writing that survives, what else do we know of Plato's life after Socrates, after the challenge? Another clue comes from the word either Socrates or Plato coined: philosophy. The etymology of the word provides the clue – the love (*philia*) of wisdom (*sophia*). Wisdom was, of course, the thing that Socrates sought. But he had a particular relationship to it: he knew that he would never gain it. Empirically he knew this because he had spent his life engaging fellow Athenians in key questions about how to live, and no-one had ever told him anything that could not be refuted. Politicians, he realised, were particularly easy to trip up. Poets tended to make the mistake of thinking that their gift with words meant that they had a gift for truth. And craftspeople, though undoubtedly good at making everything from sculptures to shoes, confused expert knowledge in these areas with expert knowledge about other matters too. Socrates knew that he could not answer his own questions any better than they, so he concluded that wisdom eludes us all. His only distinction was that he knew it of himself whereas others were ignorant.

However, that he knew it made all the difference. For knowing you lack something as valuable as wisdom, leads to a longing and a love for it. Hence being called a philosopher.

In the *Symposium*, Socrates recounts a story told to him by the priestess Diotima about the origins of Love that illustrates the meaning of this longing. She said that when Aphrodite was born, the gods held a party. Poros (meaning 'way'), son of Metis (meaning 'cunning') was there, got drunk and fell asleep in the garden. Meanwhile, Penia (meaning

'poverty') passed by, and discerning a cunning way out of her poverty, slept with Poros and became pregnant. Love was the result.

Diotima goes on to describe Love in ways that exactly describe Socrates: both are poor, ugly and shoeless; both long for something they lack, but are endlessly cunning in the pursuit of what they love – wisdom. Thus, concludes Diotima:

> He [Love] is in between wisdom and ignorance as well. In fact, you see, none of the gods loves wisdom or wants to become wise – for they are wise – and no one else who is wise already loves wisdom; on the other hand, no one who is ignorant will love wisdom either or want to become wise. For what's especially difficult about being ignorant is that you are content with yourself, even though you're neither beautiful and good nor intelligent. If you don't think you need anything, of course you won't want what you don't think you need.

A way of life

The value of understanding that one lives in this in-between state is that it engenders the desire for insight, illumination, intellect and intuition. Ultimately, of course, such a life will never achieve its goal – the expression of the inexpressible. However, the life it nurtures is hugely valuable, and is, moreover, the most valuable life that anyone can lead. The beginning and end of that life is to embrace human limitation and construct ways of exploring this lack ever more profoundly. So, paradoxically, the very acceptance of the limited means of the human condition makes for endless creativity. This is a way of life that is, in fact, very familiar to the artist. A composer takes the twelve notes of the scale and by pushing their harmonic permutations to the limit creates music. A painter takes the seven colours of the spectrum and with infinite shades and textures creates work. In the words of the Pet Shop Boys, the remarkable thing about human beings who embrace their limits is that they 'make such a little go a very long way'. When Plato said, 'I am a philosopher', he meant it in the same sense as the artist today who says, 'I am an artist'. It is a passion that is a vocation, informing the daily habits and general orientation of a life.

I knew the artist Glynn Boyd Harte. He was remarkable not just for his prolific output, that ranged from fine art, to commercial design, to avant-garde music but also for his manner of life. No doubt this could be affected at times. But I recall his son once saying that his father's great gift to him was to have taught him to see. At times this could be annoying, as when even the lunch table had to be interestingly arranged. But there is a parallel here with the Socratic way of life. Philosophy, like art, infects every area of life. As Plutarch wrote of Socrates:

> Socrates did not set up grandstands for his audience and did not sit upon a professorial chair; he had no fixed timetable for talking or walking with his friends. Rather he did philosophy sometimes by joking with them, or by drinking or by going to war or to the market with them...[3]

Another thing to notice about this way of life is that it cannot be conducted alone. It is not some autonomous search for integrity, nor the right verbiage, as if what counted was the ever more abstract articulation of a gnostic or esoteric discourse. The way forward is found in the struggle to live it with others. Seneca wrote this in the Roman period:

> The living word and life in common will benefit you more than written discourse. It is to current reality that you must go, first because men believe their eyes more than

their ears, and then because the path of precepts is long, but that of examples is short and infallible. Cleanthes [the Stoic] would not have imitated his master Zeno if he had been merely his auditor; but he was involved in his life, he penetrated his secret thoughts, and he was able to observe first hand whether Zeno lived in conformity with his own rule of life. Plato, Aristotle, and that whole crowd of sages which ended up going in opposite directions – all derived more profit from Socrates' morals than from his words. It was not Epicurus' school which made great men of Metrodorus, Hermarchus, and Polyaenus, but his companionship.[4]

Disciplining the desire

Having taken that on board, it should be noted that this 'creative longing' as a way of life is not without discipline. In fact, quite the opposite, as anyone who has tried to grapple with a Platonic dialogue from beginning to end will realise. Plato represents Socrates as so disciplined in his thought that it often seems like he is splitting hairs. People who bumped into him in the street frequently found the going tough. They made such comments as, 'talking to Socrates is like being stung by a ray'. Others, seeing him coming, simply stepped in the opposite direction; they knew he was only going to ask them something and that the experience would be demanding.

This discipline was in part about learning the techniques and history of philosophy. But it had a higher purpose too. The point of Socratic dialectic, the conversations that Plato worked up into the masterpieces we read today, was not just self-expression but self-transformation too.

Think, first, of having as one's sole goal that of self-expression. The parallel here, from Plato's time, is found in the argument he had with the sophists. The sophists were the masters of rhetoric. The truth of what they said did not matter: the manner in which they said it did; and winning the argument was all. Plato's objection to training that resulted in this way of life was that it led to a dangerous relativism. Plato was a relativist of sorts, of course – the person who is a relativist because they know that their wisdom is limited – but the sophist's relativism was different. It assumes any position can be defended or attacked with equal validity.

Plato objected to the sophists partly because of this 'walking on air' and 'nonsense' but also because they were disingenuous; he thought that they knew that their 'anything is philosophy' relativism was bogus (any first year undergraduate philosopher learns how to refute it: if everything is relative then so is the doctrine that everything is relative!).

However, he also objected to the sophists because they undermined the creative imperative in philosophy to remake oneself. The fundamental reason that their relativism was so corrosive was that it belittles the task of self-transformation. We might say that it is inauthentic.

For example, a good test of whether self-transformation is in play, as opposed to brute self-expression, is provided by the tone of the collaboration. Self-transformation is most likely to happen when amity not enmity holds sway, since only then can the parties trust each other enough to be vulnerable enough. Socrates described the right attitude as including goodwill and a willingness to speak freely. It does not require individuals to be knowledgeable about the matter in hand so much as have a passion for wanting to know more about it. And the most promising collaborations will be between individuals who, in the process, become friends – a product, as it were, of being as honest as they can, particularly when it comes to their self-awareness.

Inspirational friendship

This idea of the philosophical endeavour as being associated with profound friendship is, I think, very powerful. However, it can easily be lost in the ways friendship is frequently discussed today. For example, friendship can be treated rather sentimentally – as in, 'I'll get by with a little help from my friends.' The trouble with such sentimentality is that it is focused on the self not on the transformation of the self: the friend, in this picture, comforts and coddles the ego, not confronts and cajoles it. Alternatively, friendship is thought of as an undemanding relationship. If lovers make you sleepless, and families make you scream, then friends are the people you relax with. Just what it might be to work on one's friendships is therefore something of an enigma – though the answer is to be found in the effort required to be honest with yourself and another.

'Love is the attempt to form a friendship inspired by beauty,' was the Stoic expression. It might be shuffled around to say, 'Love is the attempt to form beauty inspired by friendship'. This happens because the relationship comes to embody its passion in a certain way. The fervour and enthusiasm is not primarily directed at each other, as is the case with lovers. Rather, it is directed towards the growing interests that emerge as the friendship does too. It is a passion for the things that the friends are now working on together.

Such a distinction between an erotic passion that focuses solely on an individual to a shared passion for the creative life is well captured in an observation made by C.S. Lewis. He noted how lovers are typically depicted gazing into each other's eyes, whereas friends portrayed together usually look straight ahead. Artists, we might add, look at the world together. And their greatest joy is then to look back at each other, not to declare a self-obsessed love, but to declare: 'Do you see the same truth?'[5] When artists can say, 'yes', to each other, an idea is on the way to being realised.

Nietzsche is another philosopher who pondered the part of friendship in a creative way of life. What he concludes is that with friends, a new passion becomes possible.

> Here and there on earth we may encounter a kind of continuation of love in which this possessive craving of two people for each other gives way to a new desire and lust for possession – a shared higher thirst for an ideal above them. But who knows such love? Who has experienced it? Its right name is friendship.[6]

One can think of other examples of this kind of friendship. It is what happens when philosophers or intellectual friends share a passion in their thoughts, reading or insights; or when friends who are interested in science together delight in the wonder of nature or mathematical entities – strange as that may seem. I find my own connection with this friendship when I think about the dynamic between myself and a friend, Guy Reid, who is a sculptor. He has a great gift for carving human figures in wood that have the uncanny appearance of being almost alive. When I first met Guy I found this ability of his quite intimidating since any creativity I possessed seemed woefully pedestrian in comparison. It was a privilege just to write an occasional press release for him when he was having a show. But as our friendship developed, I allowed myself to be inspired to pursue my own creative hopes in writing. He awoke a passion in me. I recall going to a literary festival to catch a whiff of the creative energy in writers I admired and at the festival being very conscious of my friendship with Guy. The friendship, I realised, was telling me something: 'Get on with it!'

Renewing the vision

Another aspect of this passion is shown in what Socrates meant by another one of his famous comments, that 'virtue is knowledge'. This can be taken mistakenly to mean that knowledge is knowledge of virtue – perhaps the good or the beautiful. But really it means that knowledge is 'an inner disposition in which thought, will, and desire are one'[7] – in other words, it is the kind of integrity or attitude that we think someone has when we say they are wise.

The idea that virtue is knowledge also relates back to the idea that the creative is a lover: and it adds the crucial point that this desire is oriented in the right direction; or as a Freudian might put it, creativity is libidinal but it is libidinal energy carefully channelled. The most famous description of this aspect of the way of life comes later in the *Symposium*. Diotima, again, tells Socrates that the first real steps that the philosopher will make comes when they fall in love with someone who they think is beautiful. Soon, though, they will realise that the love they have of this particular person is odd, since the world is full of beauties. This is not to advocate promiscuity! Rather, it is to be awakened to a general sort of beauty – corporeal beauty. This, then, leads to another step in which, to the love of corporeal beauty, is added the love of immaterial things that are beautiful – perhaps beautiful ideas. Once awakened to this, the individual takes another step, to the love of wholly abstract things. Then finally, they come to love beauty itself – peak experiences that achieve nothing less than the transformation of life.

This, then, highlights another part of the reason why self-transformation is so important. In a life of self-transformation, love will lead to constantly renewed vision, whereas in the life of mere self-expression what tends to be the result is perpetually indulged lust.

The contemporary philosopher Pierre Hadot has characterized the effort of self-transformation as a 'spiritual exercise'. The point of the Socratic way of life was not just to learn refined ways of expressing things but to take yourself out of your old ways of thinking and into radically new ways; resisting the temptation to impose your view of the truth, and instead discovering new truths for yourself by being able to put yourself in someone else's place. What happens then is that the two achieve something that separately they could not. The Greek word is *askesis*, to take yourself out of yourself (or lose yourself). Two, or more people, would engage with the aim of transforming one another.

Plato outlines various kinds of spiritual exercise at different points in the dialogues. One would obviously be intellectual engagement. He also appears to have preferred sexual abstinence. Another has to do with sleep: 'terrible and savage' dreams provide material for reflection. However, the great test of the worth of the philosopher was their attitude towards death. Death is the supreme subject for contemplation because it is the absolute moment of self-transformation. Someone who does not fear death, therefore, does not fear the most profound effects of the choice of life they have embarked upon. Socrates was the model here: when he drank the hemlock, he faced death with consummate serenity: iconography represented in the many paintings entitled, 'The Death of Socrates'.

Innovate not imitate

Plato's dialogues are much more than philosophical treatises. They contain discussions of the great subjects of philosophy – from art to virtue, from science to the soul – but they are philosophical dramas too, encouraging us to enter the drama, and adopt the way of life.

However, and this is one final suggestion that might interest the 'navigating' artist too, they encourage us not to imitate but to innovate. It might be thought that the best way to respond to Plato was to become Platonic but the dialogues deliberately undermine any stable idea of just what a Platonic stance might be. Take the doctrine of the Forms. This is the idea that we can only know what a table is, for example, because in the realm of Ideas there is a Form of Table to which we can relate the multiple tables we see on earth. It also powers the idea that Platonic philosophy is most interested in that which is transcendent; the world of phenomena is but a secondary issue, or so it is said.

What this account of so-called Platonism misses is that whenever Plato introduces the Forms into a discussion he also ridicules it. And often in the most irreverent ways. In the *Symposium*, the Form of Beauty is the Beatific vision described at the end of Diotima's ascent of love – from bodies, to abstractions, to Beauty itself. However, the next thing that happens is that Alcibiades bursts in, completely drunk. Apart from being an infamous character, he was also famously handsome. The implication in the dialogue is: here is an example of your Form of Beauty – the debauched, dancing, Dionysian Alcibiades. So much for the summit of your Platonic philosophy!

More prosaically, others who encountered Socrates tried to imitate his way of life literally. But they too are ridiculed. One such character in the dialogues, for example, stops wearing shoes because Socrates goes always about barefoot. He is laughed all the way to the forum.

The point then, is that Plato needs to tread a fine line between presenting an engaging account of Socrates' way of life without initiating a cult of Socrates the man. He wants his readers to respond to Socrates as he does himself. His response was his philosophical way of life. The question he poses is: how will *you* respond?

Conclusion

I would like to suggest that creating a way of life, as well as art work, is key to the process of navigation that takes an intuition and makes it manifest. If that is right, then Plato is himself a guide along the way.

He is such a guide because he too is making a creative response – in his case to Socrates. This was the man who believed that wisdom is not found in what you might claim to know or believe, but in an ever deeper understanding of your limits. As mortals, human beings are 'in-between' creatures, not blind like the animals who cannot know that they don't know, nor omniscient like the gods. However, this status brings with it a great gift: it engenders the desire to explore, a love of understanding, and the passion to express it. This is the sense in which Socrates, and his followers, are philosophers. It is also, I would say, the source of the creative drive.

Plato did, of course, engage in intellectual debate but more importantly, he developed a way of life that was nothing if not creative: paradoxically perhaps, the very commitment to not knowing, launched him on a journey. His great achievement was to follow the man who was arguably the most inspiring man ever to have lived with a life that was inspiring again.

Plato's dialogues capture that spirit for us; looking at that pattern of life evokes reflection on the creative process. It is disciplined and resourceful. It is aimed at self-transformation as well as self-expression. It is a collaborative venture with passionate friends. Its aim is to innovate not imitate. It takes courage that behind every attempt is the knowledge that human beings are limited and conscious of those limits. At the end of the day, it is a life of love – a love that takes you out of yourself.

Of course, the realisation of a work of art is, in practice, full of hard and dull labour too but always, finally, the instrumental gives way to the idea. To borrow from C.S. Lewis again, art is unnecessary, like philosophy, like friendship... it has no survival value; rather it is one of the things that give value to survival.

1   Friedrich Nietzsche, *The Gay Science*, transl. by W. Kaufmann (New York: Vintage Books, 1974) p.232

2   The phrase used by Friedländer. See Paul Friedländer, Plato *An Introduction* trans. by Hans Meyerhoff (Princeton: Princeton University Press, 1969) p.128

3   Plutarch, *Whether a Man should Engage in Politics When He Is Old*, 26, 796d

4   Seneca, *Moral Epistles*, 6, 6

5   This exclamation comes from Emerson's essay on friendship. See Ralph Emerson, *The Essential Writings of Ralph Waldo Emerson* (New York: Modern Library, 2000) p.201-214

6   Nietzsche, *op. cit.* p.89

7   Pierre Hadot, *What is Ancient Philosophy?* transl. by Michael Chase (London: Harvard University Press, 2002) p.65

Expectant Waiting

Rosemary Lee

Navigating

Rosemary Lee

Navigating the Unknown cannot help but conjure in me images of ships of souls lost on a dark sea, Homeresque epic journeys of life changing significance, or, on the other hand, playing Poohsticks. For these watery analogies and fishy stories bear with me. I am an East Anglian girl and the grey North Sea's presence as comforter and destroyer is never too far away from my consciousness.

Imagine being eight years old, swimming determinedly and with an ounce of breathless fear, back and forth between the groynes, aware of the invisible mighty force of the tidal pull, drawing you in or out. Beneath you, down in the murk may be a flat fish with its eyes not quite turned to the top of its body, little frills ribboning the sand over its back (or does it think it is its front). As if that would stop you stepping on it – only swimming determinedly feet OFF the bottom. Or try to float, motionless, on the cold salty swell, but your breath is still snatching. Relax, give in, ride on the slapping volatile waves and see where you end up when you daren't not look any more or your nose is full of stinging water. You are too far from the shore, kicking hard to defy the sucking undertow, you struggle to find your depth again, tip of toe on the sludgy sea bottom. This time is it a jellyfish that might brush your thigh?

These were my first tastes of navigating the unknown, in the watery realm at least. The balance of respect for the unknown and forging into it seems to be encapsulated in my sensory memories of swimming as a small child. Strangely, or maybe not so strangely, these feelings mirror my experience of the more intangible unknown I search for and encounter now, when making work.

A moment

It's crisp bright outside, the edges sharp the surfaces tangible,
waxed rose leaf, splintering fence,
soft white fat cat,
alarm trills of the blue tit find no hindrance in the clear air.

It's dark inside, cavernous;
thoughts on tiny silent boats
lose themselves,
drifting in the gloom,
their bright lights finding some hidden hindrance.

Rosemary Lee

Navigating the Unknown cannot help but conjure in me images of ships of souls lost on a dark sea, Homeresque epic journeys of life changing significance, or, on the other hand, playing Poohsticks. For these watery analogies and fishy stories bear with me. I am an East Anglian girl and the grey North Sea's presence as comforter and destroyer is never too far away from my consciousness.

Imagine being eight years old, swimming determinedly and with an ounce of breathless fear, back and forth between the groynes, aware of the invisible mighty force of the tidal pull, drawing you in or out. Beneath you, down in the murk may be a flat fish with its eyes not quite turned to the top of its body, little frills ribboning the sand over its back (or does it think it is its front?). As if that would stop you stepping on it – only swimming determinedly, feet OFF the bottom. Or try to float, motionless, on the cold salty swell, but your breath is still snatching. Relax, give in, ride on the slapping volatile waves and see where you end up when you daren't not look any more or your nose is full of stinging water. You are too far from the shore, kicking hard to defy the sucking undertow, you struggle to find your depth again, tip of toe on the sludgy sea bottom. This time is it a jellyfish that might brush your thigh?

These were my first tastes of navigating the unknown, in the watery realm at least. The balance of respect for the unknown and forging into it seems to be encapsulated in my sensory memories of swimming as a small child. Strangely, or maybe not so strangely, these feelings mirror my experience of the more intangible unknown I search for and encounter now, when making work.

A moment
It's crisp bright outside, the edges sharp the surfaces tangible,
waxed rose leaf, splintering fence,
soft white fat cat,
alarm trills of the blue tit find no hindrance in the clear air.

It's dark inside, cavernous;
thoughts on tiny silent boats
lose themselves,
drifting in the gloom,
their bright lights finding some hidden hindrance.

Rosemary Lee

Waiting for an idea

The empty virtual page here now as I write; the empty notebook at the start of a project; the empty space of the studio. They seem so inert and inanimate, so dead it would take a monumental shift to mark them. Or do they seem as if they are waiting for me; there, with no judgment, offering themselves to me to enter into? Ready when I am, ready for transformation, present, shimmering and alive. This reminds me of an empty theatre the morning of a tech day: sometimes I see the stage in all its blankness, all its flaws revealed by the harsh working lights, other times I see it as a site of possibilities to house transformation and change.

It can go either way; how you view that emptiness. The page and the studio may be the manifestations of your state of mind: a threat, or an ally; a forest of possibilities or a barren wasteland. Regardless of which it seems to you, your choice is to dive into that emptiness, forge your path, get busy, or wait with it and for it. By this I mean wait for the moment of transformation to occur.

Writing a story feels to me like fishing in a boat at night. The sea is much bigger than you are, and the light of your little lamp doesn't show you very much of it. You hope it'll attract some curious fish, but perhaps you'll sit here all night long and not get a bite... So you set off in your little boat, your little craft of habit, intention and hope, and bait your hook, and drop it in the water, and sit and wait, calm and relaxed and aware of every ripple, every faint swirl of phosphorescence, every twitch on the line, until...

Philip Pullman

Rosemary Lee

Waiting for an idea

The empty virtual page here now as I write; the empty notebook at the start of a project; the empty space of the studio. They seem so inert and inanimate, so dead it would take a monumental shift to mark them. Or do they seem as if they are waiting for me; there, with no judgment, offering themselves to me to enter into? Ready when I am, ready for transformation, present, shimmering and alive. This reminds me of an empty theatre the morning of a tech day: sometimes I see the stage in all its blankness, all its flaws revealed by the harsh working lights, other times I see it as a site of possibilities to house transformation and change.

It can go either way, how you view that emptiness. The page and the studio may be manifestations of your state of mind: a threat, or an ally, a forest of possibilities or a barren wasteland. Regardless of which it seems to you, your choice is to dive into that emptiness, forge your path, get busy, or wait with it and for it. By this I mean wait for the moment of transformation to occur.

Writing a story feels to me like fishing in a boat at night. The sea is much bigger than you are, and the light of your little lamp doesn't show you very much of it. You hope it'll attract some curious fish, but perhaps you'll sit here all night long and not get a bite... So you set off in your little boat, your little craft of habit, intention and hope, and bait your hook, and drop it in the water, and sit and wait, calm and relaxed and aware of every ripple, every faint swirl of phosphorescence, every twitch on the line, until...

Philip Pullman

Philip Pullman, 'Isis lecture' delivered 1 April 2003 at Oxford Literary Festival. Archived online at <www.philip-pullman.com> [accessed 1 December 2005].

Rosemary Lee

Space

I am in an empty beautiful studio. I feel a sanctity in the tabula rasa, the unspoilt nature of emptiness and silence. It is to me the essence of beauty, quiet stillness. So why disturb this fragile sacred place? Isn't anything I do just going to mess it up? To move would be to shatter this moment with a clumsy timing and spoil the emptiness with the presence of my form in this space. To balance this deep (and until now secret) belief, I try to find a way of compromising. Maybe if I wait for the silence and emptiness to reveal itself to me (or should I say in me), maybe if I truly taste it, surrender to it, yield, I will find the truth. Then the first mark will be one in absolute keeping with this time and place. Often though, this thought paralyses me.

Rosemary Lee

I am up at dawn, the soft light oozing forth imperceptibly. The ground is saturated with dew and I sense the fauna in the shadows of the woods. The others are noisy, filling the space with unwanted sounds and clumsy movement. What right have we to invade this quiet place, what gives us permission to step here let alone try to dance here? What pride, what lack of humility! I retreat under a bush for every dawn improvisation and rail at this folly and asking forgiveness from the place and the time that we invade with such insensitivity. I wait but cannot move for a week, as no move I make seems in keeping with this place and time. No move seems true or worthy of this stillness. I feel sickened to be part of this.

I am up at dawn, the soft light oozing forth imperceptibly. We walk silently out across the marsh to the sea. The herons rise noiselessly beside us, looming from the dykes and the cattle watch us pass. A barn owl swoops close by and continues to hunt. We quietly go on alongside them, their actions largely unchanged, ours ridiculous. I do as I am told with great inner reluctance. I crawl through the wet grass with the urgency of a mother turtle struggling inland to lay her eggs, I bury myself, face down in the peaty goose-shit marsh land. Somehow I can do this, somehow I am not disturbing the quiet place and time. Somehow this is acceptable and I feel accepted. I feel part of a continuum and very humbled.

Space

I am in an empty beautiful studio. I feel a sanctity in the tabula rasa, the unspoilt nature of emptiness and silence. It is to me the essence of beauty, quiet stillness. So why disturb this fragile sacred place? Isn't anything I do just going to mess it up? To move would be to shatter this moment with a clumsy timing and spoil the emptiness with the presence of my form in this space. To balance this deep (and until now secret) belief, I try to find a way of compromising. Maybe if I wait for the silence and emptiness to reveal itself to me (or should I say in me), maybe if I truly taste it, surrender to it, yield, I will find the truth. Then the first mark will be one in absolute keeping with this time and place. Often though, this thought paralyses me.

I am up at dawn, the soft light oozing forth imperceptibly. The ground is saturated with dew and I sense the fauna in the shadows of the woods. The others are noisy, filling the space with unwanted sounds and clumsy movement. What right have we to invade this quiet place, what gives us permission to step here let alone try to dance here? What pride, what lack of humility! I retreat under a bush for every dawn improvisation angrier at this folly and asking forgiveness from the place and the time that we invade with such insensitivity. I wait but cannot move for a week, as no move I make seems in keeping with this place and time. No move seems true or worthy of this stillness. I feel sickened to be part of this.

Rosemary Lee

I am up at dawn, the soft light oozing forth imperceptibly. We walk silently out across the marsh to the sea. The herons rise noiselessly beside us, looming from the dykes and the cattle watch us pass. A barn owl swoops close by and continues to hunt. We quietly go on alongside them, their actions largely unchanged, ours ridiculous. I do as I am told with great inner reluctance. I crawl through the wet grass with the urgency of a mother turtle struggling inland to lay her eggs, I bury myself, face down in the peaty, goose-shit marsh land. Somehow I can do this, somehow I am not disturbing the quiet place and time. Somehow this is acceptable and I feel accepted. I feel part of a continuum and very humbled.

Rosemary Lee

I am told the choreographer's art is to deal with bodies in space and time and what I am realising as I write, is that waiting is inextricably linked to those phenomena. I wait to truly know the place, space I am in, be it a workshop or a site I am to make work for and I wait in order to try to find the right time to make a movement.

The pressure of finding the right movement for the context in site-specific work can be exhausting. In order to make that choice I find I need to wait in the context, preferably alone. That waiting may be better described as being in the space. I need a quiet time to meet it much like one needs that to meet an animal – breathing into its nostrils: it's a type of communion. If I feel I have not achieved that communion then any work I make is superficial and disconnected. I suspect the less time I give myself for this process, the more dissatisfied I am with it and its outcome. After much work that has been context driven, I have recently been drawn back to making work in a void. The void for me is the closest spatial symbolism to our inner world, a void for possibilities, thoughts, feelings to drift into and a void where one senses ones aliveness more fully. It is limitless, fathomless, containing everything and nothing (though not salty or tidal in this case).

I think of a black box theatre space as a void, though of course it is far from neutral. As a performer in the blackness I feel that heightened sense of my own presence and my utter solitude. I suspect the audience also sense their own heartbeat and breathing in those dark moments of blackout before the show – that no man's land between the chatter, the settling and the unfolding of another world.

This intimacy with themselves and perhaps with the performers as they watch, can be held and supported in that void. It is a paradox, I realise, but it is about suspension (suspension of disbelief among other things). They may experience, perhaps, a state of expectant waiting.

I am told the choreographer's art is to deal with bodies in space and time and what I am realising as I write, is that waiting is inextricably linked to those phenomena. I wait to truly know the place, space I am in, be it a workshop or a site I am to make work for and I wait in order to try to find the right time to make a movement.

The pressure of finding the right movement for the context in site-specific work can be exhausting. In order to make that choice I find I need to wait in the context, preferably alone. That waiting may be better described as being in the space. I need a quiet time to meet it much like one needs that to meet an animal – breathing into its nostrils: it's a type of communion. If I feel I have not achieved that communion then any work I make is superficial and disconnected. I suspect the less time I give myself for this process, the more dissatisfied I am with it and its outcome.

After much work that has been context driven, I have recently been drawn back to making work in a void. The void for me is the closest spatial symbolism to our inner world, a void for possibilities, thoughts, feelings to drift into and a void where one senses ones aliveness more fully. It is limitless, fathomless, containing everything and nothing (though not salty or tidal in this case).

I think of a black box theatre space as a void, though of course it is far from neutral. As a performer in the blackness I feel that heightened sense of my own presence and my utter solitude. I suspect the audience also sense their own heartbeat and breathing in those dark moments of blackout before the show – that no man's land between the chatter, the settling and the unfolding of another world. This intimacy with themselves and perhaps with the performers as they watch, can be held and supported in that void. It is a paradox, I realise, but it is about suspension (suspension of disbelief among other things). They may experience, perhaps, a state of expectant waiting.

Suspension

Even though the cloudswing is in perpetual motion it goes nowhere – it swings between two suspension moments at either end of the swing – hence my sense when I am on it that I am waiting, almost at times stranded…

Matilda Leyser

Matilda Leyser aerialist and actress. Extracts from unpublished correspondence with Bryony Lavery, 2005, about her experiences on the cloudswing (a rope swing).

Suspension links time and space inextricably. When you wait you are in suspension, between two places, the past and the future, behind and in front, on a threshold. We linger in doorways, on corners, on beaches, timelessly between places; it's no surprise. We want to catch a glimpse of what is beyond but may not yet want to leave what we know behind. This subtle tension is what cradles the suspension. This place of suspension, being stuck between this instance and what is beyond is not always a comfortable place to be. We are neither here nor there and Neither Out Far, Nor In Deep, as Robert Frost titled his insightful poem.* Fear can keep us trapped in this place, in limbo, and decisions can feel insurmountable. Even as I write this I feel a familiar squirming sensation, remembering how difficult those threshold places can be.

*Robert Frost, The Poetry of Robert Frost ed. by Edward Connery Lathem (New York: Holt, Rinehart and Winston, 1975) p.301

Rosemary Lee

Playing in the threshold of the door to my room as if the landing was a transitory place that would lead me somewhere new but we, the dolls and me, never got anywhere. Always playing cruise ships, dressing the dolls for their dinner with the captain, but never ever reaching a foreign land. This game was always ultimately frustrating, boring, tedious, always packing but never arriving anywhere, endlessly waiting for the unknown to appear. Why couldn't we get there?

Suspension

Suspension links time and space inextricably. When you wait you are in suspension, between two places, the past and the future, behind and in front, on a threshold. We linger in doorways, on corners, on beaches, timelessly between places; it's no surprise. We want to catch a glimpse of what is beyond but may not yet want to leave what we know behind. This subtle tension is what cradles the suspension.

      This place of suspension, being stuck between this instance and what is beyond is not always a comfortable place to be. We are neither here nor there and Neither Out Far, Nor In Deep, as Robert Frost titled his insightful poem*. Fear can keep us trapped in this place, in limbo, and decisions can feel insurmountable. Even as I write this I feel a familiar squirming sensation, remembering how difficult those threshold places can be.

*Robert Frost, *The Poetry of Robert Frost* ed. by Edward Connery Lathem (New York: Holt, Rinehart and Winston, 1975) p.301

Even though the cloudswing is in perpetual motion it goes nowhere – it swings between two suspension moments at either end of the swing – hence my sense when I am on it that I am waiting, almost at times stranded…

Matilda Leyser

Matilda Leyser aerialist and actress. Extracts from unpublished correspondence with Bryony Lavery, 2005, about her experiences on the cloudswing (a rope swing).

Rosemary Lee

Playing in the threshold of the door to my room as if the landing was a transitory place that would lead me somewhere new but we, the dolls and me, never got anywhere. Always playing cruise ships, dressing the dolls for their dinner with the captain, but never ever reaching a foreign land. This game was always ultimately frustrating, boring, tedious, always packing but never arriving anywhere, endlessly waiting for the unknown to appear. Why couldn't we get there?

Time

Rosemary Lee

Time

Wait and the moment passes by, go too early and the act feels clumsy and inappropriate. These days as an idea dawns or begins to connect I find myself trying not to clutch at it. I wait for it to drift into clearer view before I try to actively decipher it. This seems risky as things slip away. I try to remain calm and not get over-excited at the sight of a dawning idea, hoping it will appear more fully formed if I touch it less with my mind. Ideas are more fragile these days and more prone to disintegration.

When I am up there my focus is on a precise, split second in time – just now – just this exact threshold place of the dead point…as if up there is a place to find infinity inside the pause.

Matilda Leyser

Time and timelessness are connected. This instant and eternity are struggling within us. And this is the cause of all our contradictions, our obstinacy, our narrow-mindedness. Our faith and our grief.

Arvo Pärt

Arvo Pärt, *Tabula Rasa* quoted by Wolfgang Sandner in accompanying booklet (London, ECM, 1985)

Rosemary Lee

I am a young dancer walking the circle, the audience and my tutor Bonnie Bird are watching me. It is silent. I walk and walk this circle, I am pacing, I am forging, I am full of anticipation, there is a right time to jump into the circle. When is the right time? When is the moment to jump into the fire? When, when should I leave this circle and jump? I feel as if I am paper to the flame and will be engulfed at any moment. Can anyone else feel the intense heat? Will I miss the moment of truth?

Are you going to
find a fish? Well
there are things you
can do to improve
your chances: with
every voyage you
learn a little more
about the bait these
fish like, and you're
practised enough to
wait for a twitch on
the line and not
snatch at it too
soon; and you've
discovered that
there are some
areas empty of fish,
and others where

Philip Pullman

There is a visceral sense of the rightness of the moment that I try to stop my emotions clouding. To sense it one needs an element of distance coupled with acute attentiveness. When waiting alone, sensing the rightness is much more difficult since there is no visual activity to work with but when working with people dancing I feel more able to ride the timing of a situation, to steer it in a fruitful way that will uncover the most potential – mine its grove like a seam of precious ore. I am trying to do the same with each individual I work with, making choices about the timing of when to commit, when not to, when to coax, when to wait, when to surprise and when to be inevitable and predictable.

One's hunger and desire can get in the way of the best ideas and solutions but similarly there is a danger that inactivity or lack of attentiveness produces nothing. There is expectant waiting that is both static and dynamic and there is kidding yourself you are waiting. The art of managing that delicate balance into a dynamic state is one that I would love to work on daily.

I suspect that choreographers are still thought of as doers who work quickly rather than contemplators who work slowly. After all they devour space and time.

Rosemary Lee

I am teaching. They are restless, their bodies have not found the quality I am trying to conjure in carefully chosen words and sound. They are pushing onward and outward and there is no depth in the embodiment of the yielding quality I am after. Should I let them suffer in this awkward state of agitation like horses in the stable or should I release them? Wait, trust, gently let them resign themselves to the fact that they are to stay in this place. If I am lucky the room will change like a subtle lighting cue and the participants will, through their acceptance of staying find new depths in this yielding only to then fly higher when they rise from the floor.

There is a visceral sense of the rightness of the moment that I try to stop my emotions clouding. To sense it one needs an element of distance coupled with acute attentiveness. When waiting alone, sensing the rightness is much more difficult since there is no visual activity to work with but when working with people dancing I feel more able to ride the timing of a situation, to steer it in a fruitful way that will uncover the most potential – mine its grove like a seam of precious ore. I am trying to do the same with each individual I work with, making choices about the timing of when to comment, when not to, when to coax, when to wait, when to surprise and when to be inevitable and predictable.

One's hunger and desire can get in the way of the best ideas and solutions but similarly there is a danger that inactivity or lack of attentiveness produces nothing. There is expectant waiting that is both static and dynamic and there is kidding yourself you are waiting. The art of managing that delicate balance into a dynamic state is one that I would love to work on daily.

I suspect that choreographers are still thought of as doers who work quickly rather than contemplators who work slowly. After all they devour space and time.

Are you going to find a fish? Well there are things you can do to improve your chances: with every voyage you learn a little more about the bait these fish like, and you're practised enough to wait for a twitch on the line and not snatch at it too soon: and you've discovered that there are some areas empty of fish, and others where they are plentiful.

Philip Pullman

Rosemary
Lee

I am teaching. They are restless, their bodies have not found the quality I am trying to conjure in carefully chosen words and sound. They are pushing onward and outward and there is no depth in the embodiment of the yielding quality I am after. Should I let them suffer in this awkward state of agitation like horses in the stable or should I release them? Wait, trust, gently let them resign themselves to the fact that they are to stay in this place. If I am lucky the room will change like a subtle lighting cue and the participants will, through their acceptance of staying find new depths in this yielding only to then fly higher when they rise from the floor.

Presence

Rosemary Lee

Presence

I was heartened to find the connection between the word 'wait' and 'watch'; and then between 'watch' and 'awake'!

This is precisely my point – I am hoping by waiting to become more awake and hence to be present.

Whenever I write about dance it comes back to one thing: being present. I try to skirt about avoiding it so as not to come to the end of an article too quickly but all roads lead to presence and why not celebrate that fact? In order to achieve the "supple state" as Joan Skinner (founder of Skinner release technique)* describes it: I would say one needs to let go of – assumption, habit, expectation, disappointment and negative judgement. You could say these are all time-based, lodged in the past or imagined future and you cannot truly ride chance or contingency when these obstacles persist.

*Joan Skinner, founder of Skinner Release Technique, comment made in dance class, c.1991

Wait ….to watch, attend, F. guetter to watch, to wait for, fr. OHG. wahta a guard, watch, G. wacht, from OHG. wahh[=e]n to watch, be awake. [root]134. See Wake, v. i.]
1. To watch; to observe; to take notice. [Obs.]

"But [unless] ye wait well and be privy, I wot right well, I am but dead," quoth she.
– Chaucer.

2. To stay or rest in expectation; to stop or remain stationary till the arrival of some person or event; to rest in patience; to stay; not to depart.

All the days of my appointed time will I wait, till my change come.
–Job xiv. 14.

Webster's Revised Unabridged Dictionary,1913

If pressed to say what they are actually doing in a meeting for worship, many Quakers would probably say that they are waiting – waiting in their utmost hearts for the touch of something beyond their everyday selves. Some would call it 'listening to the quiet voice of God' – without trying to define the word…

…Others would use more abstract terms: just 'listening' (though no voice is heard), or 'looking inward' (though no visions are seen), or 'pure attention' (though nothing specific is attended to). The word 'inward' tends to recur as one gropes for explanations.

Richard Allen

Richard Allen, *Silence and Speech* (London: Britain Yearly Meeting, Quaker Books, 2004)

Rosemary Lee

Rosemary Lee

I was trained to be a 'thinking dancer', but at present I feel I have to try to hide from my thoughts, try to outwit them, to get away. It is almost as if I have to run from myself, or is it my intellect in order to find a place of unknowing again, a place of waiting, a place of presence. I am too self-conscious, I am my own worst enemy and my own worst pupil. How can I become unknowing in order to sense discovery again? Thinking is altogether too conscious, too navigational, too frontal, too in your face. Thinking seems at loggerheads with sensing, with allowing.

In an Alexander lesson years ago I was encouraged to look at a picture of a lemon on the wall to take myself further away from trying to think about releasing. I was trying too hard. Then my body was left alone and it could find its own knowing without my cerebral consciousness trying to steer.

Similarly I see a dancer thinking, with a furrow between her eyes and I try ways to ease that consciousness back a bit further from the forehead to give her space, time, to flow onward along a more… a more what… authentic… effortless… deeper… genuine… truthful… instinctive journey? (I tread in dangerous water here with such words.) What I mean is she is able to sense herself more, to flow, be more connected to her own movement, able to be less behind or ahead of herself. She is in the present and has presence; this for me is an asset both aesthetically and experientially.

When one is truly present one is experiencing the here and now, space and time equally. Presence for me is the radiance of being alive.

What better place for all roads to lead to.

Sensation is the language of dance

Nancy Stark Smith

Nancy Stark Smith, dancer and teacher of Contact Improvisation, comment made in dance class, c.1995

You can't bulldoze your way into the unconscious consciously.

Michael Donaghy

Michael Donaghy, poet, in conversation with author c.2002

Rosemary Lee

Discoveries

Waiting seems similar to a state where one is not steering, one is rudderless but not lost – a state where discovery is possible.

I am searching at times and at other times actively trying not to search so that things can creep up unawares. The idea, the dawning, the solution is often more of a discovery than a creation.

It is said that in order to see the stars of the Pleiades more clearly you need to look at them using your peripheral vision, and not look at them directly. That reminds me of running away from myself so as not to look so directly, think so directly, entering the side door of my mind. Perhaps that is the same as lateral thinking.

I am thinking of the analogy of Poohsticks again – the twig being taken by the stream, the unknown, dwelling in the uncertainty of where next. One of the advantages of being the Poohstick, at least at certain points in the process, is that like the stick I will encounter many surprises along the way. My path is unfolding as I go, governed by my environment. I must have the lightest of touches. I am 'going with the flow' (an overused phrase and one that is little thought about). I am waiting for something to happen rather than determining it. This state, though, is far from passive: it is a state of acute attentiveness and relaxation. Transformation can happen in an instant, but it can take a lifetime to achieve the state in which that change can occur.

Something of the inaudible music that moves us along in our bodies, from moment to moment like water in a river. Something of the spirit of a snowflake in the water of the river. Something of the duplicity and the relativity and the merely fleeting quality of all this. Something of the almighty importance of it and something of the utter meaninglessness.

Ted Hughes

Ted Hughes, Poetry in the Making (London: Faber and Faber, 1967) p.124

Ted Hughes

I am talking about whatever trick or skill it is that enables us to catch those elusive or shadowy thoughts, and collect them together, and hold them still so we can get a really good look at them.

Ted Hughes

Rosemary Lee

We return to the studio feeling guilty that we have not used it all day, its potential to be filled with activity and dancing was left untapped. I am wrestling with my guilt, trying to trust that talking and then walking alongside the river for miles together was of equal value to working in the studio. The dancers begin an improvisation based on their walk, I turn on a track of music I sense might work. There it is! The foundation of the dance unfolding before me, there is everything I need, the source of a thirty-five minute dance effortlessly emerging. Walking and talking whilst being outside was unconscious and necessary waiting.

Discoveries

Waiting seems similar to a state where one is not steering, one is rudderless but not lost – a state where discovery is possible.

I am searching at times and at other times actively trying not to search so that things can creep up unawares. The idea, the dawning, the solution is often more of a discovery than a creation.

It is said that in order to see the stars of the Pleiades more clearly, you need to look at them using your peripheral vision, and not look at them directly. That reminds me of running away from myself so as not to look so directly, think so directly, entering the side door of my mind. Perhaps that is the same as lateral thinking.

I am thinking of the analogy of Poohsticks again – the twig being taken by the stream, the unknown, dwelling in the uncertainty of where next. One of the advantages of being the Poohstick, at least at certain points in the process, is that like the stick I will encounter many surprises along the way. My path is unfolding as I go, governed by my environment. I must have the lightest of touches. I am 'going with the flow' (an overused phrase and one that is little thought about). I am waiting for something to happen rather than determining it. This state, though, is far from passive: it is a state of acute attentiveness and relaxation. Transformation can happen in an instant, but it can take a lifetime to achieve the state in which that change can occur.

Something of the inaudible music that moves us along in our bodies, from moment to moment like water in a river. Something of the spirit of a snowflake in the water of the river. Something of the duplicity and the relativity and the merely fleeting quality of all this. Something of the almighty importance of it and something of the utter meaninglessness.

Ted Hughes

Ted Hughes, Poetry in the Making (London: Faber and Faber, 1967) p.124

I am talking about whatever trick or skill it is that enables us to catch those elusive or shadowy thoughts, and collect them together, and hold them still so we can get a really good look at them.

Ted Hughes

Rosemary Lee

We return to the studio feeling guilty that we have not used it all day. Its potential to be filled with activity and dancing was left untapped. I am wrestling with my guilt, trying to trust that talking and then walking alongside the river for miles together was of equal value to working in the studio. The dancers begin an improvisation based on their walk, I turn on a track of music I sense might work. There it is! The foundation of the dance unfolding before me, there is everything I need, the source of a thirty-five minute dance effortlessly emerging. Walking and talking whilst being outside was unconscious and necessary waiting.

Rosemary Lee

I am struck by how one's relationship to the forces of nature provides both wonderful support and numerous analogies for one's experience of navigating the unknown. With a deep breath I venture to say that this more intimate foot to earth, face to wind, hand to rain and heart to fire relationship is being lost. As we move towards more virtual relationships in many areas of our lives we replace the more elemental ones of our ancestors with great benefits and immeasurable tragic losses. After writing this I have a strong urge to clamber into the rough waves of the North Sea (the comforter in this case) and drown my sorrows for what is lost.

I am standing in a wet field in the misty rain along with some freshly shorn forlorn looking sheep looking at a Henry Moore sculpture. What is it that makes this work; a smooth, metal, curved interlocking piece, seem so right? It is as if it is meant to be here, content in time and space at this exact moment and forever. I am humbled and rather envy those sheep, being in the presence of this quiet, oracle-like form. Made so recently but it could have been moulded over millennia.

I am struck by how one's relationship to the forces of nature provides both wonderful support and numerous analogies for one's experience of navigating the unknown. With a deep breath I venture to say that this more intimate foot to earth, face to wind, hand to rain and heart to fire relationship is being lost. As we move towards more virtual relationships in many areas of our lives we replace the more elemental ones of our ancestors with great benefits and immeasurable tragic losses. After writing this I have a strong urge to clamber into the rough waves of the North Sea (the comforter in this case) and drown my sorrows for what is lost.

Rosemary Lee

I am standing in a wet field in the misty rain along with some freshly shorn forlorn looking sheep looking at a Henry Moore sculpture. What is it that makes this work; a smooth, metal, curved interlocking piece, seem so right? It is as if it is meant to be here, content in time and space at this exact moment and forever. I am humbled and rather envy those sheep, being in the presence of this quiet, oracle-like form. Made so recently but it could have been moulded over millennia.

When I am waiting I am in some senses in service, as in the work of a
waiter, serving. What interests me, and what I explore, is the human condition and
the world we inhabit both temporal and earthly, both subtle and tangible. I relish
the connection between the subtle unseen body and the flesh and bones of our mass:
the known and the unknown, the visible and the invisible. The threshold between
these is that creative place I want to linger in. The material I work with is not only
the tangible – the metered time, the measured space, the present dancer in the here
and now. It is the intangible – the dimensionless, the subtle energy, the invisible flow,
the spirit. It is what is beyond words, plans and rational thought. These subtle
mysteries that I strive to serve and make evident are worth waiting for, for a lifetime.

Rosemary Lee

When I am waiting I am in some senses in service, as in the work of a waiter, serving. What interests me, and what I explore, is the human condition and the world we inhabit both temporal and earthly, both subtle and tangible. I relish the connection between the subtle unseen body and the flesh and bones of our mass: the known and the unknown, the visible and the invisible. The threshold between these is that creative place I want to linger in. The material I work with is not only the tangible – the metered time, the measured space, the present dancer in the here and now. It is the intangible – the dimensionless, the subtle energy, the invisible flow, the spirit. It is what is beyond words, plans and rational thought. These subtle mysteries that I strive to serve and make evident are worth waiting for, for a lifetime.

Rosemary Lee

Special thanks to Niki Pollard, Charlie Kronick and particularly to Matilda Leyser for their feedback and editorial suggestions.

Expectant Waiting

Rosemary
Lee

As you look at this page,

sense the subtle pull of gravity in your body and sense its opposite

Rosemary Lee

As you look at this page, sense the movement of your torso in response to your breathing

As you look at this page, sense the hairs on the back of your neck

Rosemary Lee

MAGMIES

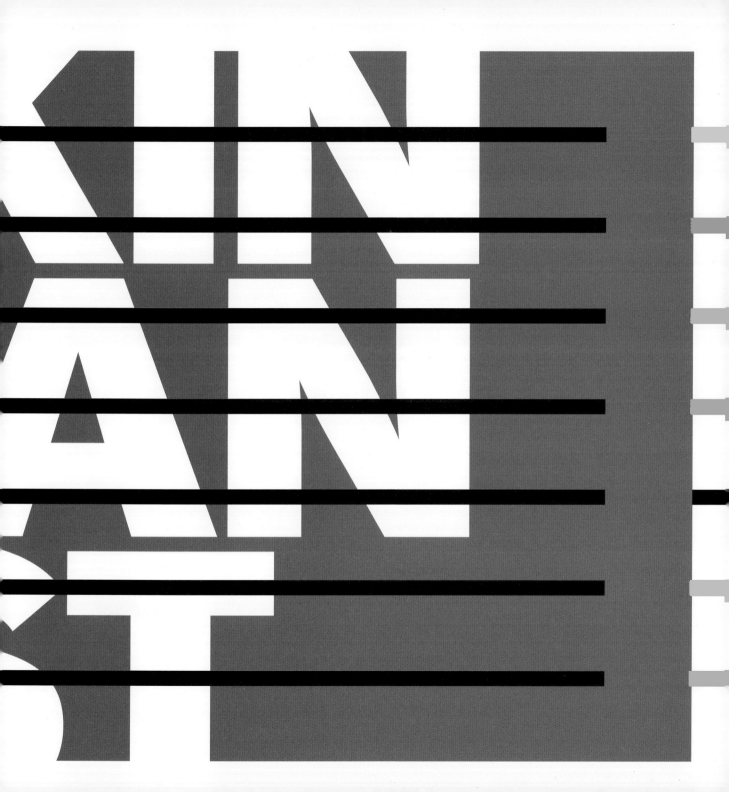

All
Aboard

Jane Watt

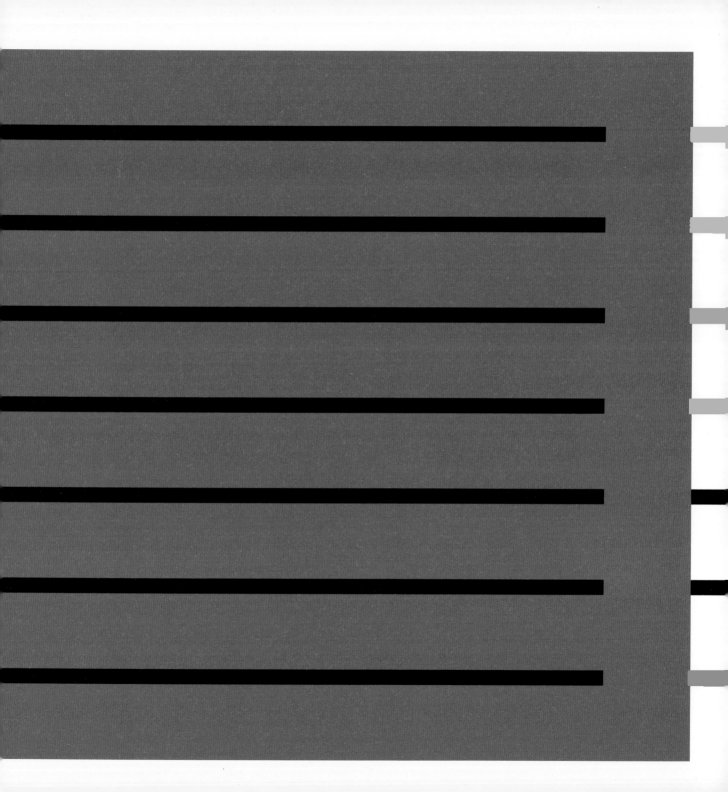

Rosemary Lee states at the beginning of 'Birth, Death and What Lies in Between', a conversation between the six ResCen Research Associate Artists about issues of 'making manifest', that:

> When we first talked about working on this book, *Navigating the Unknown*, I had an aversion to the idea that the third section would be called 'Making Manifest' because it implies a linear path attached to making a work.

Rosemary's stance has similarities with geographer, and one of ResCen's guest seminar speakers, Doreen Massey's assertion that life, and if we apply it to this example, creativity and art practice, is not a lateral (and essentially temporal) trajectory, so favoured by (Western) historians. It is not necessarily a logical, plotted graph, nor a journey from A to B starting at one moment in time and ending so many minutes, hours, days or years later. Rather, as Doreen Massey proposes, we exist, work and create in 'a sphere of multiplicity' and 'co-evalness' which allows 'that ability to see others as standing in another place simultaneously with you and looking back at you equally'.[1] Doreen Massey's position of co-evalness echoes a dialogic position, or approach. The dialogic perspective, proposed by the Russian philosopher Mikhail Bakhtin at the beginning of the twentieth century, is described by the Bakhtin scholar Michael Holquist as:

> …the name not just for dualism, but for a necessary *multiplicity* in human perception. This multiplicity manifests itself as a series of distinctions between categories appropriate to the perceiver on the one hand and categories appropriate to whatever is being perceived on the other. This way of conceiving things is not, as it might first appear to be, one of binarism, for in addition to these poles dialogism enlists the additional factors of situa-tion and relation that make any specific instance of them more than mere opposition of categories.[2]

Bakhtin's notion of co-being, or co-existence, is more than a relationship between two points, as each person, or idea is situated in time and space. This acknowledgement of more than one positioning, in terms of point of view, physical location and experience is one which has been central to the ResCen ethos and approach to research.

So what does this actually mean in terms of the artist's creative process, the impact on their work, on the people with whom they collaborate, and ultimately the audience? In 'Geo-Choreographies: Self as Site', which arose out of a series of discussions Shobana Jeyasingh had with Susan Melrose about issues of location in her work and process as a chore-ographer, Jeyasingh vividly describes her own sense of the dynamic in dance:

> I often have the movement of a windscreen wiper in mind. Not a linear, nor even circular, or any of those classical geometric shapes, but a restless movement across and back – even when it goes to the furthest extreme, you know that it will come back. A constant possibility of getting back to the beginning, or of being aware of a range of possibilities, rather than simply of arrival or departure.

As she points out, the advantage of this stance is 'being aware of a range of possibilities'. It means that simultaneously there can be many alternatives, many manifestations which 'co-exist'. Again, Doreen Massey articulates this within a wider geographical context: 'What I'm trying to get at is an ability to live life in the knowledge that [yours] is but one story among many. There's [sic] a zillion other stories going on at the same time right now, always right now….'[3] This 'now' has parallels with the notion in performance practice of being 'in the moment'.[4] There is a heightened awareness about that point of time and space, an awareness of one's own, and others', physical and emotional presence. Jeyasingh also highlights that the range of possibilities are not just at the beginning or end points – a departure point which leads to one arrival point on a single journey – but rather an awareness of a shifting dynamic, a potential for change, a restless movement. This sense of movement implies journeying, travelling.

Over years of discussing aspects of their creative processes, many of the Research Associate Artists have been aware of stimulating their imaginative and creative thoughts on train journeys. Graeme Miller often mentions going on 'gratuitous train journeys'.[5] The fact that he describes them as 'gratuitous' suggests that he makes train journeys not necessarily for the purpose of going somewhere, nor perhaps for even consciously being creative, or having creative thoughts but as an activity which allows space for thought, *if* it happens. The pressure is off. He doesn't have to perform, he doesn't have to be anywhere at any particular time. Whilst other artists may be taking the train for another reason – a meeting, a rehearsal, or performance – the train environment and the scenery that rushes by outside the window create a space which is neutral, transitory, without expectation (apart from the expectation that the journey is finite and that there is a destination to be arrived at). The train needs to be moving for this state to be induced, if the train breaks down, or remains stationary for too long, it doesn't work. In a ResCen round table discussion, 'Picture the Sound of a Dripping Tap' about imagination in the creative process, published in *Engage*, Jeyasingh points out that '… being in a car or on a train with scenery whizzing past makes me suddenly lose all sense of where I am. My body thinks I am being occupied; I am in a kind of suspended animation which allows a kind

of productive dynamic or imagination'.[6] Here it is the actual act of moving that induces creative thought.

Jason Wilson discusses notions of journeying in poetry and travel writing in his essay 'Travel, Writing and the Unknown', and gives us the Spanish poet Antonio Machado's perspective:

'Traveller, your steps/are the journey and nothing more', where intense temporality, the now, is where the traveller always is. Machado's acute insight is that the traveller is the journey.

Again, we have the 'now', and a state of being that can produce an intensity of awareness, experience and thought. Whilst the act of journeying can be seen to induce creative thoughts and allow imaginative ideas to take flight, Wilson later asserts that: 'it's not the factual journey but its recreation in the mind afterwards… creativity is this later struggle more than the experience of a trip. It takes place afterwards, in the study or library, alone, sitting still'. Wilson's essay examines the journeys of a number of poets, travel writers and in particular Bruce Chatwin's journey to become a travel writer. He points out that it is the journey, and the subsequent creative struggle to select, embroider, animate experiences and moments on that journey that 'is worth more than arrival, the finished product'. The assertion is corroborated independently by Graeme Miller in his fake advert for the now defunct Network SouthEast with its slogan 'It is better to journey than to arrive'.[7]

So here, there is a dilemma: the journey may stimulate creative thoughts and new ideas, it may produce heightened awareness of oneself, new experiences of new people and places. There may be a sense of excitement, enjoyment, a physical sensation that is attached to speed and movement, not stopping or resting in any one place for long enough to think beyond the now, but the journey is not the only part of the (creative) story. The 'later struggle' is the problem solving: fitting the memories, ideas and practical elements together in order to make the story, performance, or work, manifest. This requires lateral thinking, invention, projecting forward to see how things might fit together. It requires pragmatism and practicalities, two elements which do not necessarily fit in with a romantic image of the wandering creative traveller.

Graeme Miller shows in his chapter 'Two into One: One into Two' that problem solving and setting up tasks can, in fact, be the entire creative process of generating content, structure and work *ex nihilo*.[8] Unlike the majority of the contributions in this publication, Graeme has not written an essay, nor has he presented, or drawn on conversations about an aspect of his creative process. Instead, 'Two into One: One into Two' is a text and visual manifestation of processes he uses in order to create content and structure in his own work, his work with collaborators, and with students. In his Dis-Introduction he writes: 'Artists' theories, or at least mine, seem to lie in the toolbox, not the bookshelf. They emerge from practice then get applied to new work'. Thus the pages of 'Two into One' reveal a selection of his tools. They allow the reader a direct insight into ways in which this particular creative process comes to life, makes manifest. Miller comments that:

> I am fascinated that what emerges is no-one's idea. It made itself up. That might suggest that creation and composition do not require us to make stuff up and that as 'makers' we are not really making, but stage-managing and cultivating circumstances to *serve* creation.

The cultivation methods – in this instance a series of tasks – remain the same, the circumstances – time, place, people – change and produce different results each time. Again, we come back to the 'now'. Each time it happens *now*. Each time it will be slightly different. Central to this process is a belief that artists are resourceful, quicker to react and good at lateral

thinking.[9] There is also an openness and willingness to play.[10] The sociologist Richard Sennett remarks in *The Fall of the Public Man* that 'To play requires a freedom from the self; but this freedom can be created only by rules which will establish the fiction of initial equality in power between the players'.[11] Graeme illustrates this through his fascination of binary structures putting A and B together. Sometimes A and B are set out to mirror each other, on other occasions they start as two different points and through the course of the task, they begin to work in unison. At other times they are opposing forces – like in an arm-wrestling match. Here the binary points are positioned dialectically. As Bachelard highlights in 'The dialectics of outside and inside' in *The Poetics of Space*, such opposing, conflicting forces of these two positions 'are always ready to be reversed, to exchange their hostility. If there exists a border-line surface between such inside and outside, this surface is painful on both sides'.[12] The 'pain' that Bachelard speaks of, in this context, is one of intensity and tension. The tension that Miller sets up in his examples in 'Two into One' create a vibration between binary positions and it is this that can be used creatively to produce narrative, and to make content manifest. If the tension slackens, or ceases then the narrative ends. If it becomes too painful, it can break, or die.

In a discussion with composer Peter Wiegold at the ResCen conference *Nightwalking* in 2002, Miller noted that:

> … as soon as you put two people on a stage, or you put two musicians together, there's immediately a kind of structural necessity going on, and the thing you might find to contain that will immediately start to produce results.[13]

The creation of a structure, a parameter in which to work, or rules with which to approach an environment, or situation create the content, and sometimes the work itself. Perhaps the most well known example of this way of working is in the writings of Georges Perec. Perec was fascinated with classification systems, and used severely restrictive linguistic rules such as palindromes, and lipograms (a text which excludes one or more letters). His most well known lipogrammatic work, *La Disparition*, is a novel written without using the letter most frequently used in the French alphabet: the letter E.[14] His fascination with using such systems could be seen merely as a way in which to challenge his skills in problem solving, to raise the stakes, make things a bit more difficult. But perhaps, more pertinent to this context, it is a way in which new thoughts, or reactions, are allowed to surface. By having rules, or something with which to react, new and unexpected ways of thinking, looking, or reacting emerge. These very manifestations of the rules become the narrative.

In Perec's later essay 'Species of Spaces' he notes that:

> When nothing arrests our gaze, it carries a
> very long way. But if it meets with nothing,
> it sees nothing, it sees only what it meets.
> Space is what arrests our gaze, what our
> sight stumbles over: the obstacle, bricks,
> an angle, a vanishing point. Space is when
> it makes an angle, when it stops, when we
> have to turn for it to start off again.[15]

Perec's stumbling articulates an unexpected point, one which is not known, but also implies an openness, or belief that something will be stumbled upon. Jason Wilson's citation of Baudelaire's 'Le Voyage': 'To dive to the bottom of the abyss, hell or heaven, who cares? / To the bottom of the unknown to find the new' also implies that not only is there a 'bottom' but that it *will* render something new. It is this belief that allows the artist to jump into the unknown, to begin again. Shobana Jeyasingh notes in 'Birth, Death and What

Lies in Between' that: 'In classical dance, when one is working with conventional vocabulary and 'ideal' shapes, it is possible for the choreographer to almost instruct the dancer verbally and get the desired result because they both know the ideal that they are striving for. In contemporary work, one allows for more interruptions, accidents, contributions…'. She continues: 'I don't think there are rules as such for my practice… perhaps one just gets better at coping without rules – to relax more and trust one's instincts more'.

Trust is the essential element here, trust of 'one's instincts' and also trust of the people with whom one is working. The writer and organisational theorist Charles Handy[16] points out in *Understanding Organizations* that trust and control are married to each other acting like two weights balancing on a scale: if trust is less, the need for control will be more; if trust is more, there will be less need for control.[17] This simple counterpoint equation shows the sensitive balancing act that occurs within relationships between a manager and his staff.

Jeyasingh recalls in 'Geo-Choreographies' how:

> In the past I may have almost had to seduce
> [the dancers] into my way of seeing, or try to
> find a way of keeping my vision as a choreog-
> rapher separate, making sure that their vision
> for themselves is also being realised while
> doing what I want them to do. So that does
> fracture my own vision in the making process.
> Interestingly, sometimes a dancer might be
> on a completely different journey from my own
> but I find that I can use that different journey –
> it can provide a different layer in the work.

A journey is usually associated with encounters with a series of people, points and/or locations. In 'Geo-Choreographies' Jeyasingh discusses her loss of sense of space and a feeling of dislocation through her childhood memories. Most vividly, she describes her experience as a dancer in Britain: 'I found the walk from the dressing room to the wings, dressed in my [Bharatha Natyam] costume, usually through some draughty municipal corridor, particularly bizarre and unsettling. There was a mismatch of arrival and departure'. She goes on to say: 'I think my choreographic journey began with trying to make sense of that feeling of alien-ation: to find a different way of mediating myself as performer; to make a different bridge between the performer's personal reality and their reality on stage'.

The awareness of a personal reality – whether strongly rooted to one location, or an experience of multiple (and sometimes very different) points – is one that is necessary if the journey is to be drawn upon, and reported. Jason Wilson asserts that: 'There's no travel writing without someone leaving home… travel writing reports back to those who stay at home, the armchair readers, the public'. In leaving home there is a sense of departure, in reporting back there is also a feeling of dislocation, an awareness of what is back home, but also distance – distance to the place, and distance to one's audience.[18] In Alistair Hannay's collection of thoughts *On the Public* he states that: 'Being able to form a public is not merely a matter of numbers, there is also distance to account for: the distance between performer and audience'.[19] Whilst this distance can be emphasised through the positioning of the audience, the artist's awareness of the audience's viewpoint, or potential experience, is, undoubtedly a factor within the manifestation of the work.[20] The poet Michael Donaghy discussed this with Rosemary Lee at the Nightwalking conference in 2002:

> When you write a letter to someone or a love poem to someone, to someone in particular or send a telegram, you know who you are talking to. But in poetry as a literature, printed form, you really have no idea who your audience is. What you are doing is you have

to set up a fiction, a working fiction that is your audience…[21]

Graeme Miller has a particular way of approaching this:

> I pretend that I have an audience which is entirely made up of me. But it's me in various badly fitting wigs, disguised as other people. The emphatic premise is somehow what is necessary so that my internal world gener-ates the whole thing, including this audience. Somehow, by some fluke, a lot of the time it seems to work out that the very thing you hope to effect upon your inner puppet audience actually seems to work on a real audience.[22]

Ghislaine Boddington has also articulated seeing an imaginary audience and performance space:

> When I've got something to aim at – a looming deadline – I see the context. Even if I don't know the space I'll make it up. I'll visualise the technical rehearsal…. In my head I see the space and if I am using moving audiences, how they will move around. I see how one element will balance against another.[23]

Here, Michael Donaghy, Graeme Miller and Ghislaine Boddington all talk of the imaginative tools which are part of the artist's creative process and are used towards creating the public manifestation of the work. The imagined audience, whether passive or active individuals, are necessary elements, not just for the final product to become public, to be talked about, critiqued and be born, but also a vital element within the artist's own creative thought process in making the work. They are not a faceless mass. Even in Graeme's case where they are all Graeme Millers, they have (at least on the surface) different appearances, disguises and characters. Whilst the artist might try to imagine, anticipate and manipulate how the audience might react, recent neuroscientific research by Daniel Glaser has shown that the audience's own knowledge and experience – in this particular research, knowledge of movement – directly informs how they receive visual information about the dancers that they are watching. If you have had a physical experience and knowledge about a particular way of moving, then your brain will be more active when you are watching someone else making the same movements, than if you had no physical knowledge or experience.[24]

This two-way exchange between the work and viewer whether she is an anonymous, armchair reader, staying at home experiencing the journey through the medium of the travel book, or perhaps an audience member at a performance, conjures up simultaneously experienced locations of space and time. She is physically in the 'here' and 'now' of the armchair, or the performance space but, if the story is any good, she will experience a travelling sensation of being in the 'there' and 'now' of somewhere else.

Whilst the manifestation of these elements might seem like the end of the journey, the arrival at the destination, the final product, Jeyasingh points out in 'Birth, Death and What Lies in Between' that 'I don't think a dance work is ever finished. There are too many variables in the human body. You can put a frame around six dancing bodies – the proscenium arch, the site, lighting – but what happens inside it is always shifting.' This means that for the artist, there can be a sense of continuation, being able to revisit, and refine.

So although there is a performance, a product, the work can continue to change. It may be a shifting point for the artist, but what about the audience? The audience member usually sees the performance, or product of the artist/writer's work, once.[25] It starts and ends at a specific time. It may be different from the performance of the previous night or, indeed, the next night, but that is of no consequence to the viewer. For her, that particular performance is her own, and only physical experience of it. Errollyn Wallen has talked of this experience from the composer's point of view: 'I think one of the best things about being a composer… is however long you've got, forty minutes, you've got people captive and you're taking them on a journey and you're manipulating them.'[26] Then curtain falls, the lights go up, they leave the building and return home.

Despite the artist perhaps viewing the work in the long term as never finished due to the variable factors such as different performers, venues and times in which the work could be made in the future, each time a new work is premiered, or even restaged, there is usually one inescapable factor: the deadline. Errollyn has articulated her relationship to this imposed aspect of the creative process: 'Emblazoned on my mind in gigantic theatre lights is the word FINISH. I must. There's a palpable fear in my belly, and I wake up in the middle of the night sweating music'.[27] So this type of ending is a vital part of the creative process, essential if the work is to be made manifest to an audience, or viewer. There must be an end, an arrival at a destination at some point, even if the artist decides that this is not the final stop. At this point there is, what Graeme Miller describes in 'Birth, Death and What Lies in Between' as a 'ritual death':

> I think of live performance as a ritual death which I experience in the curtain fall, when the last note is complete. It is a valedictory moment, a parting of something, and I know the thing itself is connected to its afterlife at that point.

In response to this point Ghislaine Boddington points out that this 'ritual death' can be experienced by the artist as a very physical phenomenon and, in some cases, the result of an addiction to the adrenaline high of performance which quickly drops at the death, or the curtain fall. The fact that Miller refers to this as a 'ritual' and Boddington talks of 'addiction' suggests that it is, in fact, not *the final ending*. There will be another life and another death and so on.

So, there is life after death, at least after the ritual death we are talking about here. Once it is over, the process (usually) begins again: restaging; touring; new work; new commission. Or, another way to look at it is through the eyes of Graeme Miller: 'If we observed an orchestra from its final note to the dressing room it would turn the end into the beginning'. The arrival becomes the departure point. Perhaps then, rather than it being better to journey than to arrive, it is necessary to arrive in order to journey again.

1   Full transcript of ResCen seminar with Doreen Massey 'Making Space', 12 January 2005, <www.rescen.net>

2   Michael Holquist, *Dialogism: Bakhtin and his world* (London: Routledge, 1990), p.22

3   Massey <www.rescen.net>

4   See Rosemary Lee's chapter 'Expectant Waiting' p.158

5   Full transcription of ResCen seminar with Guy Claxton, 'Intuition and the Artist', 8 May 2003 <www.rescen.net>

6   Jane Watt, ed., 'Picture the Sound of a Dripping Tap: perspectives on imagination in performing arts', *Engage*, 16 (Winter 2005), p.34

7   These two citations echo Robert Louis Stevenson's assertion that 'To travel hopefully is a better thing than to arrive' in his essay 'El Dorado' in *Virginibus puerisque* (London: Thomas Nelson & Sons, 1881).

8   See Graeme Miller's *Ex Nihilo* web pages at <www.rescen.net> for examples and more detail about this ongoing concern.

9   See Graeme Miller, 'Country dance' in *Architecturally Speaking: practices of art, architecture and the everyday*, ed. Alan Read (London and New York: Routledge, 2000), pp.109-117 (p.117).

10 See transcript of ResCen seminar 'The Artist: working?... playing?', 20 April 2004, <www.rescen.net> for more discussion of this topic.

11 Richard Sennett, *The Fall of Public Man* (London: Faber and Faber, 1993), p.319

12 Gaston Bachelard, *The Poetics of Space*, trans. Maria Jolas (Boston: Beacon Press, 1994), pp.217-218. First published in French under the title *La poétique de l'espace*, by Presses Universitaires de France, 1958.

13 Full transcript of Peter Wiegold and Graeme Miller podium discussion, *Nightwalking*, 27-29 September 2002, <www.rescen.net>

14 Georges Perec, *La Disparition*, (Denoël, Les lettres nouvelles, 1969). Gilbert Adair's prize-winning English translation, *A Void*, was published in 1996 by Harvill Press.

15 Georges Perec, *Species of Spaces and Other Pieces*, trans. by John Sturrock, (London: Penguin, 1997), p.81. Espèces d'espace [Species of Spaces] was first published in French by Editions Galilée, 1974.

16 Charles Handy was one of ResCen's first guest speakers to contribute to a seminar day in March 2003 at ResCen.

17 Charles Handy, *Understanding Organizations*, 4th ed. (London: Penguin, 1999), pp.283-284

18 The term 'home' is a very emotive, and sometimes controversial one, as it implies solidity, tradition and family, not all of which are present, or indeed desirable in one's life and creative process.

19 Alistair Hannay, *On the Public* (Abingdon: Routledge, 2005), p.32

20 This argument favours the more traditional stance of audience as viewer, and not as interactive participant. Although Hannay refutes this: 'What is called audience participation may seem to belie this, but typically it does not. On the contrary, audiences invited to participate in a performance are nothing like the performers themselves, part of whose performance is to co-opt members of the audience to get them to do what they, the performers want' (Ibid). However, here, Hannay's argument still appears somewhat limited as he includes an expert performer within the performance mix.

21 Full transcript of Michael Donaghy and Rosemary Lee podium discussion, Nightwalking Conference, 27-29 September 2002, <www.rescen.net>

22 Full transcript of ResCen seminar 'The Motivation of the Artist' 25 May 2004, <www.rescen.net>

23 Watt, ed., p.34

24 See full transcript of ResCen seminar with Daniel Glaser 'Mis-Seeing: vision, experience and prejudice in the creative process', 17 November 2004, <www.rescen.net> and <www.icn.ucl.ac.uk/glaser> for more details of this research.

25 The exception to this is the loyal, and sometimes fanatical fans of popular musicals such as *Cats*, *Phantom of the Opera*, and *Les Miserables* who go to see the performance dozens of times.

26 In an unpublished ResCen conversation with Graeme Miller, October 2005.

27 See Errollyn Wallen's pages on <www.rescen.net>

Graeme
Miller

Follow someone

else's nose

Graeme Miller

Ghislaine
Boddington

Shobana
Jeyasingh

Richard
Layzell

Rosemary
Lee

Graeme
Miller

Errollyn
Wallen

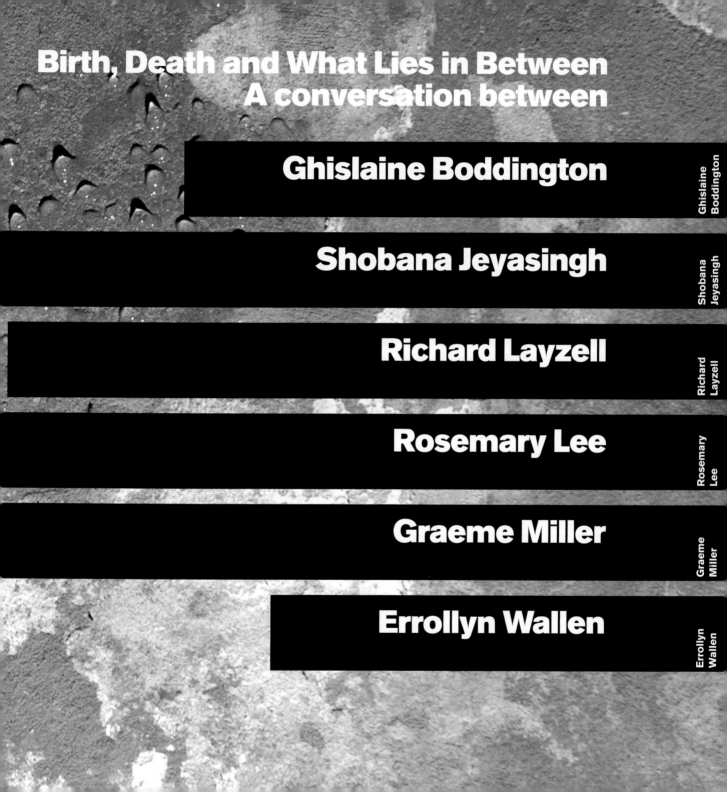

Birth, Death and What Lies in Between
A conversation between

Ghislaine Boddington

Shobana Jeyasingh

Richard Layzell

Rosemary Lee

Graeme Miller

Errollyn Wallen

Errollyn
Wallen

Graeme
Miller

Rosemary
Lee

Richard
Layzell

Shobana
Jeyasingh

Ghislaine
Boddington

Rosemary: When we first talked about working on this book, *Navigating the Unknown*, I had an aversion to the idea that the third section would be called 'Making Manifest' because it implies a linear path attached to making a work. For me, making manifest happens throughout the process of creating. The first making manifest is the idea actually becoming conscious in my brain. I'm in a constant state of trying to communicate that first sensation of feeling the idea throughout the subsequent process. Then there are many steps along the way that make it manifest: like putting it onto paper; or telling somebody it. Then it is realised, in choreography, in a dancer's body, and then on the stage. There's a transition point each time between my brain and communicating with the dancers, or between the dancers dancing it and my notes in my notebook. It's not just about a finished product, or the act of getting the work, or idea, out there in the public eye.

Graeme: What I like about making manifest, and why it suits me as an idea, is that it suggests that something already exists. The content often lies in the gaps and the shadows. That's where the readable, visible traces that I allow into the world are. As an artist, I'm like a kind of broker of hidden content, I'm making the thing manifest, but the thing, by implication, exists even if I weren't to make it manifest. The way I work is often to fool around on the surface until I find the content that's hidden. What I'm making manifest may not be apparent until I start trying to make it manifest.

Richard: Maybe making and manifest go together. From the position of the visual artist, nothing is manifest until it's visual, until it actually appears in some form. Once the drawing is there, or the object starts to appear, then it manifests itself visually into the world. So, it would be hard for me to separate the appearance from the making. They are interwoven. There is often another person – like a potential commissioner or a client – involved in this process and they are always asking me to show them an example. Somehow, that demonstration of a manifested thing clarifies what the work is about.

Ghislaine: I think of the word 'manifesto' in relation to manifest. A manifesto is setting a mission statement. A mission means you have a message; you've got something to say, a need to communicate. It implies a direction, or a passion, or something that you have to put across. It is a debate that is created: a dialogue beyond yourself.

Errollyn: It's an act of commitment isn't it?

Ghislaine: It is. It's putting something in place that will create a reaction because other people will think differently. And that's what, surely, most artists would want to happen. From the first inkling of an idea or concept, I am busy working, in my body and mind, on how it can 'come out', be made manifest. It does not leave me alone, it nags inside me, insistent on being released. As an artist my need is to find the way to release it, to issue it into the world, to push that debate. The way I do this is by juggling and testing it – the form, the context, the feel and further into the process, the performers, the site, the audience. All these elements must be considered from multiple angles and it is the juggling and ultimate jigsawing of these elements that enables the emergence of a manifestation. It is a cause with a need to create an effect.

Shobana: Manifest does suggest some sort of product – visible or experienced – otherwise it would be more like conceptual art. In dance, especially, it needs to have some sort of visible or objective existence. As Rosemary says, choreography

Errollyn
Wallen

Graeme
Miller

Rosemary
Lee

Richard
Layzell

Shobana
Jeyasingh

Ghislaine
Boddington

Errollyn Wallen | Graeme Miller | Rosemary Lee | Richard Layzell | Shobana Jeyasingh | Ghislaine Boddington

becomes manifest through the dancers' bodies, through the relationship to its other parts – like the music, design, lighting – and most of all through its relationship to its audience. Sometimes, when you present forms to an audience, like Indian classical dance, or ballet with its specific codes, that have no context in common, then it can almost feel like the dance cannot manifest itself. It cannot communicate itself and remains opaque or unrealised. So, yes, manifest seems to have within itself the act of communication: a responding spectator or audience, a listener to the narrative. However the communication does not necessarily have to be uniform. This is particularly true of time-based art forms which need an audience to make themselves manifest. It takes for granted the existence of an observer, a relationship, an exteriority. Perhaps then, making manifest is a process of communication, without a tangible product at the end?

Richard: I was thinking, while you were talking, that even if I'm making the idea manifest, if the person I'm manifesting it to cannot visualise it then it's not a manifestation. If it's so befuddled and personal that it doesn't make any sense, then I guess that's not really making manifest.

Graeme: Maybe this is where the idea of refining comes in? Maybe there are degrees of focus, or degrees of clarity? So the idea of a befuddled piece of work suggests that part of making manifest is about pulling something out of the mist to relative clarity. Refining is about distillation, which is about the removal of unwanted material. It happens over time. It's a thing you can do once, or several times. It's a repetitive process. It's important to know what you're after, or what remains true. It's important to know when to change what you're looking for.

Shobana: For me, the process of refining is something that keeps happening over a very long period of time and is very much a part of the beginning as well as the end. So it is not the case of a finished product being refined. I find that talking to collaborators about the concept at the very beginning is a

kind of refining. Often what is communicated changes drastically when you put the choreography on stage for the first time with all the other elements of production and then again at each meeting of the audience and the dance.

Errollyn: When I talk about refining, I think of it as revisiting something with different eyes and ears, and with a different perspective. As Graeme said, refining is another journey which is to do with looking at the essence of the work. As that essence becomes clearer to me, I know what the extraneous things are. So there is sense of knowing, but also a sense of coming to the work again, almost half blindfolded, to something that I missed earlier on. It's all with the purpose of attaining clarity.

Richard: I can see how the idea of refinement might be really closely interlinked with making manifest. I'm working on a second prototype for a work at the Science Museum. The first one didn't do what we wanted it to do and I thought I'd just give up on it. However, I put some images down on a piece of paper which I thought could work. I could not figure out the drawing until I physically made it. That was a refining process. The piece does work now.

Graeme: 'God is in the detail.' There are times when I think I work in rough. If I don't know what I'm going to say I can mumble it, pull the sharp out of the vague. But on the other hand in making manifest there's also this element about writing everything in best. Don't write it rough, because until you write it in best with the full detail you won't know what sort of creature it is. An idea that I used when I worked as part of a theatre cooperative was to reach a point where something is 'self-tightening'. Self-tightening is a critical stage where if something's left to it's own devices (in this case, a group of performers), it'll either tend to pull itself up, and in, energise itself, and start to find new detail, or, it'll tend to stay the same, or start to sag. So the trick is always to get a piece of work up to a self-tightening state. An example would be within the interaction of individuals in a performance group who all have enough knowledge and ownership of a work to be able to play it differently every night: they have something to suggest that can evolve and work in details. At this stage, as the outside eye or director, I don't need to say a word.

Ghislaine: The concept of dramaturgy (which is not well acknowledged in performance in Britain although this creative role has a long tradition in Germanic theatre arts) is to act as a bridge between what the

Errollyn Wallen

Graeme Miller

Rosemary Lee

Richard Layzell

Shobana Jeyasingh

Ghislaine Boddington

Ghislaine
Boddington

Shobana
Jeyasingh

Richard
Layzell

Rosemary
Lee

Graeme
Miller

Errollyn
Wallen

artists are making, what they want to communicate, and whether it is going to reach its audience. When I work as a dramaturg, quite often I'm involved throughout the process but the first research inputs and last three or four inputs I put for consideration just before the piece goes live are often the most imperative: it might be about the entire research, the topical contexting of the whole performance, or maybe the tiniest shift, or detail, like the movement of an eye, for example. Refining, for me, is necessarily continuous throughout the creation and production process.

Shobana: We now seem to be talking about the idea of perfection, the measuring up to an ideal (which is an 'interior' word). There is something very Platonic about the word 'manifest' in this context, as if the ideal is conceptual and the making manifest is the realisation of this ideal in the most perfect exterior way possible. In classical dance, when one is working with conventional vocabulary and 'ideal' shapes, it is possible for the choreographer to almost instruct the dancer verbally and get the desired result because they both know the ideal that they are striving for. In contemporary work one allows for more interruptions, accidents, contributions. The manifesting process is delegated. In dance, of course, the 'self-tightening' that you talk of Graeme is in operation from the start since the script is written with the dancers' participation and with their consent. I am always aware of having their permission to draw on their expertise. Whatever ideas I may start off with, the first stage is gaining entry to the dancers' imagination and bodies. This does not necessarily mean that they have to have the same journey as I do. Often they don't.

Errollyn: Refining is not always about making things perfect because sometimes work can be over refined. Refining can be about putting the rough back in.

Ghislaine: Yes, I wasn't saying that it was about perfection, rather about contextualising and clarifying one's message.

Graeme: It's a kind of finishing process. Refining is different to editing. Editing is the building of material from something that already exists in some way, whether you've found it or generated it yourself. I suppose an editor in literature will work with a poet's, or a writer's, work, removing and organising, shaping, structuring it and detailing it. You need all those elements there. I think editing is a fantastic process. I often edit found material. The material is deliciously impersonal and it allows the power of editing to make work and to make all sorts of implications and suggestions.

Richard: What's the difference between editing and refining?

Rosemary: I would say we need all these words because they do tend to come at slightly different points in the process. To me, editing comes before refining. Editing is usually to do with taking away and refining might be to do with adding. I know that's a generalisation. I refine the edit.

Graeme: I know that sometimes I refine something until it's yards too long, it's over detailed. At that point, I need a ruthless editor, it could be myself, to go in and throw out every third word, to get rid of the gaps, and bring in 'a bit of rough' as you say, Errollyn, to re-animate this thing.

Errollyn: Editing implies a process of detachment doesn't it? You start by being involved with something and then you see what you've got and you move away and you become ever more detached to the point where you feel like someone else – separate to the creator.

Rosemary: I wanted to come back to the word refinement in terms of our processes and our age. Certainly, talking to other choreographers at similar stages in their careers,

Errollyn Wallen | Graeme Miller | Rosemary Lee | Richard Layzell | Shobana Jeyasingh | Ghislaine Boddington

Errollyn Wallen · Graeme Miller · Rosemary Lee · Richard Layzell · Shobana Jeyasingh · Ghislaine Boddington

we'll often think we're refining our practice more and more, we have a more refined practice, we know what we're working on, we know our areas of interest.

Errollyn: Yes, I feel that I have more of an awareness of my practice and as things emerge, I have something like a checklist, a way of asking 'does this fulfil this criterion?' Nobody can teach me that, I have to find those rules myself.

Richard: Sometimes I use this fantasy idea that I'm the most highly skilled and experienced person in the room. I know my practice so well that I'm impervious and can demand acknowledgement of that. So I guess that I don't have rules exactly, but if I wanted to write a list of all these imaginary qualities I could do that.

Shobana: I don't think there are rules as such for my practice. But with time, hopefully, I get better in recognising what I am about. Rules suggest something objective and visible to others with the possibility of being reproduced in all situations. I don't think that what I learn from one piece is very useful in the next because the questions that I want to ask have changed. Perhaps one just gets better at coping without rules – to relax more and trust one's instincts more.

Graeme: So a technique could be having faith in having no technique?

Richard: Yes, absolutely, and belief.

Graeme: So it's knowing what you can draw on, knowing what works, or that you can get sufficiently lost?

Richard: Or even just adopting a kind of confident manner that makes people think 'Oh yes! He must know what he's doing because of how he sounds'.

Ghislaine: What you're saying is you believe enough in your own experience.

Richard: Yes, it doesn't always work, and it's relatively recently that I've realised and used this way of thinking. I know that I can be very

Errollyn: I feel that part of the attitude that one needs to make good work is to be humble and doubtful. But then when I'm out there in front of the performers and the public I have to pretend that I'm sure about the work. A lot of people only form an opinion if somebody tells them this is good or bad, so often there's only the artist that has to stand up for the work. And if the artist is being truthful they'll say: 'I don't really know because I don't quite understand the nature of the universe…' But people don't want that, they want to know that you embody this total expertise.

Errollyn: But what I'm saying is if I'm in a rehearsal situation, the performers want to know every little detail, every answer. I've seen it. It's better to give an answer in good faith and check it later than to say that you don't know. This is because time is short in rehearsal. You have to be very quick, on top of it, and show that all along the way you've been committed to every move. There's a certain amount of psychology involved.

defensive, but by not being defensive, and instead being sure, people do respond to it.

Richard: But if you declare that your uncertainty is essential to how you develop the work, as part of your process…

Graeme: Seeing yourself involved in doing a series is one way of dealing with this. Every piece of work that I made used to feel like the last thing I'd ever do. It took me ages to realise I was re-doing old work. There are enormous similarities in all my works. I really admire people who find new ground within the same type of work, they're actually just redefining what new ground is.

Richard: I'd like to discuss the so-called quest for originality. Is there a virtue in saying well actually I just make the same piece of work over and over again? The reason I'm particularly interested in this is that I've recently been under some pressure to develop a number of events called *Project IS* in Bristol in a short space of time. I wasn't conscious that three of the proposed works relate closely to previous pieces in terms of imagery I've used. I feel that this is fine, but I was a bit shocked that these were unconscious ideas, or links, within my work.

Richard: Exactly. You could say that through the process of repetition, which involves refinement and repetition and modification, they are eventually getting to an original place?

Shobana: I am sure that all my dance works basically address the same thing but I do not see that as repetition. Without being aware of it, most of my

Errollyn Wallen
Graeme Miller
Rosemary Lee
Richard Layzell
Shobana Jeyasingh
Ghislaine Boddington

Errollyn
Wallen

Graeme
Miller

Rosemary
Lee

Richard
Layzell

Shobana
Jeyasingh

Ghislaine
Boddington

titles are to do with location: *Making of Maps; New Cities Ancient Lands; Configurations*. However, when I make the works, they never feel like old territory. One of the things that I'm told is 'this looks so different to your last piece!' It is like I'm asking the same question but each year the answer is articulated differently. Even in a piece in which I use a lot of repetition, I am always amazed at how little one needs as raw material in order to exploit its elements endlessly. With time-based arts the use of repetition is a very important skill since you need to fix certain things in the onlooker's memory.

Rosemary: At the moment, I am in the middle of revisiting, or reviving a dance piece for three dancers called *Beached* that was originally made in 2002 and performed at Bluecoat, Liverpool. It is a strange process because it feels like I'm starting from the centre of the process and progressing out, rather than feeling that I'm at the very beginning. It's already had its afterlife. I've already turned it to face the audience and now, I'm wrenching it back towards myself again. That process brings up all kinds of good, as well as difficult, things. The information that I start to give the same dancers is information that I wouldn't have given them when I first worked with them. So I feel that I'm in the wrong stage of the process when I revive it again. It's a very peculiar feeling, like re-folding myself. As Graeme would say: 'You can't refry an egg!' We do all kinds of things to try to get back to the original – go back to the original tasks and my notebooks – but I've refined once and now I'm refining again. So I'm distilling it again and then looking to see what debris is left at the edges. So then I take parts out, or change it, which shakes up the whole work.

Graeme: But is what's shaking it up the fact that everybody's lives have moved on?

Rosemary: Oh yes, of course there's that as well. But I'm not trying to go back to that point in time exactly. I've chosen to start a new process because I think we have to although we still need to fold back a little bit in order to remember. It was originally made for, and in response to, those dancers and now they've moved on. So it's trying to embrace their development, their maturing whilst being true to the piece and its maturing too. By doing the work again, it's like trying to find the piece. We've been there once and now we've got to find it again. It's just hovering there. If it was made well enough the robustness will hold all the images there, the container will have been the right container. I can see where there are leaks, so I'm trying to patch up the leaky bits of the piece. I think now we've found the piece again. A student group saw it yesterday and I quizzed them afterwards (I've never done this before): what did you see; what do you think they'd wear? They told me exactly what I had originally drawn in my notebook. So I then just opened my notebook and showed them: they designed the same costumes; they even described a drawing in my notebook. So I thought: I've done it. The piece is showing what I wanted it to show. I guess this time I've managed to make it manifest!

Shobana: I regularly revisit old work because I think it needs a re-visit for it to mature and express its full potential. Revisiting always means a new version.

Errollyn: I don't have that experience as a composer, because the work is written to be fixed so that if I'm not there at the rehearsals, or at the performance, the conductor knows exactly what decisions need to be made. So I generally wouldn't go back and recreate anything.

Richard: The night before an installation is open to the public, I panic. I might be up half the night. I'm refining. The reason I stop refining is simply because of the deadline. Once the installation is open to the private view, then I can't do any more. Once it's opened it's fixed. So finishing is sort of arbitrary, the end point is simply to do with a timeline, a deadline. Refinement could go on for another week unless that point came. That state of last minute adjustments and thinking this could be better, is not particularly pleasurable, it is not as enjoyable as Graeme said, is really pleasurable.

Shobana: I don't think a dance work is ever finished. There are too many variables in the human body. You can put a frame around six dancing bodies – the proscenium arch, the site, lighting – but what happens inside it is always shifting. I usually have the end image, or scene, at least halfway through the rehearsal period. I do not usually have all the music at this stage so the ending is suggested by the logic of the dance. The journey is towards the ending that I have set up. For me, it is less about knowing when I have finished, it is more a case of asking myself is this a convincing journey to the end that I have chosen?

Errollyn
Wallen

Graeme
Miller

Rosemary
Lee

Richard
Layzell

Shobana
Jeyasingh

Ghislaine
Boddington

Errollyn Wallen | Graeme Miller | Rosemary Lee | Richard Layzell | Shobana Jeyasingh | Ghislaine Boddington

Of course there are times when the journey modifies the end somewhat. Having said that, there are pieces that I have made where any type of classic ending seemed impossible. Some journeys stop because the music runs out or one makes endings which are about communicating the futility of endings. All endings are, in some ways, artificial, especially in non-narrative, time-based arts. They are emotional moments where a line is drawn and all options closed. A part of me always resents this!

Rosemary: For me, the idea of when a piece is finished is when I leave. If I go to every performance it won't ever be finished because I'll always be giving the dancers notes. So perhaps I have to enforce it being finished by leaving and never seeing it again.

Errollyn: If I'm working on a piece, I sometimes play a game. I'll ask myself: What if I said it was finished now, what would I feel like? Would the essence still be there? Often, as most recently, I'll have been writing a piece for three months and I'll say I've nearly finished. Then another month goes by and I'll still say I'm nearly finished. Then there's a point where I think: Right, I'm so sick of it, I don't care. Then I know it's finished.

Richard: I think the feeling of panic that I mentioned has to do with the confines of a preparation situation. For example I may have a week to install and during that period it's not just about installing, but also about: how do things look; how do they feel; how do they fit together; are they finished; is that element quite finished? There is also the issue of having to change things quite late on in the process. That state of standing back, when it's at that 'finished state' and thinking about what needs to happen now, I think that's probably more of an experience that visual artists have, that couldn't happen as a choreographer, I think you would have had to make those decisions earlier.

Graeme: Yes, I have a very different relationship to a deadline for an installation than I do for a performance. I think a lot of that has to do with what I call the 'God of the Last Minute' who looks over live performance. I think of live performance as a ritual death which I experience in the curtain fall, when the last note is complete. It is a valedictory moment, a parting of something, and I know the thing itself is connected to its afterlife at that point.

Rosemary: Yes, that's right.

Graeme: I've tended to make lots of bits of work that have a galloping rhythm to them and then they end abruptly. I love this idea of strutting and fretting for an hour on the stage, cramming a lifetime within a ritualised amount of time. A performed piece that is done in front of an audience suits the deadline well. It focuses everybody's minds at every level. It seems to build up and if things are going on course (equally, they can go badly) there's a kind of efficiency in that process. However, an installation which has a looser relationship with time – people come to it in the real world and in their own time – doesn't necessarily suit deadlines.

Richard: I agree with you completely. I have a much more satisfying relationship to deadlines and endings through performance. There's something about the acts in the present, with the audience, that gets around some of the issues relating to it not being quite right. Maybe because it has to do with the whole experience.

Rosemary: In the rehearsal process and through the tech day, I'm looking at the work and it's looking at me. Suddenly I turn the work round, and there's the audience and the work is now looking away from me. It is a really odd feeling. For me, it can have a terrible feeling of anticlimax, because it's gone. It's wrenched away from me. I want to give it to the audience, that's why I do it, but there is this wrenching away from the intimacy of me, the work and the people making the work with me.

Shobana: The choreographer Christopher Bruce talked about the disappointment that accompanies the journey from the studio into the theatre. It is always a trauma when you lose the intimacy of the studio where you have built up a community within the conventions of performance. I have now got used to the fact that things that work in the ecology of the studio do not work with the distance of the theatre. During rehearsals you are looking at the work very close up and your eyes get used to that intense and over-magnified gaze. Introspective details work very well here and the space between the dancers can seem to burn intensely. The same scene put on stage can sometimes look very un-theatrical and empty because one has not attended to the form of it, which is what hits the eye when you look at it from a distance. Subtleties which

Errollyn Wallen   Graeme Miller   Rosemary Lee   Richard Layzell   Shobana Jeyasingh   Ghislaine Boddington

Ghislaine
Boddington

Shobana
Jeyasingh

Richard
Layzell

Rosemary
Lee

Graeme
Miller

Errollyn
Wallen

communicate in the studio often look self-indulgent or closed-in on stage. However, I am always aware that I am making a piece for the theatre, or site, and not for the studio. It does not achieve completion till it has entered into the dynamics of the theatrical experience. I don't think I feel loss when I see my dance work on stage but rather it is like witnessing a new birth. The whole thing can look very different to what you had imagined, or got used to, during rehearsals but to be outside it at last, is sometimes a great relief.

Ghislaine: When working as a director on live events and installations I feel there is a weird empty void that occurs between releasing the piece from its creation time and its appearance into performance time. I hang in this void, I make myself let go of the work and give it to others. It's like giving a present to someone, but a present that you are not sure is the right one for that person, and in fact you really would prefer to keep it for yourself. This void is full of anticipation for the moment when they open your present. It is a floating space, empty, hollow, numb, and at times echoing with potential fears. It is a place of mature control, of rising panic. The void only refills and harmonises as I watch and feel the audience, or participants, emerge from the experience. In particular I have tuned my senses to the pregnant moments, the hanging minute between the end of the performance, or experience, and the reaction of the receiver. It is this micro part of the whole creation process that really tells you whether your manifestation has created the debate you wanted. Applause and facial expressions around you tell you all. But isn't the ritual death that Graeme talked about also part of an addiction, because what we're talking about is an adrenalin drop, which is actually a physical and chemical process? My whole life has been made up of these patterns of ups and drops. I've co-directed fifty or so workshops, after every one I have a two to three-day drop.

Afterwards, when I finally go home, I sometimes just wander around in my slippers for two days, I can't even think straight.

Richard: The emotional drop can be colossal at the end point and it might be made worse by the other emotional panic and fear about it not being right. So the inevitable crash is perhaps worse. But I think it's something that one learns to deal with through experience, because you know it's going to come, you know the crash is coming.

Errollyn: When I've crashed I have no interest in writing music, and I believe I'll never write another note again. So the deadline involves the death of other things too. Death of the spark, the drive, momentarily…

Graeme: To produce creative work at a steady overlapping pace with no deadlines is a very unlikely idea to me just as to live life with no births, funerals, parties, rows, or crises is unlikely. Time is one of the ways of making things, also space, you find yourself using a particular space in a certain way to intensify your life. I think artists find ways of tapping into interestingness, and I become interesting with a deadline.

Errollyn Wallen

Graeme Miller

Rosemary Lee

Richard Layzell

Shobana Jeyasingh

Ghislaine Boddington

Errollyn
Wallen

Graeme
Miller

Rosemary
Lee

Richard
Layzell

Shobana
Jeyasingh

Ghislaine
Boddington

Shobana: I am definitely someone who uses deadlines as an artistic prop. One needs the chemicals associated with seeing a deadline loom over the horizon to activate the cells. Sensible preparation, time management and terrific ideas rarely seem to go together. I stretch time like an elastic band and it is the huge rebound that seems to kick start the imagination.

Rosemary: I think I've changed with age. I think I was as a young person, but then I realised that I actually wanted a slightly more even keel. I think that's one of the reasons that I worked with film and installation because the deadlines just don't feel so fierce and it's not such a sudden drop, it's a slow fade. My work doesn't tend to stop suddenly like you were describing earlier, Graeme. Mine often peters out with a three-minute fade. So it's quite interesting there are different lines and endings to the process as well as to the pieces themselves, ones that bleed out, or sharp, clear endings.

Errollyn: I always bear in mind that people remember the last thing they've seen or heard.

Rosemary: The audience's reading of the ending and what they're left with and afterwards, the aftermath, is something over which I have much less control. It is a lovely moment when the work faces the audience, but I do still want to control it, I'm trying, right to the end, to control the after-images that will be in the heads of the members of the audience. So the ending is really important.

Ghislaine
Boddington

Shobana
Jeyasingh

Richard
Layzell

Rosemary
Lee

Graeme
Miller

Errollyn
Wallen

Two into One: One into Two

Graeme Miller

Intro

Graeme Miller

An empty-theatre ambience of sour fluorescent lights on black emulsion paint. My ten postgraduate students and I are sitting in the audience seats and I hear myself say what I said last year: 'I don't really know what I can teach you about making work. Just take the shortest route to the end'.

Having said this I am tempted to walk out the building and not return. This statement is still true, yet 'shortest route' can mean through thorn forest on hands and knees and back again. In fact, of course, I stay and share over a few weeks a vein of thinking that runs through my work over time from then till now.

This enquiry can be imagined as a line. My Central Line, the track running through all my creative work (in red) intersects and links seemingly unrelated elements and now itself becomes ever more the subject of my work. It concerns how things come into being and the forms, the prime shapes, that seem to be present at this generation. That I allow things to 'write themselves' as much as I can may be an anthropomorphic conceit that allows me to sever the embarrassment that *the moving hand* at work here is merely my own. Still, the recurring sensation that work speaks suggests that work is language, everything is language. Permeating this landscape of genesis are codes of grammar – structural motifs. Running through the heart of these is a recurrent moment aligning itself with its echoing other selves – a fault line. The line connects moments of division when a single thing becomes two. Encoded in the same moment is its reverse as two elements resolve into one. 'When Two Become One' sing my inner Spice Girls. They refer to conjunction – a cellular merging in human biology and precursor of cell division. They probably aren't singing about Conjunction; a crucial stage in the Alchemical formula, but this stage and its sister, Separation are key stages in transformation. The biological and alchemic moments, as well as those we might detect in real creative processes, share a hard to catch, almost secret, quality. That is not to say they do not exist, or do not exert a force. It is just that they happen in real space, in real time, in complex organic systems. It is only recently that high quality imaging has been able to capture the secrets of the womb and return an image of the moment of cell division.

I will presume we are in the business of transformation and will lead my students through a playful series of practices and observations that follow the same axis that links cousin-moments where two become one and one becomes two. Over the next weeks the empty stage will become a Memory Theatre – a philosophical space in which to browse through the Singular and the Binary in particular and the whole idea of self-generating material in general. This year, I say as I said last year, that at best, by considering these pre-structure structures, you may pick up tools (for overcoming inertia, breaking open dynamics, shaping, containing and especially making something out of nothing) which may shorten, or make more effective, your own routes to your own ends. I still believe this is true.

What I write is interspersed with what I say and tasks I suggest and the index." 1

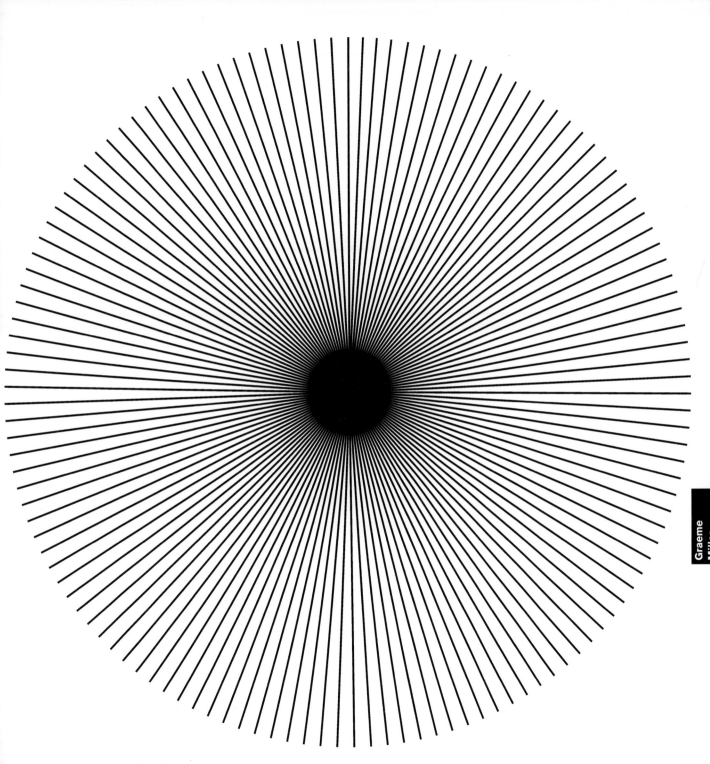

Graeme
Miller

Singular

Graeme
Miller

It is an acid green regularised catering apple from the cafeteria chiller-cabinet. We place it in the space – a philosopher's object more than something you would actually want to eat. This is thinking for makers. I am taking it for granted that you are makers… Put an apple on a table in as clear a space as possible and watch it for a long time. The invitation is to talk. What is a singular thing? What qualities does it have? The talk repeatedly veers to some inherent instability. A resistance to neutrality. A desire to relate. The apple absorbs. It absorbs the fluctuations in our concentration. It marks time then? It absorbs the space around it. It seems to disappear just when it is most visible. *2-5 Then the apple radiates. The apple is a kind of lighthouse beaming its own objecthood. The apple is big in the space then small. The apple must be breathing. The apple keeps trying to relate to things; its name 'apple' and apple-related ideas like its taste. It is hard to keep them at bay. We look at the large quantities of space and time we have given this. We have added some nothing, some spatial nothing and some temporal nothing. A kind of frame made by the object itself at the centre, then?

I talk, scanning *The Anxious Object**6, and Keith Critchlow's exposition of the origin of number and form in Islamic geometry.*7-18 You don't need to write this down, this is thinking on your feet. I skim through The Singualrity* 19 and creation *Ex Nihilo.**20

So what is a single event? Do a single thing on stage. Not so easy. What doesn't work? Things that go on for too long, that seem to have a beginning, middle and end. Things too indistinct from their surroundings. And what does work? The sudden, short, unrepeatable. Make a fistful of coins hit the floor. Comic, violent, emphatic. Imagine a piano falling from the ceiling. Imagine its aftermath. Or its anticipation or lack of it. The single event, like the single object has such high valency it draws us, it's immediate environment and anything else it can relate to, into its field.*21 A cuckoo in the nest. A penumbra of potential. I draw an exclamation mark.*22 This tool for emotional intensity and symbol for danger looks like a thing and its long shadow or an impact and its splatter.*23

An individual stands in the middle of the stage and feels infinitely lost in the middle then expands to entirely fill it, then retreats again (a kind of psychic breathing) without actually doing anything. See from the outside if it is possible to detect this shift. Actually we couldn't really. Shame, but there is a value to placing a person in the apple's position. People are objects too, but when the object breaths, blinks, they seem to generate more narrative. We are narrative monkeys and we project anthropomorphic attributes to our objects. I will encourage this attribution of characteristics to the material and tools of making performance, because it is useful. The singular event and the singular object *can be* anxious, self-assured, pulsing and expectant and we should use them as if they are. *24-25

Graeme
Miller

Frame Academy

Graeme
Miller

A leads B around the space, B with their eyes shut, A looking for something for B to 'photograph'. When A says, B briefly opens their eyes. It is an exercise many people do, for different reasons, but this morning I want to experience framing. In a sense the A persona is the photographer and the B persona the camera.*26-30 Having someone in tow, having a means of preserving against time, an artificial memory, affects the perception of A too. Allow discovery. We talk.

The extraordinary in the ordinary. Retaining the image much later for both A and B. Sampling. The removal of material from a quotidian continuum. Not so much *ex nihilo* as *ex tedium*. What is being removed here? One answer is the invisibly familiar, the other is time.

Follow your nose around the space blinking occasionally. Get into a rhythm of walking and gradually let the rhythm of your blinking fall in with your step. See how far apart you can make these flashes. It is something I did as a kid and has more of a thrill when it involves other pedestrians and traffic. It is also a way of thinking about time. Further ahead we will think about rhythm and tempo in structuring and in generating material but for now the experience of the frozen frame and the act of (literally blind) faith which fills the gap which I try to share. When your blinks become fast and regular enough we experience frame animation, and the entoptic fill-in makes a plausible and seamless reality. The single frame though, caught like this in the head and not presented on a wall, on a page, in Space, exerts uniqueness and gives importance to the material because it is starved of Time. Snapping – subtracting time and a way of adding Nothing. Adding Nothing a way of creating a surrounding field that is suitably empty. A kind of petri dish zone ready to be infected by the questioning of whatever is introduced into it.

Graeme
Miller

Cliffs

Graeme Miller

A single person goes up on 'stage' or assumes position in a charged up observed space and get ready. Prepare to do something but stop at the moment you would do it."31 She seems poised on the edge of…unzipping something at the back, taking her hair down, throwing herself forwards, stretching…a cliff of uncertainty, a pool of possibility."32 Talking to theatre photographer Pau Ros, he says he tries to find the moment just before something happens rather than the obvious moment itself. So beginnings are happening all the time. Watching preparation the starting line becomes the finishing line. If we observed an orchestra from its final note to the dressing room it would turn the end into the beginning. Shifting the frame suggests these start/finish lines are lines of division which may be written into material to produce new emphasis and new meaning. Within a work are a thousand little births and deaths usually happening too fast to perceive, masked by their own effectiveness and often distributed according to their musical effect. We observe someone holding their breath."33-34 We talk about the anticipation and the aftermath. The pregnancy of the moment. I talk about pre-narrative – a state where narrative is attracted to structure, where we read into shape, because we are Narrative Monkeys. We talk about suspended time, tampering with time and rhythmic time. I try to get across that all these ideas are connectable rather than connected in any single, predictable, or *right* way. Let these things just wash through you and you will retain what you find useful.

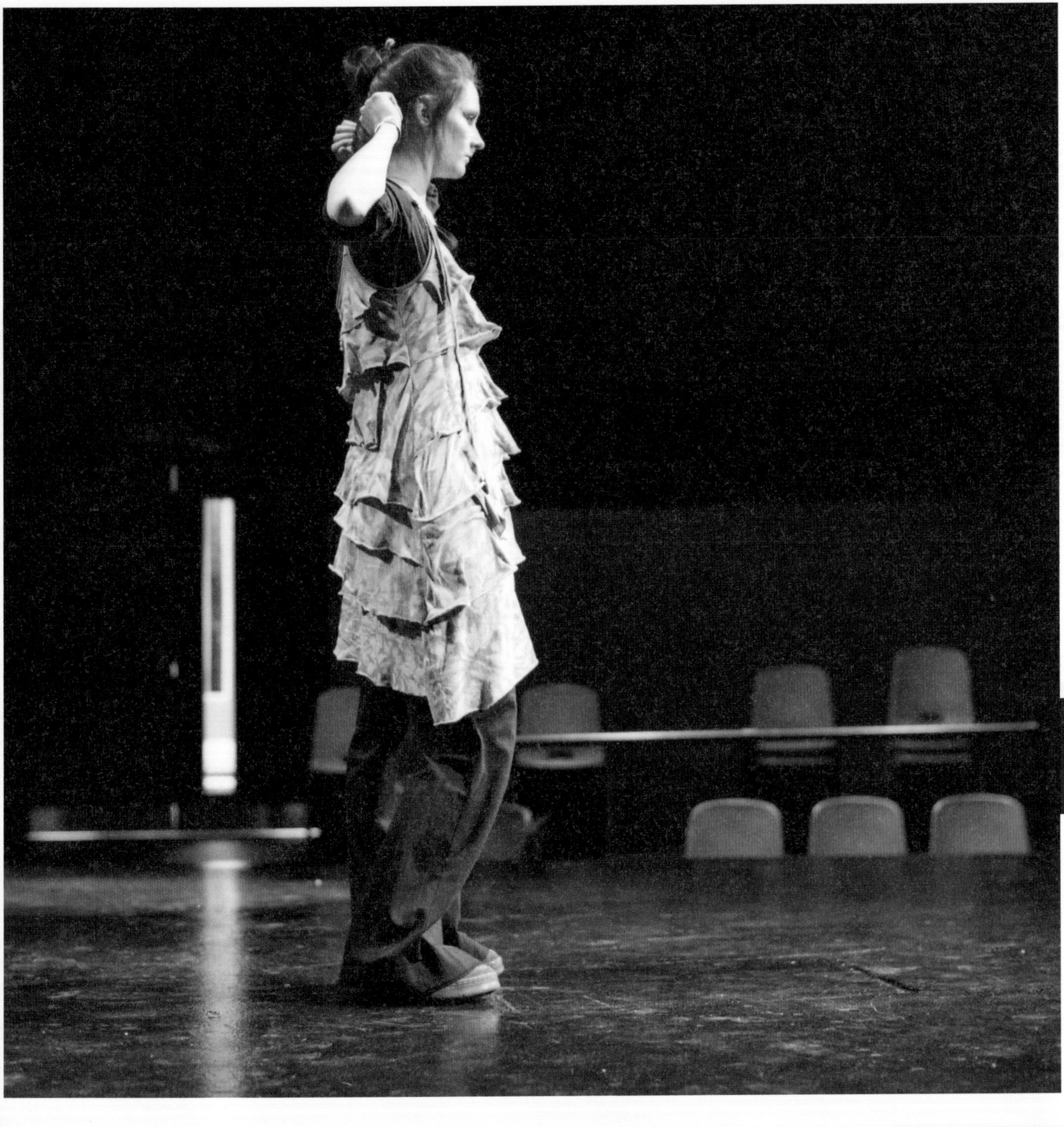

Unison

Graeme
Miller

I explain the rules of copying. These are such that we can begin by following an individual, then a sequence of individuals, then we kick the ladder away and follow no one at all. It takes half an hour or so to get there – which is relatively quick; eventually they experience leaderless authorship. When each individual is obsessively following everyone else and doing this as accurately as they can, The Flock becomes the hand that writes and although no-one is coming up with ideas, the whole group is confidently enacting a constantly changing string of behaviour delivered in absolute unison. For the shift into this un-led authorship to work at all they have to be strictly accurate, but open to chaos and surprise. Imagine that the stage is an intelligent space, that it is directly transmitting your instruction. Believe momentarily that what you do next is the inevitable consequence of what you have just done. It doesn't take much for the whole house of cards to tumble to the ground or the sequence to grind to a halt, but they keep it up for minutes enthralled in their instructions.

I never get tired of watching this. I try to explain why. It is, in part, something that places the viewer so utterly in the same moment of invention as the performer. It shares something of the thrill of defiance of gravity that the sustained rally has between two racquets. We sense the criticality of what is before us and we sense the performers' denial of it. We have privileged access to a sustained moment of creation and it's as if the teetering state is allowed to widen enough to become a navigable stream.

It is like watching evolution sped-up. The action that emerges may be as quiet as pools of algae, as flamboyant and cataclysmic as the fast-forward age of dinosaurs, but is inevitable. The action is a life-form that results from the exact circumstances of its time and place and is the unique consequence of what precedes. This suggests that whatever we make as artists can only be what will emerge from the pre-conditions of the conditions in which we make it.

This whole exercise is being written in unison. There is something about unison that gives such confidence to anything that it is forced to become something. Why else would a whole choir deliver it? It suggests importance within the slightest thing and leads us to find that importance. Also, unison works by sandwiching slightly inaccurate copies together. It is slight discrepancies that add timbre and weight, not just 'volume' to the action. Once again the Singular is breaking into being. In fact, it is the slight differences and inaccuracies of copying, and the artefacts produced by phasing*35-36 that create the seeds around which new behaviour will accrete amplifying itself in fractal echoes.*37-39

It is like opening a window on the core of invention – endoscopy revealing the beating heart. That mechanism seems to rely on doubling, not only by copying in the moment, but by repetition. The performers are navigating a fine channel where the binary emerges, the single track splits and then joins again. Prima Materia separates and conjoins. It may produce Gold.

I am fascinated that what emerges is no-one's idea. It made itself up. This might suggest that creation and composition do not require us to make stuff up, and that as 'makers' we are not really making, but stage-managing and cultivating circumstances to *serve* creation. You can distance yourself from the self-consciousness of authorship by ascribing your work creative powers.

You can use this even if you don't really believe it. You can lean on a sort of dispersed intelligence especially that of performers. It's for your toolbox.

This sustained blurt of ideas from the outside occurs before they really have time to recover from experience they have had on the inside.

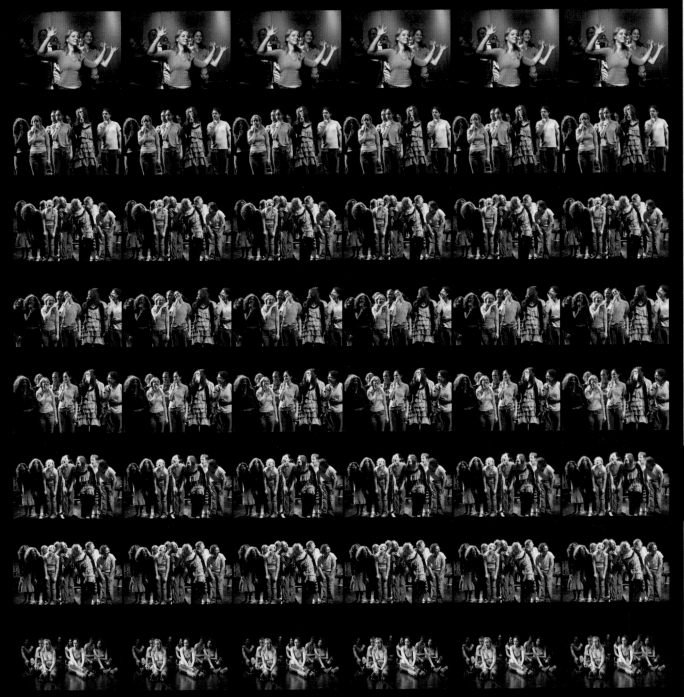

Twins

Graeme
Miller

You are twins. You speak at the same time. You always agree with each other. Tell us about…(suggestion?)…your bedroom.

Here they stand. Bookends. Four eyes defy you to return their gaze. Wrongfooted, you try to scan rapidly between them. (Twin-watchers look like a high-speed tennis crowd). The double delivery is ghostly, slow and tortuous. Unplanned words seem to ooze from the crack between them, from the fold onto the page.

Twinned activity is the last post of Unison before returning to the Singular and this delivery steers us back into the fertile hinterland*40 between the first two numbers. Here is the same authority of mutual underlining. The implied agreement of the stereo image backs up the unplanned speech.

The fold that runs down this mirrored outpouring is the fountainhead of material that seems to come from nowhere. Focus in on this bow-wave (cutting the unplanned) and you notice that in fact the words form around the slight inaccuracies at the beginning of each word. The twins jostle to comply over the first phoneme and roll the sound around in their mouths like toffee. A 'p' or a 'b' will lead them to different words and the different words, to different sentences.

In this branching world, conformity is fuelled by chaos and division multiplies possibility.

B copies A a second later as accurately as possible. B gradually closes the gap on A until they are speaking/doing simultaneously. Do this as long as you can before B overtakes and now leads with A echoing.

This is more or less impossible, but it is worth doing*41-47 as a way of drawing out the moment when no-one is leading, not least as an idea. Faster delivery than the twins and when they are neck-and-neck the speech and gesture aberrate and throw up artefacts. As the two separate lines merge and before they cross, something like a moiré pattern emerges.*48 A couple of weeks later we will watch Norman McClaren's 1961 animation, *Lines Horizontal*. An exposition of internal rules where crossing lines generate new material and new direction.

We talk about what time is doing here. The birth of echo. The beginning of rhythmic time.

our bedroom is covered

in green

wallpaper there

is

a window on

the ceiling

in the wardrobe

there

is a

robot

every single

day

the robot comes out

to serve us

coffee

and

biscuits

on the walls

are pictures

of dead

rabbits and some other

small rodents

our bedroom is covered

in green

wallpaper there

is

a window on

the ceiling

in the wardrobe

there

is a

robot

every single

day

the robot comes out

to serve us

coffee

and

biscuits

on the walls

are pictures

of dead

rabbits and some other

small rodents

Graeme Miller

Divergent/Convergent

Graeme
Miller

The Mid-Atlantic Ridge is a divergent boundary.*49 It is a hot unfathomable crease in the Atlas from which new material pours. It fans out to the West as it does to the East, slowly adding journey time from Paris to New York.*50

The Rorschach ink blot presses ink from its fold.*51-52 It is only the mirrored image which invites narrative from these stag-headed vulvic butterflies.

The fertilised human egg first divides hours after conception.*53 These two cells may become identical twins. Human cells divide every 15-20 minutes.

In the skate-park, in the snow, the halfpipe is a rounded trench built to accelerate and energise the aerial performer. They use nothing but their own energy and the grammar of the u-shaped valley.*54

I have an idea to try this in authoring on stage. Using a sustainable physical language, start along a line drawn down the centre of the space. Make a move to the right, reflect this to the left only each time extend this mirrored pattern out to the sides always building on what you have already done. Work outwards form the centre line.

Actually it didn't work. I don't know why. We talk failure, mirroring. The seeds of question and answer. The beginning of rhythm. Emergent inner dialogue and additive structures. I fantazise about what should have, could have happened.

The next exercise did work, so we talk. About reflexive structures. The mirror at the heart. Placing of endings to face beginnings. Unpacking and packing away again. Multiple mirrors, running gags. Emergent monologue and subtractive structures.

Behind you is the imagined corner of a room or the real corner of a room. Write on each wall in turn, speaking what you write. Allow your gesture and words to reflect each other. As you move backwards, what you speak and write becomes shorter and you will move faster between each wall. This will intensify until you cannot move or speak.

The ridge carries its own grammar. It marks the apex of energy and the maximum potential. It affords a view into both its valleys. Crossing a ridge in either direction marks a point of reversal. The traverse slows into momentary suspension against gravity.*55

A zygote is a single cell that is the result of fertili-sation. Two haploid cells merge into a single diploid cell containing two copies of each parent's chromosomes.*56

I took my kaleidoscope apart and found it was just a few mirrors in a plastic tube. The mirrors brought the patterns of plastic shapes together. I thought it was a collide-oscope.*57-58

The Himalayas*59 follow a convergent boundary. Matter rolls into its neighbour faster than it can be absorbed back into molten oblivion. Its constant meeting causes fracture, eruption, uplift. Geological dialogue.*60

DRAWNONWARD

DRAWN I NWARD

Graeme
Miller

Swing

Graeme Miller

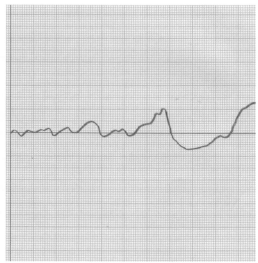

Two people arm wrestle for a good long bout.*61-65 They play for real if they are well matched, or otherwise they just act it out (well). Others observe. Someone transcribes a graph of the action along the timeline as it swings from A to B.

We talk about how the line across the table sets up a narrative potential. The balanced aggression before they begin is hinged on the line. Observers, like punters in a two-horse race, creating the potential of imbalance by their implied bidding. Just add time. A narrative of swinging fortunes unfolds hinged on the timeline. We look at the graph. This has a conversational form. Each gaining of the upper hand is a kind of riposte to the other's former dominance. Drama is a kind of dialogue; dialogue, a kind of drama. This could be the graph of a drama, a battle between good and evil. It could be a musical score. What would the poles be then?*66 We talk about translation. Translate one axis for another. Translate one state for another. Stolen structures.*67-68

A circle of people take turns to say either the word, 'fortunately', or 'unfortunately'. They should put no expression into what they say. Everyone should listen and be aware of the timing.

It takes time to get this one right. The instruction about removing expression is important. Eventually the right degree of flatness is achieved and the round continues with its own logic and pace. Short inter-cut swings of state between good and bad luck subsume to longer runs of either fortune or misfortune. Here an interesting thing happens. A run of five 'unfortunatelys' builds a tension and expectation of a return to 'fortunately'. The opposite is also true (things are going too damn well…). The deadpan words seem to be linked elastically to the opposite state.*69 The further they swing the more poignant the reversal seems. It contains the ghosts of a narrative. This is the lottery session of The Fates and it is as if somewhere far off lives are being altered. The seam of the narrative is a bi-polar hinterland where story emerges from shape.

PROGENY

A describes an event.
B describes another event.
C describes a third event which is the consequence
    of these two.

Alternatively, C describes an event which happens between
these two.
C discovers something which embraces these two –
an atmosphere, a location, a title.

A woman drops
a knife down
a drain.

The same knife,
now rusty, is
lying on a desk.

HINGES

A describes a situation.
B describes another using the words
    'but then…'

Alternatively, B can use other formats that indicate
reversal/change: 'then gradually…'; 'however…'

A small
woodland sits
on the horizon.
It is very still.

But then the
sound of
a helicopter
begins.

HALVES

Take a thing that doesn't exist yet and cut it in half.
A begins 'the first half is…', or 'in the first half…'
B tells of the second half.
C determines what it is.

Alternatively just put good combinations of first and second
halves together without questioning what they are.

In the first half
the women
seem to be
quite passive.

In the second
half…

Graeme Miller

LAYERS

These are stories, pieces of music, dynamic situations.
A determines either the top or bottom layer.
B follows with the other.
C may find what it is.

Glittery fast and sparkling

Dark and slimy

1

index of gratuitous cross reference

2

3

focus on the centre of the circle, the image shimmers because our eyes are constantly moving. our brain tries to put old and new images together.

4

5

an image attached to contact lens by a stalk will seem to disappear. in a way it is not there unless we ourselves move in time or space in relation to it.

6

The Anxious Object
Art Today and its Audience
Harold Rosenberg

7

8

9

10

11

12

13

Point:
origin of action, thought, form
Source

14

Line:
departure and measurement of space Direction

15

Arc:
makes boundary
Source externalised

16

Circle:
unity Centre, boundary and domain

17

Circles diverge
number and form emerge…

18

Read:
*Islamic Patterns:
An Analytical
and Cosmological
Approach*
by Keith Critchlow

19

general relativity shows that under certain assumptions, an expanding universe like ours must have begun as a singularity

20

EX NIHILO

21

22

23

24

ap - ple whir - ring si - lent - ly in

find in the wind - mills of your

25

26

the shutter in a film projector works in such a way that what we experience of a film in the cinema is half darkness

27

28

29

30

31

32

33

observe a single person holding their breath as long as they can

34

hold your breath as long as you can when you breathe out you will utter a single word but you will not know what it is until you have said it

35

36

listen to one of Steve Reich's phase works in its entirety

Graeme Miller

37

38
clouds are not spheres, mountains are not cones, coastlines are not circles and bark is not smooth, nor does lightning travel in a straight line.

Benoit Mandelbrot

39

40
BY Rachel Carson
AUTHOR OF *The Sea Around Us*
The Edge of the Sea

41 · 42 · 43 · 44 · 45 · 46 · 47 · 48

49
{ }

50 · 51 · 52 · 53 · 54 · 55 · 56 · 57 · 58 · 59

60

61 · 62 · 63 · 64 · 65

66 the sound of a gas boiler igniting

a toy train running on a square track

Graeme Miller

67
take the structure of a single sporting event. transcribe it graphically onto a piece of paper

68
describe the performance they might represent (convincingly)

69

70
21 CONJUNCTION

71
22 SEPARATION

72

Dis-Introduction

Graeme Miller

As the weeks pass I try to conduct my students along a slot where, when held in suspension, the moment or the space seems poised to join or split. Examine these moments in Big Close-Up and they have a teetering shadowy quality. Start to connect the connections and run from example to example of two-into-one-into-two-ness in art, then add to those the reflected structures in matter, nature, music and the seams of coincidence run in a maze of refraction. It is a panorama best taken at speed where the texture of mirroring starts to recede into generality again.

In between these extremes of view lies, not a theory, but something more like a philosophical riff. Artists' theories, or at least mine, seem to lie in the toolbox, not the bookshelf. They emerge from practice then get applied to new work.

A technique shared within Impact Theatre Co-operative in the 1980s was known as *gratuitous cross-referencing*, a method applied to a mixed bag of devised material at the eleventh hour to make it seem more thought-out than it really was. What was remarkable was that this cheap spell of repeating and reflecting in the final structure actually worked – revealing often what we really wanted to say and sometimes what lay beyond our intentions. That this worked at all opened my perception that narratives make shapes and shapes themselves can be used to generate narrative. That this works at all conditions my making to risk my faith in the material and find the form that *it* suggests. That it is possible to generate resonant material from what is either found or unplanned has led me to shift the frame to increasingly include these moments of creation *ex nihilo* in my pieces because that, in a way, is what they are about. If I were to stop making work today, the work I have already made and my knowledge of how it came about would leave me sensing ourselves as creatures inhabiting a rhythmic universe, momentarily composing ourselves and our reality. That this hard-to-grasp but encompassing view can be converted into an artist's tool for levering something into being, does not diminish it. In fact the tools that work require a measure of faith to work dependably. This perhaps is why the tour of these ideas is taken at the gallop, with the amount of gratuitous cross-referencing an invocation requires…

When stuck, consider:

Splitting hairs, installing mirrors, the use of hinges and folds, of cutting, joining and juxtaposition. The following of seams, ridges. Balancing the unbalanced, unbalancing the balanced. Dividing and dividing again. Echoing what is already echoed then joining merging, melding, co-joining again. Convergent river-systems that diverge again at their delta. Reversal, retreat, reflection, refraction. Conjunction.*70 Separation.*71 Consider the axes, the fences, the cliffs, the rifts, or soft, blurred, cracked, frayed or razor-sharp borders that run in time, that run in space and define any two part invention.

Halve the bloody thing or just double it. Double it then bring the halves together to find out what it was in the first place. Frame it then shift the frame, reveal the singular, unrepeatable, self-defining moment, object or view. Inhabit that decisive moment. Stare at it until it reveals its atmosphere, its presentiment or its aftertaste. See it reveal its evil twin, its mad cousin, eccentric aunt, ghost. Qualify. Append. Add. Subtract. Bi-polarize…

Don't worry, just copy. Move the shallows about until you find the depth.*72

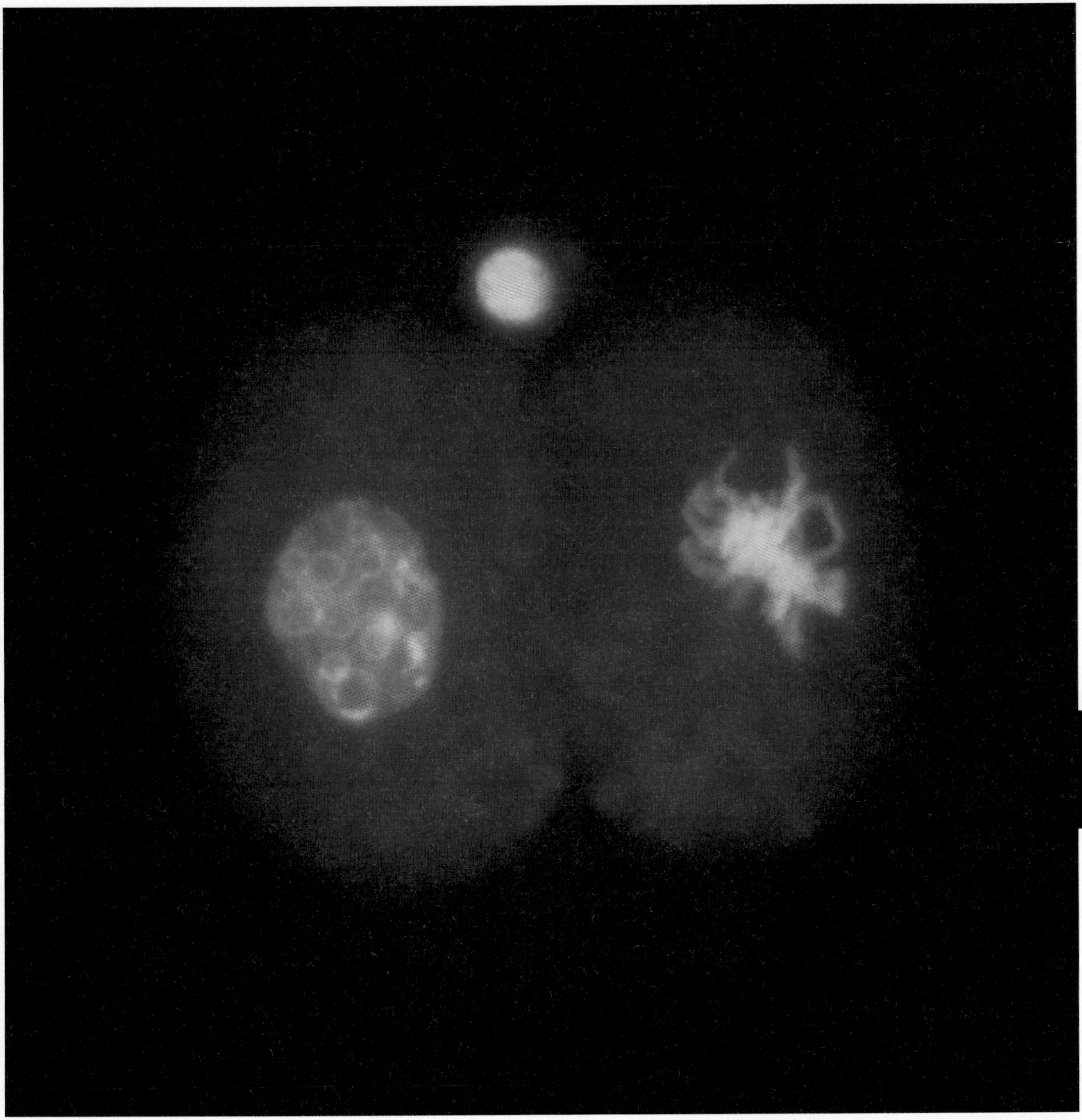

Travel, Writing and the Unknown

Jason Wilson

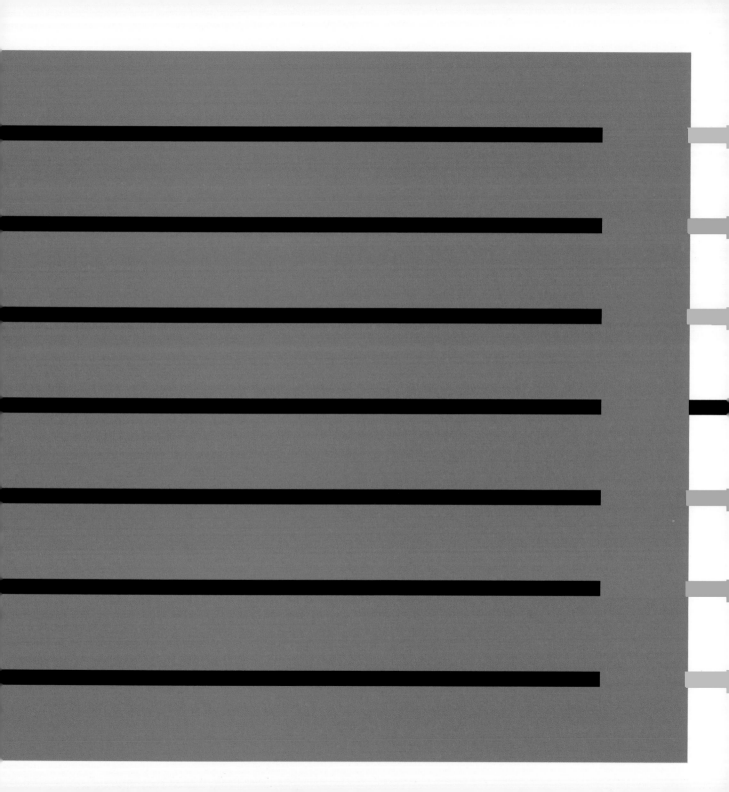

Charles Baudelaire's poem 'Le Voyage', written in 1859, ends with the oft-cited, manifesto line that incorporates the title of this collection, about plunging into the unknown to find something new:

> Plonger au fond du Gouffre, Enfer ou Ciel, qu'importe?
> Au fond de l'Inconnu pour trouver du *nouveau*.

> [To dive to the bottom of the abyss, hell or heaven, who cares? / To the bottom of the unknown to find the new].

Art critic Dore Ashton has warned that these two lines are so important 'that they threaten to become unexamined modern clichés'.[1] This poem made Victor Hugo cry out about a 'frisson nouveau'. It made Baudelaire one of the foundation poets of modernism.

This closing poem of the second edition of *Les Fleurs du Mal*[2] is a parable about the creative process where travel over the earth's oceans is also symbolic, the inner psychic seas. The poem postulates, in its rich rhymes, a map-loving child day-dreaming of sailing off on the waves of life. Baudelaire's reasons for leaving include abandoning his 'patrie infâme' [vile fatherland], horror of one's cradle and love for a tyrannical Circe (we will return to Homer later). We leave home so as not to be changed into beasts (Circe's curse). But such neurotic reasons for escape are not what count. The true voyagers, read: artists, leave for leaving's sake, light-hearted, on the move, on the road – the parable is archetypal, from Odysseus to Kerouac. These artists-travellers (I'm forcing the analogy) seek something intangible like a cloud. Baudelaire was fascinated by drifting, ever-changing clouds as metaphors of art and temporality. These true voyagers know that their own desires change, are 'unknown', without names.

Baudelaire picks out a specific boat, with three masts[3] as his self-image, seeking Icarus, the Eldorado, imagined Americas (the Columbus analogy of sailing off the world's edge). In typical Baudelairean fashion, the bitterness of home life, the poison of this prison, drives the poet to daydream, for these travellers drag their alienation with them. No actual cities ever contain the mystery of the appeal of exotica. This journey will reveal, Baudelaire continues, the same horror show, women enslaved, men as lewd tyrants, the hangman, blood, despots, the people worshipping the whip, religions and chatting humanity. That's the 'amer savoir' [bitter knowledge] earned by the actual journey. And it's this 'bitterness', the split self that never loses awareness, that makes Baudelaire modern, not the dream of escape. Not even the artist can escape time and death. So he leaves for China over the sea of darkness, here outer and inner oceans merge and the poet has no choice but to 'plunge' into the abyss, not caring whether it's heaven or hell, to find in the deep 'inconnu', something *new*.[4]

From this parable-poem, we can establish obvious overlapping insights – life stinks wherever you are and only death awaits, so dive into your inner seas and discover what will become your account of this journey, which is the poem itself. In outline, Baudelaire offers a psychological preparation – face reality – and a praxis that justifies the life trip, the long rhyming poem. However, Baudelaire was not just concocting a verbal metaphor. He had actually sailed on a three-mast East Indiaman, and suffered the hazards of shipboard life as a twenty-year old who wrote his first poems on board. He had been sent on a long journey to Calcutta by his stepfather, General Aupick, to cure him of 'literature'. But when, after the worst storm the captain had experienced, the ship lost one of its masts and limped into Port Louis harbour in Mauritius (once named Ile de

France), he jumped ship. He stayed two weeks, wrote some lovely sensuous poems about the local creole or white women and was disgusted by watching a public flogging of a black female slave. After a month on the nearby island of Bourbon (today Réunion), he sailed back home again. Baudelaire was on board a sailing ship in some of the world's worst oceans, with sailors dying of scurvy, on an outward journey that took nearly four months from when he left Bordeaux on the 9th June 1841 to when he reached Port Louis on the 1st September. It is this merging of an actual voyage with its narration that I will now explore.

If Baudelaire was right, that travellers drag their home with them wherever they go, it hints that travel doesn't change you, an anti-idealist position, a critique of the proverb that the grass is greener over the garden fence. That awareness, that irony about travel, is the modern condition. Nothing changes, except that during the journey itself the same 'you' confronts new sensations. So we approach our first definition of travel as a metaphor of a life journey; passing time forces you out of home. W. H. Auden's early poem 'The Journey', a secret tribute to Baudelaire, opens with the lilting line 'To throw away the key and walk away'; a rejection of the past, a journey without baggage or prejudice – 'Travellers may sleep at inns but not attach'. Attachment is almost a Buddhist curse. The traveller must cut the umbilical cord tying him to home, to tradition, to family, to place. Auden closes his poem with the phrase, 'the old life done'.[5] Indeed, he remained a nomad all his life. Auden proposes Ulysses as his model, avoiding return to Penelope his wife at home in Ithaca. Homer's *Odyssey* narrates this nineteen-year enriching postponement of getting home as Odysseus meanders around the Mediterranean basin. Even when he arrives home incognito, he decides to stay for one night of love-making with his wife and sets off again. The Greek-

Alexandrian poet C. P. Cavafy explores Homer's parable in his 1911 poem 'Ithaca'. Rae Dalven translates from the demotic Greek: 'Pray that the road is long, / full of adventure, full of knowledge'. Odysseus will arrive, but 'do not hurry the voyage', for 'you' (the poet, the reader) have already understood that returning home is death.[6]

One modifying thought on this journey comes from Antonio Machado in a short poem that opens 'Caminante, son tus huellas / el camino, y nada más' ['Traveller, your steps / are the journey and nothing more'], where intense temporality, the now, is where the traveller always is.[7] Machado's acute insight is that the traveller is the journey.

My reading of this weaving of Baudelaire, Auden, Homer, Cavafy and Machado is that the journey itself, the creative struggle, the process in time, is worth more than arrival, the finished product, for the artist. While for the public, the finished product is all there is. That is, the final product frees itself from the artist, the journey is over, and it exists in the public domain. In the case of a poem, any text, the end result belongs to the reader. So there's a journey and its consequence, a poem, a text. Travel writing encapsulates this dilemma for it involves an actual journey and, usually later, its writing up, its shrinking into prose.

The curt term 'home' functions as the magnetic pole of all travel and travel writing. Its brevity crams in notions of infancy, custom, safety, love, the known, prejudice, nation, familiarity and more. There's no travel writing without someone leaving home, whether prodigal son or rebellious daughter. Travel writing reports back to those who stay at home, the armchair readers, the public. All the rhetorical strategies of travel writing – similar to those of fiction – play with this stay-at-home, exaggerating danger, the traveller as hero and heroine daring fate and obliging the envious home reader to turn the pages and remain attentive. A boring journey cannot end up as a boring travel book. That's why travel writing as a truth genre is inherently flawed.

There are further reasons. Countless people travel, but only a few write their experiences up, publish and are read. Why are these journeys 'written' up? Paul Theroux wrote his diary up at the end of every day as he took a train down from Boston to Buenos Aires, yet his book *The Old Patagonian Express: by Train through the Americas*, 1980, is more than his notes. So the why relates to being a writer before travelling. The writer's attempt to catch the flow of time has always been note-taking. All writers are inveterate note-takers. These notes capture thought itself, and act as reminders in the mental war against memory loss and oblivion that is mind life. The end products that arise from notes are a touching up, a selection and seek to intensify the prose and above all else, to combat language's inherent Platonic status. To try and fake particularity and uniqueness are the skills of any writer. In travel writing, diary quotations, dates, maps, glossaries and photographs are also part of the struggle to capture the 'real'. Thus, for myriad reasons, 'home' stifles the imagination and drives the writer 'abroad'. Paul Theroux acknowledged this: 'I do not think it is an exaggeration to say that I began to write seriously because I left home'.[8] Think of Joyce's 'silence, cunning and exile' in Trieste, Cortázar and Beckett in Paris, Nabokov in Montreux, Greene in Antibes, Gombrowicz in Buenos Aires… the list is endless. V. S. Pritchett claimed, after his years abroad in Spain that 'I became a foreigner. For myself that is what a writer is – a man living on the other side of a frontier'.[9] 'Home' is also where all the most destructive passions lie in wait, as Freud pointed out in his 1925 essay 'Das Unheimliche', with his term 'unheimlich' (literally 'unhomely'), that uncanny inside the locked cupboard at home. Freud writing

about his longing to visit Rome:

> My longing to travel was no doubt also the expression of a wish to escape … like the force which drives so many adolescent children to run away from home. I had long seen clearly that a great part of the pleasure of travel lies in the fulfillment of these early wishes, that it is rooted, that is, in dissatisfaction with home and family.[10]

A writer who embodies these protean notions about home, travel and the freedom of creativity is the late Bruce Chatwin (1940-1989). His first book *In Patagonia* of 1977 led to a renewed interest in travel writing, a special number of the literary magazine *Granta* in 1984, and the incorporation of travel writing within post-colonial studies.[11] 'Travel' seemed to have turned into 'tourism' and the earth had lost all its blank spaces on the map, so that travel writing had become a form of nostalgia.[12] Chatwin's book inaugurated a new sub-genre. He combined actual travel with all the skills of fiction, essay, anthropology, and history, blending intense subjectivity – the traveller's enviable ego – with readability and speculation, shifting in and out of the self into otherness. What impresses with Chatwin is his literary cunning, as we'll see.

In a duet with his friend Paul Theroux at the Royal Geographic Society in London that was later published as *Patagonia Revisited*, 1985, Bruce Chatwin characterised himself as a 'literary traveller'.[13] In fact, as has often been noted, Chatwin told Michael Ignatieff that he resented being labelled a travel writer.[14] In this first book *In Patagonia*, 1977, Chatwin had justified himself as a writer by exaggerating a personal quest to Patagonia. The book is packed with cameos about Patagonian oddballs, including Butch Cassidy and Antoine Tounens, the King of Patagonia, and historical incidents like the anarchist uprising and massacre, written in a sensual prose that self-consciously proclaimed that here was a poet constrained to prose, creating imaginative effects through careful, exact words. An example is the strong verb 'smeared' in the following description of a shop in Epuyen: 'Only in the shop a single electric bulb smeared its thin yellow light over the green walls and lines of bottles and packets of maté'.[15] Not only the verb, but Chatwin's sprinkling of colour adjectives (yellow/green) catches his chromatic, visual style (close to his pleasing colour-matching photographs). Note the naked colour adjectives in his memory of the desert around Timbuctoo: 'I remember the desert wind whipping up the green waters; the thin hard blue of the sky; enormous women rolling round the town in pale indigo cotton *boubous*; the shutter on the houses the same hard blue against mud-grey walls...';[16] his biographer Nicholas Shakespeare quotes from Chatwin's notebook 'Writing is the painting of the voice'.[17]

However, beyond this visual-verbal precision, a controlling plot in this original book offers the reader more than impressions of random travel in Patagonia in 1974. Chatwin cleverly knew that his book mirrored a deeper pattern: 'for the oldest kind of traveller's tale is one in which the narrator leaves home and goes to a far country in search of a legendary beast', where the far country was Patagonia, and the beast was a mylodon, an extinct sloth from South America.[18] Behind this formal echo there's a version of Joseph Campbell's monomyth from his *Hero with a Thousand Faces*, 1949:

> The mythological hero, setting forth from his commonday hut or castle, is lured, carried away, or else involuntarily proceeds, to the threshold of adventure. There he encounters a shadow presence that guards the passage. The hero may defeat or conciliate this power and go alive into the kingdom of the dark... the hero journeys... tests... a supreme ordeal... reward... apotheosis... the return... The hero re-emerges from the kingdom of the dead. The boon that he brings restores the world.[19]

Chatwin explained to Ignatieff why he thought that the metaphor of the voyage lay at the heart of all storytelling: 'It's not simply that most stories are traveller's tales, it's actually the way these epics are patterned into a voyage structure'.[20] Chatwin's own source for this voyage structure was the aristocratic scholar Lord Raglan's paradigm of twenty-two categories for defining a hero in *The Hero*, 1936, that opens with a young man who goes on a journey, finds a people threatened by a monster, saves them, rescues a girl, and marries into riches and power, a fairy tale pattern of a journey. Given Chatwin's self-conscious reference to this pattern, we can ask why Chatwin as narrator remained such an enigma at the end of the book. Had he returned from the underworld of Patagonia changed, had he defeated the monster, had he found riches and power, or a boon to save the world? Was there a genuine self-revelation? Chatwin himself was aware of the way this hero-paradigm mocked him. Sitting in the Royal Geographic Society in London, he referred back to his own 'spurious' quest, and the irony hurt him: 'My piece of dung wasn't exactly the Golden Fleece, but it did give me the idea for the form of a travel book'.[21] (Instead, then, Chatwin returned home with a book in mind; he had metamorphosed into a writer, not a hero with a bride, but with future fame ensured.)

After Chatwin's death in 1989, Paul Theroux puzzled over the way Chatwin had presented himself in the supposedly factual travel book *In Patagonia*, asking: 'How had he travelled from here to there? How had he met this or that person? Life was never so neat as Bruce made out. What of the other, small, telling details which to me give a book reality?'.[22] He later criticised *In Patagonia* for jumping around, 'it's full of fictions'. Behind his imputation is a notion of telling the truth (not fiction or lies) that is never *neat*, not only in travel writing but also in real fiction. He had also posthumously accused Chatwin of not having come clean over his homosexuality. One answer to Theroux's critique would argue that self-consciously following the Raglan/ Campbell paradigm pushed *In Patagonia* beyond being a travel book into a self-mocking quest novel. This is the first book of a writer who later was forced into writing a novel when a second travel book in 1980, *The Viceroy of Ouidah*, failed. Chatwin did not believe in a generic difference between travel and novel; he told Argentine critic Christian Kupchik that *In Patagonia* played with sequence like a novel: 'All that is in the book happened, although, of course, in another order. In its final version I tried to avoid both the chronological organisation in a straight line that is so traditional in travel books and the fixed narrative perspective...'.[23] A cunningly crafted book, it seems. According to a critic, Nicholas Murray, Chatwin concocted a new term for his work, 'searches';[24] his attempt at a new genre. And then, there was the process of editing a long manuscript down to its published version, as recounted by Susannah Clapp.

It is extraordinary that so many critics have followed in Chatwin's footsteps to prove that he lied and invented. The first was John Pilkington's *An Englishman in Patagonia*, 1991. He noticed that Chatwin exaggerated, 'lacks credibility' and invented details to enliven his narrative, creating effects to escape the dull reality of travel. Pilkington's conclusion: 'Like Flaubert, Chatwin never tired of exploring Aladdin's Cave of theatrical possibilities which life offered up. He seemed to define the world not only by its wisps of reason but by its potential as

melodrama'.[25] Argentine Adrian Giménez Hutton's *La Patagonia de Chatwin*, 1998, is constructed on the same plan as Chatwin's, with interviews, much reading, re-telling the same stories about Butch Cassidy, Tounens the King of Patagonia, the anarchists etc., and trekking all over Patagonia in the 1990s. Hutton constantly corrects little details that Chatwin embroidered for literary effect. He interviewed the Argentine historian of the Patagonian rebellion, Osvaldo Bayer, who resented Chatwin's using his laborious archival research. Bayer categorised Chatwin as 'historically illiterate'.[26] Also on Chatwin's trail was his official biographer Nicholas Shakespeare who interviewed people Chatwin had included in his travel book; his conclusion is that Chatwin 'does not subtract from the truth so much as add to it'.[27] Clearly, Chatwin worked the borders between travelogue and fiction, without letting his readers know. Chatwin was followed in 1998, for a fourth time, by the Catalan writer Enric Soler i Raspall in his *Per la ruta 40: a través de La Patagonia de Chatwin*.[28] Chatwin teased Igniateff, and these readers: 'I once made the experiment of counting up the lies in the book I wrote about Patagonia'.[29] The best summary of Chatwin's relationship to travel facts is from Argentine critic María Sonia Cristoff who wrote in 1999: 'His book is not witness to all that a place is, his book tells the story he wants to tell'.[30] That is, it's not his actual factual journey, but its recreation in the mind afterwards, and Chatwin's urge to make it exciting, thanks to literary cunning. What this suggests is that travel can be tedious, but travel writing cannot; that Chatwin made sure his travels were not boring. The liveliness and creativity of the traveller's mind ensure that the mundane travels become secondary.

The same point applies to a writer's biography; it's not what he or she lived, but what they make of their lives through bouts of creativity. For example, we learn very little about the secretive, enigmatic Chatwin, always 'teasingly absent' in Shakespeare's phrase.[31] An early clue emerges from the Blaise Cendrars' epigraph to *In Patagonia*: 'Il n'y a plus que la Patagonie, la Patagonie / qui convienne à mon immense tristesse' [Nothing but Patagonia, Patagonia / fits my immense sadness]; a poet's lament fusing empty Patagonia with inner desolation, and a new etymology for Patagonia, the agon, the agony. What this 'sadness' could be is never explored explicitly in the book. Chatwin avoids introspection, associates it with a closed room, with home. The narrator Chatwin is like a camera, always looking outwards, clinching vivid snapshots. Shakespeare quotes Chatwin: ' "I'm not interested in the traveller. I'm interested in what the traveller sees" '.[32]

Chatwin took two books with him in his backpack to Patagonia.[33] One was by the Russian poet Osip Mandelstam: his short *Journey to Armenia*, 1930, another clue to Chatwin's own poetics. Chatwin confessed to Kupchik that Mandelstam has become his 'bible'.[34] Mandelstam wrote laconic, condensed speculations on what happened to him while travelling. He involves his reader in an intensely visual prose that respects the reality of Armenia but that jumps about freely, moodily. His notes are a manifesto for the writing of a travel book. Mandelstam: 'Set off for a foreign country prepared to visually probe its cities and graves, to collect the sounds of its speech, and to inhale its most noble and intransigent historical spirit'.[35] Chatwin followed suit; always testing vision with language, listening to the people met en route, immersing himself in their specific history, not ranting on about himself.

Mandelstam thanked the travelling naturalists for having taught him how to truly see, lifting 'the gray shroud of coachman's ennui covering the Russian landscape'. These natural scientists opened a 'new door into a bright and active field'.[36] Travelling allowed them to pursue what Mandelstam called the 'proximate', the telling detail, through attentive observation of landscape. A traveller had to also be a geographer, a botanist, an ethnographer. Mandelstam decided: 'Whoever was not bold enough to travel, did not dare write'.[37] Chatwin took up this challenge about travel, writing and the telling detail. At the age of thirty-seven he became a published writer, after travelling to Patagonia. Mandelstam also taught Chatwin that reality's continuum should be matched by a prose of 'broken series', laconic fragments, not copying reality mimetically, but trapping it in words (the fragmentary Cubist form of *In Patagonia*). Mandelstam: 'travel is absolutely essential ... the artist's greatest reward is to explore and exploit the worlds of thinking and feeling people other than himself'.[38] The self of the poet-traveller vanishes in confrontation with others; such is the debt to the great travelling naturalists like Humboldt and Darwin.

What Chatwin drew from Mandelstam was an intense visualization at the expense of self-confession, a respect for reality, and dialogue (allowing others to speak). If Chatwin is a poet like Mandelstam it comes not from verse but from travel; attempting the shock of fresh perception, naturally. Blaise Cendrars, the poet from the epigraph, wrote in his *Feuilles de Route*: 'When one travels ... one is making poetry'.

It seems pleasingly inevitable that the other book Chatwin took with him was Ernest Hemingway's first book of laconic short stories, *In Our Time*, 1925; a writer who also blends fiction with travel and 'who knew a thing or two though it's fashionable to put him down'.[39] The legend has him as a man of action, a daring journalist constantly risking his life on the front in Spain or among the bulls or elephants, yet the fiction tells us of control and concision and typewriter rhythms. It's this artistic care that links Hemingway with Chatwin, as well as the refraction of Hemingway's subjectivity into his characters.

Chatwin's 'disappearance' from the surface of his text, then, was a conscious stylistic decision, learnt from the naturalists, Mandelstam and Hemingway. Chatwin's theory of nomadism (developed in *The Songlines*, 1987), when translated back into personal terms, suggests the need to move, to travel to avoid definition, to escape what he called class stereotypes, the 'immense relief' of being on the move,[40] generated by his 'horreur du domicile' (a term he borrowed from Baudelaire's posthumous notes, *Mon coeur mis à nu*). His theory was both evolutionary (standing up, walking, migrating) and spiritual: 'all the great teachers – Buddha, Lao-tse, St Francis – had set the perpetual pilgrimage at the heart of their message and told their disciples, literally, to follow The Way'.[41] In Puerto Deseado in Patagonia, Chatwin discussed bird migration with a local scientist, casually alluding to 'our insane restlessness'. The idea of the solitary wanderer, the nomad outside society, homeless, was his mask. The nomad showed Chatwin how to free himself from those who categorised him at home (especially his sexual identity) and this spread to his refusing generic pigeonholes as a writer as well.

In *In Patagonia* Chatwin walks alone the twenty-five miles to Lake Kami, crossing beaver-ruined torrents, falling into black mud, and being dive-bombed by condors. It is the most realistic travel section in the book, the closest to the great nineteenth-century naturalists. The section reads as if jotted down in his moleskin notebook, crisp with details. Then he notices the fresh spoor of a guanaco: 'Sometimes I saw him up ahead, bobbing over fallen trunks, and then I came up close. He was a single male, his coat all muddied and his front gashed with scars. He had been in a fight and lost. Now he also was a sterile wanderer'.[42] This bizarre identification between narrator and guanaco – that 'also' – as sterile wanderers is a confession; sterile because anti-family, anti-procreation, a misfit male, a nomad. Chatwin couldn't abide the idea of home, he could even have made up his guanaco in order to talk about himself. This 'restlessness' has nothing to do with Chatwin's biographical practicalities, such as having married and owning a cottage, a home in the Black Hills. In order to write, he had to travel, *dixit* Mandelstam.

It is striking how controlled *In Patagonia* is; style and narrative pattern predominate over the accidents and boredom of travel, and half the book deals with what happens to others, library trawling, historical anecdote. Chatwin is skilled in drawing attention to the words and incidents, not himself. Chatwin managed to avoid psychology and realism, and indulged in erudite details with rigour and concision where words count as much as their referents. Chatwin is not a transparent travel writer like a Theroux; he writes to hide himself. Susannah Clapp: 'Chatwin hardly wrote a confessional line in his life'.[43]

The ending of *In Patagonia* is on a narrative high. Chatwin walks from Puerto Consuelo to the cave where he hopes to recover another piece of mylodon skin. He finds the cave dry, glistening with salt. Then he saw 'some strands of the coarse reddish hair I knew so well. I eased them out, slid them into an envelope and sat down, immensely pleased. I had accomplished the object of this ridiculous journey'.[44] The key term is 'ridiculous' (he used 'spurious' later in London with Theroux); Chatwin was not a mythic hero, had not changed. Instead he had written a clever travel book with style.

Chatwin's freshness comes from having invested a poet's craft in travel writing. Craft translates as an awareness of his materials; the sounds of words, the rhythm of sentences and of punctuation and what's *not* written, that inner music of language that a poet manages. Freshness can also partially be explained by diverting reader expectations, as

German poet Hans Magnus Enzenberger remarked concerning Chatwin's 'sublime disregard for the categories of fiction and non-fiction';[45] what Chatwin called 'searches'.

What we learn about 'creativity' from travel writing is that there is travel and there's travel writing. Most journeys – including life's journey – are not usually logged, despite copious diaries, so that when somebody writes up their journey they are faced with the dilemma of writing itself, that is conventions, clichés, the very inflexible nature of language, the absence of plot and the need to engage the unknown armchair reader. Creativity is this later struggle more than the experience of a trip. It takes place after-wards, in the study or library, alone, sitting still. What travel writing reveals is that you cannot write without the direct experience of a journey, but that writing-up is a second journey in words and memory. The experience of writing, the imagination, counts for more than travelling. Once again Baudelaire from 'Le Voyage': 'L'imagination qui dresse son orgie / ne trouve qu'un récif aux clartés du matin'; in the clarity of dawn, nothing but a reef, while in the mind, or dreaming at night, the orgies. That opposition between reality and desire lies at the roots of travel writing and any praxis of creativity. Chatwin, instigator of a new boom of ironic travel writing, was a self-conscious, cunning poet-in-prose. Baudelaire's 'Le Voyage' remains the Urtext of post-Romantic writing and creativity because it states both that there's no escape from the life journey towards death and that a quest for novelty is what matters, hence that 'amer savoir' of any creative person's biography. A thirty-four-year old journalist and art expert set out as a solitary traveller in Patagonia but secretly wanted to be a writer, returned home to work – the real work – on a book and was reborn as 'Bruce Chatwin'.

1 Dore Ashton, 'Essay' in Jeffrey Coven, *Baudelaire's Voyages: The Poet and his Painters* (Boston & London: Brown and Co., 1993), p.20

2 This edition was published in 1861; the first edition was 1857.

3 This was probably a type of boat called an East Indianman.

4 Charles Baudelaire, *Oeuvres*, texte établi et annoté par Y-G Le Dantec (Paris: La Pleiade, 1931), pp.144-149

5 W.H. Auden, W. H. Auden. *A Selection by the Poet* (Hammondsworth: Penguin Books, 1958), p.11

6 C. P. Cavafy, *The Complete Poems of Cavafy*, trans. by Rae Dalven, intro. W. H. Auden (New York: Harvest Book, 1976), p.36

7 Antonio Machado, *Obras. Poesía y prosa* (Buenos Aires: Editorial Losada, 1973), p.218

8 Paul Theroux, 'Memory and Creation: Reflections at Fifty', *The Massachusetts Review* (1991), p.391

9 V.S. Pritchett, *A Cab at the Door* (Harmondsworth: Penguin, 1979), p.211

10 Cited in Dennis Porter, *Haunted Journeys. Desire and Transgression in European Travel Writing* (Princeton: Princeton University Press, 1991), p.196

11 As outlined by Peter Hulme and Tim Young, *The Cambridge Companion to Travel Writing* (Cambridge: Cambridge University Press, 2004).

12 Paul Fussell, *Abroad. British Literary Traveling between the Wars* (Oxford: Oxford University Press, 1980).

13 Bruce Chatwin with Paul Theroux, *Patagonia Revisited* (Michael Russell: Salisbury, 1985), p.7

14 Michael Ignatieff, 'An Interview with Bruce Chatwin', *Granta*, Spring (1987), p.27

15 Bruce Chatwin, *In Patagonia* (London: Picador, 1979), p.38

16 Bruce Chatwin, *Anatomy of Restlessness: Uncollected Writings*, ed. Jan Brom and Matthew Graves (London: Cape, 1996), p.28

17 Nicholas Shakespeare, *Bruce Chatwin* (London: Harvill Press, 1999), p.397

18 Chatwin, *In Patagonia*, p.17

19 Joseph Campbell, *The Hero with a Thousand Faces*, [1st ed. 1949], (Princeton: Princeton University Press, 1968), pp.245-246

20 Ignatieff, p.24

21 Ibid., pp.16-17

22 Paul Theroux, 'Chatwin Revisited', *Granta*, 44 (1993), p.217

23 Christian Kupchik, 'Bruce Chatwin: los trazos del viajero', *Babel*, junio (1989), p.44

24 Nicholas Murray, *Bruce Chatwin* (Bridgend: Seren Books, 1993), p.12

25 John Pilkington, *An Englishman in Patagonia* (London: Century, 1991), p.86

26 Adrian Giménez Hutton, *La Patagonia de Chatwin* (Buenos Aires: Sudamericana, 1998), p.137

27 Shakespeare, p.318

28 Enric Soler i Raspall, *Per la ruta 40: a través de La Patagonia de Chatwin* (Barcelona: La Magrana, 1998)

29 Ignatieff, p.24

30 Maria Sonia Christoff 'El mito del escritor viajero', *La Nación on line* (1999), p.3

31 Shakespeare, p.294

32 Ibid., p.292

33 Chatwin, *Anatomy of Restlessness*, p.14

34 Kupchik, p.44

35 Osip Mandelstam, *The Complete Critical Prose and Letters* (Ardis: Ann Arbor, 1979), p.300

36 Ibid., p.391

37 Ibid., p.398

38 Ibid., p.396

39 Susanna Clapp, *With Chatwin: Portrait of a Writer* (London: Cape, 1997), p.42

40 Chatwin, *In Patagonia*, p.36

41 Chatwin, *Anatomy of Restlessness*, pp.12-13

42 Chatwin, *In Patagonia*, p.133

43 Clapp, p.207

44 Chatwin, *In Patagonia*, p.182

45 Shakespeare, p.657

Geo-Choreographies: Self as Site

Shobana Jeyasingh

with Susan Melrose

EXIT

Shobana
Jeyasingh

Over the course of several months Shobana Jeyasingh was interviewed by Susan Melrose. They discussed her experiences as a
dancer and choreographer with particular attention to the loss and
retrieval of space in her work. This essay is a distilled account of
their conversations.

...all dance work is representative of its maker's life.[1]

Building bridges

Space is such a big issue in dance in the UK: when Bharatha Natyam was first shown in the UK one of the questions everyone seemed to ask was why aren't the dancers moving more? One of the points of contrast that Bharatha Natyam offered to the British dance scene was the fact that it did not engage with space in a full-blooded way. 'Bharatha Natyam commands space, it doesn't cover it' was often offered in explanation by its early practitioners. Recently, when I saw contemporary dance in Japan, I realised that Japanese contemporary dancers seemed to be quite similar: they don't really *use* space; they don't seem to feel the need to move around in order to cover space.

Does a dancer internalise her relationship to space when she learns to dance, so that it conditions her sense of the possible in dance making? All of my own dance lessons were taught in a very small room and we never really thought about space, or that dance might need a big studio, for example. Dance needed musicians, it needed bare feet, it needed practice saris, but not a theatrical space. And this was not because we weren't trained as a touring company. I already knew, by the time I was learning it, that Bharatha Natyam was a theatre form. My dance master was also a

choreographer who would put the work in the theatre but there was never any awareness in any of us, as dancers, of a necessity to co-relate the space in the theatre with the space we learnt in. The symbolic form – which was body-based – was spatially self-sufficient. So we had no sense that we would have to translate what we were learning to a bigger space. Whatever space it was, in fact, was internal.

My very first Bharatha Natyam lesson, from my dance master's father, was in a little tiled circle in the shape of a lotus in his very traditional house. Everyone who started lessons in his house was initiated into the process by standing in this circle. So the starting point was, literally, about spatial discipline and it followed that when we thought about theatre space we did not imagine it in practical, physical terms. My teachers, in fact, had built a bigger hall in their garden but even that was very narrow. If you stretched out your arms you could feel the two walls.

If space was internalised there were other externals that were given great attention. The costume and ornament of the dance, for example, were very prescriptive and reminiscent of the finery of a Tamil bride. There is also a sense of putting on a persona from the outside. The jewellery, make up and costume transform the person

Shobana Jeyasingh
(1992)
Photo: Chris Nash

Shobana Jeyasingh

into a performer. I remember that as a Bharatha Natyam performer in Britain I would often be in a theatre with the English rain outside and feel rather uninclined to be an Indian dancer but the very act of getting costumed would motivate me and I would be raring to go. In Kathakali, this transforming process is even more striking: the performer lies down with her head on the make-up artist's lap, goes to sleep and wakes up as a character in the Mahabharatha or Ramayana.[2] It is almost as if the performer dies to be resurrected as an icon.

Where my choreography actually started from was my sense of being overwhelmed by a feeling of disjunction, between that persona that I was creating in the mirror in the theatre dressing room and everything that was around me, especially the backstage spaces and the wings. I found the walk from the dressing room to the wings dressed in my costume, usually through some draughty municipal corridor, particularly bizarre and unsettling. There was a mismatch of arrival and departure. There was something odd and even painful about putting on a highly codified persona in the dressing room and then taking that particular journey to the stage to meet an English audience. I think my choreographic journey began with trying to make sense of that feeling of alienation:

to find a different way of mediating myself as performer; to make a different bridge between the performer's personal reality and their reality on stage. Also, the discomfort that I felt as a performer mirrored my own sense of cultural discomfort.

When Doreen Massey talked about personal geography at the ResCen seminar, 'Making Space', at the Royal Institute of British Architects, London in January 2005, it reminded me of the strange education in geography that I had in my childhood. I can still remember sitting in a very hot, airy classroom in East Malaysia, right by a beach where I could see the palm trees and feel the sea breeze. We were having a geography lesson about volcanic activity and glacia-tion. The area around Edinburgh Castle was given as an example of this sort of formation. It was very strange to be in that situation at school, where I was living very much in the Eastern Malaysian landscape, but everything the teacher was offering us came straight out of a British geography book. The teacher was from Wigan, and my classmates were all Chinese. So for me, geography was closer to science fiction. This type of thing was very symptomatic of a colonial education. I was Indian, in a Chinese school, in a Malay country, and everything we learned about was like that Scottish geography lesson. So that's really the place from which I'm trying to build a bridge.

I was in East Malaysia, which was politically aligned to Malaysia itself, but there was a large Chinese population in the towns, and then there were indigenous people living in the mountain areas whom we never saw in school. It all added up to a rather mixed-up background. Until then, everything I had learned had been in Tamil, and my favourite subject had been Tamil literature. My world as a child was peopled with very culturally specific imagery – which was probably in conflict with the way I experienced life myself. As I remember it, classical Tamil poetry was very stylized, formal and academic which I found beautiful. Landscape in particular was treated in a strikingly different way to how it would be treated in English poetry, for example. All poetic land-scapes fell into five categories each with their own emotional hue and descriptive conventions. The overall sense was that it was less about the subjective feeling of the poet towards a particular tree, for example, but more about using it as a rhetorical template to luxuriate in the objective conventions of poetic language. The realities of the actual landscape (like the size of the tiled lotus where I had my first dance lesson) were not as impor-

tant as its symbolic value. The epic stories of Tamil literature (like all epics) which I was brought up on did not go for much introspection, or subjectivity. I cannot remember many soliloquies but there were rousing speeches and grand public action, such as when the heroine of the famous 'Tale of the Anklet' burns down an entire city to avenge the wrongful death of her husband despite the fact that the king, together with his queen, admit their guilt and take their own lives as an act of penitence. In contrast, reading about these favourite heroes and heroines required private spaces, rooms where one could read and forget the world. But there are no individual rooms like that in a tradi-tional Indian household, such as that of my dance teacher (my own house being more urban and professional was different). In his house there was a big communal room, where everything happened, and little rooms leading off were for the couples that made up the extended family and where they could keep their bedding and their clothes.

So, in terms of disjuncture, I suppose I was always in different locations as a child and always in some sort of artificial location: I was an Indian at a boarding school in Sri Lanka, and then in Malaysia, so I had a feeling of not being quite in the mainstream of a location. These

were, in a sense, layered locations. Even literal landscape did not escape a certain science fiction feel. In Sri Lanka, where I spent some of my childhood, we lived in what was called 'up country' among the tea plantations which still bore the influences of the many Scottish planters who had made it their home. Popular place names were Dunbar, Highlands (the name of my house), Aberdeen, even Blinkbonnie! On one occasion one of my father's Scottish colleagues gave me the library that had belonged to his son who had gone to boarding school in Britain. There were two big packing cases of books from the UK from the inter-war years, Tiger annuals and lots of Ladybird books. So I grew up reading Tamil poetry and these English children's books.

I wonder whether this layering of cultural experiences somehow 'mapped' something in me, something disruptive about place? I certainly identified with everywhere a little bit but with nowhere completely. It is a bit like having an incredible choice of clothes. Yes, you become strongly aware of difference, but also of similarities. It's not only about difference. What I always find fasci-nating is that there are threads that you can follow all the way through. I find ideas of mutation generally very interesting – for example,

Shobana Jeyasingh

there are so many words from Sanskrit that have ended up slightly transformed as English words. As a choreographer, when you find you can shuffle spaces like a pack of cards, you find spatial patterns mutating. When I think about dynamic in dance, I often have the movement of a windscreen wiper in mind. Not linear, nor even circular, or any of those classical, geometric shapes, but a restless movement across and back – even when it goes to the furthest extreme, you know that it will come back. A constant possibility of getting back to the beginning, or of being aware of a range of possibilities, rather than simply of arrival or departure.

I don't know whether there is a specifically Indian perspective which might emerge if an Indian dance critic were to look at my work. There would be things that they would recognise. There is a very small contemporary dance scene in India, but it isn't developed enough for us to identify schools of thought in contemporary dance like we see here in the UK; but certainly anyone with a knowledge of classical Indian dance would recognise things such as the 'hasta' – gestures and shapes – in my work, although they may query the way I have deployed these elements. They might feel that it was in the service of something with which they were not in sympathy, but in India there is still a huge investment in discourse, in political discourse. Bharatha Natyam has always been politicised. Its regeneration was part of the movement to political independence, so it came into prominence through political activity. My mother sent me to learn Bharatha Natyam probably because for urban Indians of her generation it was a patriotic, culturally affirming thing to. Here, in Britain, you dance within that tradition and, on top of that, you are immediately surrounded by the politics of cultural diversity – so it is a wholly politicised dance form, and that colours the way people look at it. Dancers trained in the Bharatha Natyam tradition have invested so much of their will – the will to self-respect as a colonised person – in Bharatha Natyam, and that means that it is a rather over-invested form. It has to carry that considerable burden, and it can't then just be a dance form.

Originally, Bharatha Natyam was performed by temple dancers. They had a particular position in society, and enjoyed considerable respect, but then during the movement towards Independence, Bharatha Natyam was taken from that arena and it became a means of intellectual engagement in the cities. In some ways, what I've been trying to do is to say, if we took all of that baggage away, what would we have left?

Flicker (2004/5)
Dancers from the
Shobana Jeyasingh
Dance Company
Photo: Chris Nash

I think the closest equivalent of that politicisation of dance that I have encountered is ballet in China which was introduced by the Russians along with communism. The difference is that ballet was a form alien to Chinese tradition (though extreme physical skills might have struck a chord with native martial arts and acrobatics) whereas Bharatha Natyam was a form alien only to the urban intelligentsia who adopted it. In both cases however, dance was co-opted for historical reasons. Given the amount of political baggage with which Bharatha Natyam comes, I was wondering whether my creativity as an Indian had anything, and if so to what degree, to do with a loyalty to historic Indian forms.

Inventing 'imaginary homelands'

I would argue that in making new choreographic work, in the UK contemporary dance context, you do always make the work about yourself – you can't avoid it. Whenever a choreographer puts two people onstage, it is always a metaphor, whether it is done consciously or subconsciously, and you are always projecting something about your views of society. It's an ideal, or your ideal, or your view of the ideal – and I suppose that when you are projecting an

ideal, somewhere bound up in it is its opposite.

I was thinking about this when I was reading the reviews of Mark Morris's latest work at Sadler's Wells.[3] Someone actually wrote that his work revealed a utopian idea of society, and I agree with that. It's very utopian, and I simply don't recognise society as I experience it in his work – it's communal, and what you see onstage is a warm, giving society. It would be difficult to see this degree of optimism in British dance making at present. It's not just a matter of the bodies and the way they move spatially, but also it's a matter of the way the movement rests within the music. There's a kind of wholesomeness about the bodies' relationships to each other, as well as their relationship to the space. What I mean by 'wholesome', in terms of dance technique and in terms of the way the work is composed, is that I see a lack of disjuncture, or fracturing, in it. There's something about *making* the body dance to the music which is a very wholesome activity. As a choreographer you have all sorts of other choices: you can make the body question the music; or counterpoint the music; or even ignore the music; or dance in the spaces that the music gives you. When you make a decision to *partner* the music – in a very non-combative way – then you project a consensus.

It may not be a conscious decision on his part but what strikes me most about his work is the way the space agrees with the body, one body agrees with another and they all agree with the music. It all adds up to something that can be very pleasing, very organic.

In my case however, I find such agreeableness hard to come by in the studio. Space and music seem to take on an unprovoked combative mode in the studios that I work in. Exits, for example, become much more than dancers leaving the stage. Are we going to take the theatre space and use its conventions? There are very conventional ways of leaving the stage. For example, in ballet everyone dances off, and this reinforces the feeling that this is a stylised space, and that this is the only way to leave. What that means is that in your head, you have a sense that the dancers are still dancing, somewhere out of sight of the spectators. So you imagine a cut, a reality cut, somewhere invisible between the dancer as a person and as a dancer. The person of the dancer isn't ever actually there, onstage. There's a kind of illusion – because they leave in their fluttery way.

In a play, conventionally, everyone leaves the stage in character – it would be very strange if they didn't. But in dance, the way you leave the stage can become

Flicker (2004/5)
Dancers Navala
Chaudhari and
Deveraj Thimmaiah
Photo: Chris Nash

Shobana
Jeyasingh

opposite and overleaf:
Foliage Chorus
(2004)
A site-specific work
at artsdepot, London
Dancers Kamala
Devam, Saju Hari,
Navala Chaudhari,
Rathimalar
Govindarajoo
Photo: Vipul Sangoi,
Raindesign

a very strong signifier – if you want to use it – of what dance is about. In early Wayne McGregor pieces people would simply finish dancing and walk off. Sometimes, I use that option, because there I'm thinking of it in terms of a film edit: you're not looking for continuity, so they walk off. It's a very mechanical activity – like showing the dark spaces between one frame and the next in a film, which is what it feels like when dancers simply walk off.

The choices you make about how dancers exit are very important: in ballet you keep the illusion; if they walk off, then you are saying something about that illusion. Walking off is very impor-tant. If dancers walk in and they walk off it's a very strong message. I ask the dancers to be very quiet when they walk off. Bharatha Natyam dancers have a neutral, stylised, heel-based walk, in contrast with female ballet dancers who flutter off. The spine is very straight; it's meant to be a graceful but extremely stylised way of walking, the leg lifted very high and placed with the heel down, and the foot is worked through the heel. So traditionally, classically trained Indian dancers have a particular gait. In my work we try to get away from that gait, I ask them not to do that heel-based walk, and this might explain why they sometimes seem to exit so quietly.

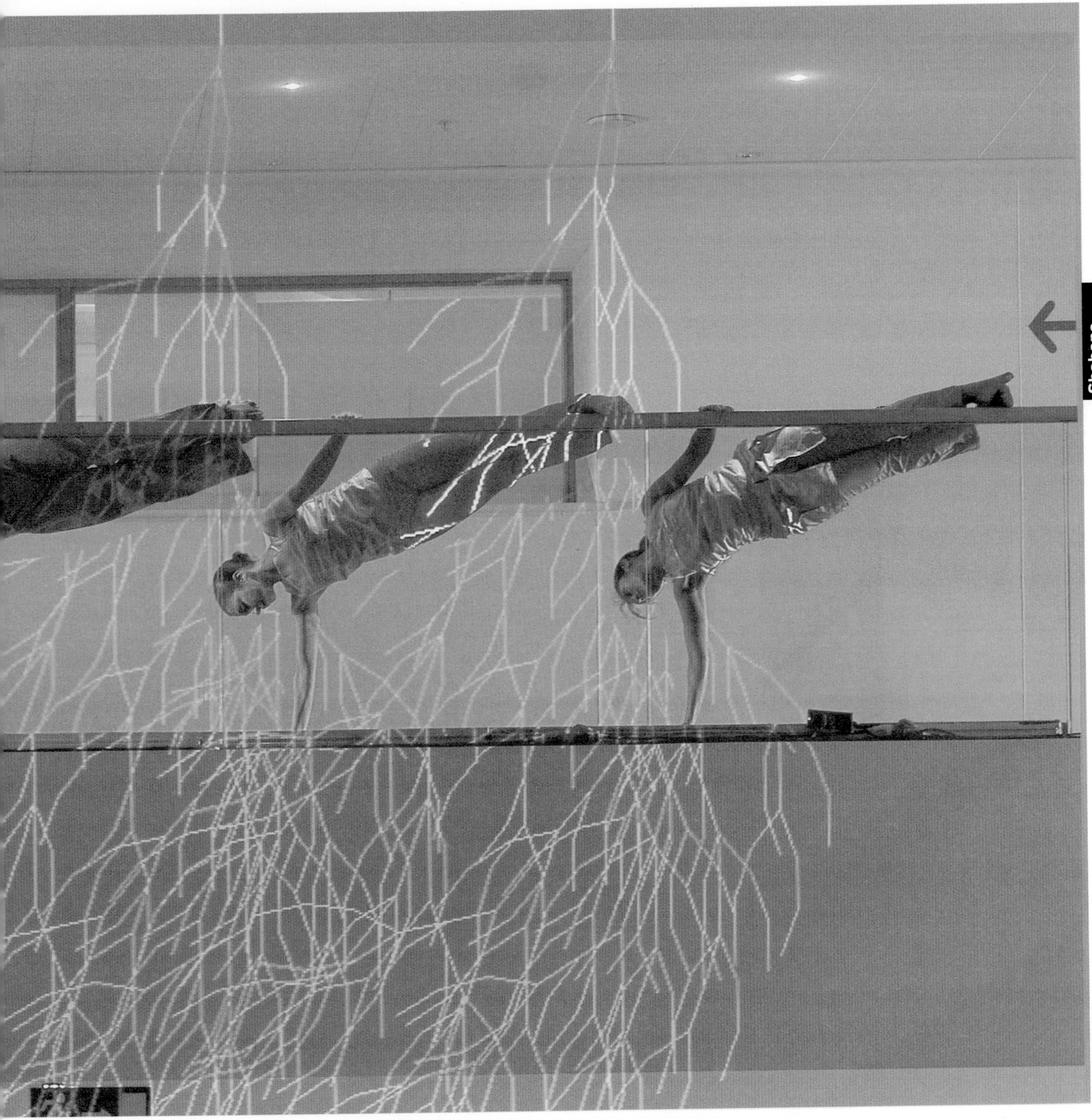

Shobana Jeyasingh

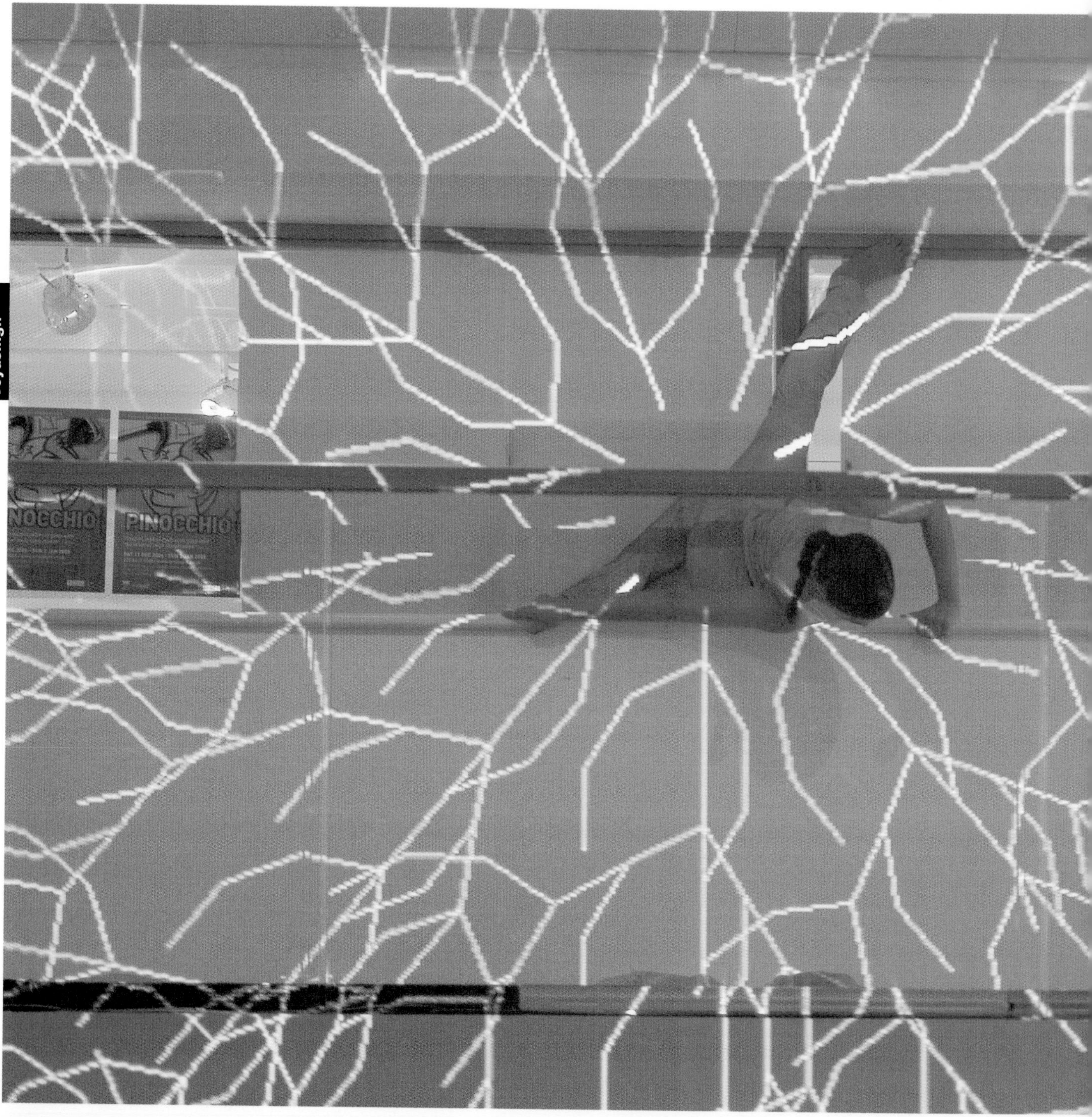

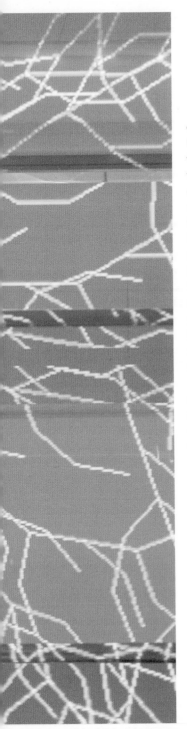

I quite like the filmic way of leaving the stage space that a blackout gives. I use it quite a lot in the middle of a piece, rather than at the end. In fact, I always wish that I could edit the material like you can with film. With live theatre, the whole thing about the mechanics of leaving, and about reconstructing your next image can sometimes be very clumsy. Sometimes I wish I didn't have to go through the mechanics of the exit. I wish that I could go straight from one shot to the next. However, the choices that one makes in this area are very revealing.

When you choose dancers from different conventions and stylistic backgrounds, apart from aesthetic differences, you also have to deal with the way these differently trained dancers use space. I find this both frustrating and interesting in equal measure. It is fascinating because the way they understand space involves a subconscious activity, and it can be frustrating because I realise sometimes that they can't actually hear what I'm saying about how I want them to do something. Dancers I work with who come from a very strong, Indian classical dance background, for example, feel a sense of incompleteness when they become aware that their whole body can't be seen by the audience. They seem to feel that not being

wholly visible means that they are not actually dancing properly. I don't think that it's just a matter of ego: 'I want to be seen!'. Instead, it is a genuine sense, for them, that 'I am dancing, but I can't communicate properly – because there is another dancer in front of me!' Often, probably subconsciously, they gravitate to places where they can see the audience and vice versa in order to feel that they can be seen. It's a bit like ballet, in the sense that there are diagonals, or straight lines, but in Bharatha Natyam, as far as the performer is concerned, the dance is traditionally *within one body*. It's very clean-edged, and all of the ornamentation of the body is highly visible. Their whole training is to enable them to communicate that clarity, that detail; so it doesn't make sense to them otherwise. Of course they don't actually say 'What's my motivation to dance, if I can't show my dance?' in so many words, but I realise that they are not completely happy in what I'm asking them to do.

I tend not to talk to the dancers in that analytical sense when I'm making the work, and I don't talk to them one-to-one in those terms. We work as a group in the studio. The motivation in the studio is so practical, and I can't explain to them the types of observations that I'm making here. All I can do in those circumstances is

Shobana Jeyasingh

to try to find a way to reassure the dancer concerned that they are still really valued, even if the audience at that moment can only see one arm. I can't really say to them that the whole of their body has to be animated, that they have to attend to the whole of their body, even when the audience sees only their arm. I can't explain that to them in those sorts of terms at the time, because in the studio we're involved in an emotional activity, not an analytical activity. Maybe, much later, a situation might emerge with one dancer where these sorts of questions can be discussed, but not when we're making the work.

When it comes to choosing the dancers, I think that you get further much faster when the dancer has a sense of what it is that you're trying to get to. An experienced dancer, like Mavin Khoo for example, completely understands the disjuncture I've been talking about, he has experienced this first hand. But sometimes I have to work with dancers who are not entirely convinced by what I'm doing, and may not even be interested in what I'm doing. What interests them is being a dancer. In the past I may have almost had to seduce them into my way of seeing, or try to find a way of keeping my vision as choreographer separate, making sure that their vision for themselves is also being realised while doing

what I want them to do. So that does fracture my own vision in the making process. Interestingly, sometimes a dancer might be on a completely different journey from my own, but I find that I can use that different journey – it can provide a different layer in the work.

When I'm making a new piece of work, I always have some difficulty in knowing, at the beginning, what the new piece is about. That comes much, much later. In the studio, I really don't know what the central thing is – it's like trying to hold something that's moving and shifting the whole time. It's like trying to hold a slippery eel in my hands, when I'm not sure that it even is an eel. But obviously I'm also choosing on a microscopic scale, I'm making small, small choices, all of the time. I might say to a dancer, 'No, don't look that way, try it like this', or I say to myself, 'I'll keep that', or I say to the dancer, 'Let's try that again'. So on one level, all of the time I am making tiny, tiny choices, but I don't know what all those tiny choices are actually leading up to. And I won't know until I recognise something – which tends to come after my technical week, when suddenly all of those tiny choices I've made have to butt up against, for example, lighting choices that I have to make – and of course everything looks completely different then. Or we listen to the music, really for the first time, maybe with musicians rather than on tape. So the big picture, when I can stand back and actually have a look, really comes when I take all of my choreographic decisions into the theatre space. Suddenly there are some really huge decisions to make very quickly, and it's actually a bit later than that when I really start to know what the work is about.

It is difficult to work in those terms with collaborators. At the beginning, all I can really do is hint at what I'm looking for. I talk to them about possibilities, and about hypotheses, and a lot of the time I don't know if they are going to work. It's in talking to my collaborators that I tend to begin to realise that if I can convince myself, then what I'm trying to do might work for all of us. It's a little test I set myself. I try to externalise something: I try out the idea on someone else, and if it doesn't sound too bad, then I think maybe it can work. But it's always a step in the dark. The dancers are such a huge part of anything I make. Once they are there, and ways of working with them begin to be resolved – and in much of my work I'm talking about seven to eight individuals, volatile sites as all human beings are – then somewhere in their bone structure and musculature, I might begin to discover an idea. I have already chosen them, obviously, but there

is a question of how far anyone can choose anything definite about a human being at any one time. I have chosen the person and dancer, and I have some sense of her or his potential, but there is such a lot of slippage – between them and the other dancers, for example – so that choice itself is a very vague sort of measure.

In terms of my own invention, sometimes I use the vocabulary of classical Indian dance extensively. It depends on the piece. Sometimes I might be working with a very good Bharatha Natyam dancer. I will tend to start working with that dancer in terms of material that she knows very well and can already deliver to a very high standard. But then I might ask her to perform a very simple task, for example, to rewind the story. Take the very simple story about a woman opening a window, and making a pattern on the floor: I say to the dancer, 'OK, you're in a film, you've produced the sequence of actions, and now you're going to rewind your actions'. This involves her performing the same set of actions, but in reverse order, and immediately the rewind itself will change the entire feeling of the thing. So she rewinds the set of actions, and we suddenly have a whole new phrase or sequence. But for this to function, I have to be working with dancers who are

happy to do that, who don't feel that in that process I'm destroying their craft.

In audition, that capacity is what I am looking for: evidence of an ability to work with the concrete through abstraction. I am looking for people who will be interested in that sort of process, who will be intrigued, but sometimes it turns out that they're not interested in that degree of abstraction. Most people, when I say something like 'rewind', emit a tired sigh! But for some it is intellectually challenging, and it is also physically challenging. When I take something habitual to them, as trained dancers, and do something else with it, then they are genuinely pleased. They relish the chance to work with the familiar in a completely different context.

In that sense, I would define my actual choreographic work as a matter of intensive, small-scale composition, at the micro level. What I mean by that is that although I say that I don't know what the work will be until a very late stage, it is true that in compositional terms, I am constantly 'making work' at the micro level. Sometimes after a whole week of work with the dancers, I end up with five minutes that will contribute to the final work. With each different dancer I have to have a different strategy to be able to get to a way of generating material which helps what I realise

Web (2000)
Dancer Anuska Lak
Photo: Chris Nash
Design:
Feast Creative

Shobana
Jeyasingh

I am trying to do at the macro level. With the Bharatha Natyam dancer, for example, I've evolved a whole basketful of tasks which they can put to use which, in turn, is likely to give me something back. I was working recently with a Kathak dancer, and I didn't really know the technique very well, so I was having to learn it by watching her, and I had to find a way to put her in situations where she could give me something that was pertinent to the dance work. I was very pleased with the piece I made for her, which drew on a classical technique that I didn't know very much about, but I found that some of the strategies I use for Bharatha Natyam dancers worked very well with her too – so perhaps the compositional strategies hold true across the different dance traditions.

In her case we went into a story, about a woman to whom Krishna gives endless sari material. We did a lot of rewinding! We took the same movements, and in fact what she was actually doing was very much in the territory of what she was used to, but the end result was completely different. It is in these intensive compositional terms that I find that I can make otherwise traditional material talk in the way I want it to talk. Sometimes of course I work with dancers who don't have that classical training, so it's a different journey, but I still

want that precision of detail. My compositional technique is always to do with precision of the detail – that's part of my story. I don't think about it because my choices are already oriented to being precise. Composition, sadly, in dance and in critical discourse around dance, doesn't get much space. It seems invisible. Often spectators want to stay at the level of *what* the body is doing, rather than how they are made to view the body, how the eye is directed. Composition, for me, is about directing the eye judiciously to what the body is doing in new and radical ways. It is a different activity to making movement on the body. It is precision in this area that carries and communicates a dance work to the audience and it is actually *on* that compositional precision that interpretation by an audience finally depends.

1   Shobana Jeyasingh, 'Imaginary Homelands…', in Alexander Carter, *The Dance Studies Reader* (London & New York: Routledge, 1998), p.47
2   Kathakali is the classical Keralese (South India) dance-drama dating from the seventeenth century. It combines literature, music and dance in the re-enactment of stories from the Mahabharatha and the Ramayana. Costumes are elaborate and face painting can take up to eight hours.
3   Mark Morris (2005), *Somebody's Coming to See Me Tonight, All Fours The 'Tamil Film Songs in Stereo', Pas de Deux and Grand Duo.*

Shobana
Jeyasingh

**Watch a dance work as if it were
a science fiction film – they both
offer metaphors about space,
time and the body.**

Christopher Bannerman is Head of ResCen and Professor of Dance at Middlesex University. He has served as Chair of Dance UK, Chair of the Arts Council of England's Advisory Panel for Dance, as a member of the Trustee's Committee of Akademi and the Dance Forum of the Department of Culture Media and Sport.

Caroline Bergvall is a poet, critic and performance artist based in London. Her most recent collection of poetic and performance pieces is *FIG (Goan Atom 2)*. She is co-Chair of the MFA Writing Faculty, Bard College, New York and Research Fellow at Dartington College of Arts, Devon. <epc.buffalo.edu/authors/bergvall/>

Ghislaine Boddington works as an artist, director and presenter internationally. As Artistic Director of sound/movement research unit shinkansen (1989-2004) and the Future Physical programme (2001-04) she focused on inter-authorship processes and the interaction of the body in digital space. She recently co-founded London based design unit bodydataspace to explore innovative interactive environments. <www.bodydataspace.net>

Guy Claxton is Professor of the Learning Sciences at the University of Bristol Graduate School of Education, where he directs the research initiative on Culture, Learning and Identity in Organisations (CLIO). He is the author of the best-selling books *Hare Brain*, *Tortoise Mind* and *The Wayward Mind*.

Shobana Jeyasingh has directed the Shobana Jeyasingh Dance Company since 1988. She has choreographed numerous award winning works and was awarded an MBE in January 1995. She holds an honorary MA from Surrey University and an honorary doctorate from De Montfort University, Leicester. <www.shobanajeyasingh.co.uk>

Richard Layzell is an artist who works in performance, video and installation internationally. Having developed a series of innovative residencies in industry, defining the role of the 'visionaire', he is working on *The Manifestation*, a major work for galleries, with Tania Koswycz. He is the author of *The Artist's Directory*, *Live Art in Schools* and *Enhanced Performance*.

Rosemary Lee is a choreographer, director, film maker, and performer. She also teaches and writes. Her creative output is diverse: large scale site specific work with mixed age community casts of up to 250, solos for herself and other performers, films for broadcast TV, and most recently, interactive installations such as *Remote Dancing*.

Susan Melrose is Professor of Performance Arts at Middlesex University. She is author of *Semiotics of the Dramatic Text* and she co-edited *Rosemary Butcher: Choreography, Collisions and Collaborations*. Her writing focuses on the need for the systematic reappraisal of 'critical orthodoxies' in Performance Studies. <www.sfmelrose.u-net.com>

Graeme Miller is an artist and composer. His work spans installation, video, stage and music, which emerged from the influential Impact Theatre Co-operative of the 1980s. Recent works include *Linked* 2002, *Bassline* 2004 and *Held* 2006. He works as a composer and sound designer for dance, theatre, and film. He also teaches and writes.

Adrian Rifkin is Professor of Visual Culture & Media at Middlesex University and formerly Professor of Fine Art at the University of Leeds. He is the author of *Street Noises – Parisian Pleasure 1900-1940* and *Ingres then, and now*. He is currently Editor of the journal, Art History. <www.gai-savoir.net>

Joshua Sofaer is an artist and writer, and Senior Research Fellow at ResCen. Recent projects include *SFMOMA Scavengers* a scavenger hunt and exhibition for the Museum of Modern Art, San Francisco. He is the author of *The Performance Pack* and *Performance and (his) Everyday Life*. <www.joshuasofaer.com>

Mark Vernon is a writer and journalist. He is the author of *The Philosophy of Friendship* and *Science, Religion and the Meaning of Life*. He writes regularly for *the Guardian* and *Management Today* and broadcasts on the radio. <www.markvernon.com>

Errollyn Wallen is a singer-songwriter and classical composer. She has received numerous commissions including from the BBC and the Royal Opera House. She founded the group Ensemble X and has performed at venues around the world. She won the 2005 BBC Radio Listeners' Award at the British Composer Awards. <www.errollynwallen.com>

Jane Watt is an artist and ResCen Research Associate. She has made a number of temporary and permanent commissions including work for Westonbirt Arboretum, Gloucestershire; the Royal Aberdeen Children's Hospital; Forces of Light Festival, Helsinki; and Edinburgh Dental Institute. She is the author of *Reflections on Networks* and for *a-n Magazine* she wrote 'Navigating Places'.

Jason Wilson is Professor of Spanish and Latin American Studies at University College London. He is the author of *Octavio Paz*, *An A-Z of Modern Latin American Literature in English Translation*, *Traveller's Literary Companion to South and Central America*, and *Buenos Aires, a Cultural and Literary Companion*.